TRANSLATING HEGEL
THE PHENOMENOLOGY OF SPIRIT
AND MODERN PHILOSOPHY
———
SÖDERTÖRN
PHILOSOPHICAL STUDIES
2012

Translating Hegel

Edited by
Brian Manning Delaney
& Sven-Olov Wallenstein

SÖDERTÖRN
PHILOSOPHICAL STUDIES
13

Other titles in this series

*Rethinking Time: Essays on
History, Memory, and Representation* (2011)
Hans Ruin & Andrus Ers (eds.)

Phenomenology of Eros (2012)
Jonna Bornemark & Marcia Sá Cavalcante Schuback (eds.)

Ambiguity of the Sacred (2012)
Jonna Bornemark & Hans Ruin (eds.)

Foucault, Biopolitics and Governmentality (2013)
Jakob Nilsson & Sven-Olov Wallentein (eds.)

Södertörn University
The Library
SE-141 89 Huddinge

www.sh.se/publications

© The authors
Cover artwork: The Stations of the Cross,
eleventh Station (Jesus is nailed to the Cross),
Rickard Sollman, 2007
Graphic Form: Jonathan Robson & Per Lindblom
Printed by E-print, Stockholm 2012

Södertörn Philosophical Studies 13
ISSN 1651-6834

Södertörn Academic Studies 53
ISSN 1650-433X

ISBN 978-91-86069-56-8

Contents

Introduction   5

On Hegel's Claim that Self-Consciousness is "Desire Itself"
(Begierde überhaupt)
ROBERT B. PIPPIN   31

The Self-Consciousness of Consciousness
WALTER JAESCHKE   55

Absolute Knowledge
TERRY PINKARD   71

From Finite Thinking to Infinite Spirit
SUSANNA LINDBERG   87

Hegel's *Phenomenology of Spirit*
CARL-GÖRAN HEIDEGREN   103

Hegel's Anomalous Functionalism
STAFFAN CARLSHAMRE   121

Hegel and Exposure
VICTORIA FARELD   131

The Place of Art in Hegel's Phenomenology
SVEN-OLOV WALLENSTEIN   147

Understanding as Translation
PIRMIN STEKELER-WEITHOFER   163

Hegel in Swedish
BRIAN MANNING DELANEY   191

French Losses in Translating Hegel
JEAN-PIERRE LEFEBVRE   213

Authors   223

Introduction

The enigma of Hegel

In 1807, one of the most ambitious, dense, and enigmatic works in the history of philosophy was published: Hegel's *Phenomenology of Spirit*. Neither a commercial nor an academic success in its own time, the book has remained with us to this day, albeit more often cited and alluded to than actually read. It is one of those works that always seem to be waiting for an adequate deciphering, that we never really have begun to read, and whose position in history remains undecided.

Thus while Hegel's Phenomenology and indeed all his later works in one sense lie behind us, like gigantic and enigmatic pyramids, as Nietzsche once noted, in another sense Hegel's Phenomenology points to a task still before us: to grasp the mature works as the origin of a philosophical modernity that fuses concept and history into the movement of thought itself, where one of the first decisive steps was taken to create an expanded concept of reason that would be able to include its own temporal becoming, its own opacities and ruptures, its own development.

In various degrees of proximity to Hegel's own philosophical vision and language, many subsequent philosophers within the Continental tradition, from Husserl and Heidegger to Adorno and Derrida, have grappled with the historicity of thinking, and in this they continue his legacy—often, paradoxically enough, in seeking to free us from a certain Hegelian shadow, from the theodicy or Parousia of history bequeathed to us by the idea of absolute knowing.[1] To some extent they all aspire in different ways to end with the Hegelian ending of metaphysics, to rethink, as it were, the completion of philosophy in light of what remained unthought or repressed

---

[1] Indeed, the Continental tradition itself can be defined by the persistence of specifically Hegelian themes, whereas the analytical tradition, at least up until a few decades ago, often omits Hegel entirely. Both of these traditions of course acknowledge the importance of Kant (although in very different ways), whereas Hegel, and specifically, his insistence on the historicity and situatedness of philosophical thinking, is where they part, at least when these two traditions narrate their respective histories.

within it. Adorno's question whether metaphysics is still possible,[2] which in principle asks about the fate of philosophy after the Hegelian consummation and the catastrophic failure to realize its promise, finds an echo in Derrida's inquiry into what the "remains" of Hegel mean for us today,[3] both of which can be taken as responses—of course quite different from, yet not entirely unrelated to—Heidegger's claim that we need to take a "step back" from the Hegelian determination of philosophy as absolute knowledge.[4] And yet, such overcoming and unhinging of the Hegelian circle may

---

[2] "Its [philosophy's] critical self-reflection may not stop however before the highest achievements of its history. It needs to be asked if and whether, following the collapse of the Hegelian one, it would even be possible anymore, just as Kant investigated the possibility of metaphysics after the critique of rationalism. If the Hegelian doctrine of the dialectic represented the impossible goal of showing, with philosophical concepts, that it was equal to the task of what was ultimately heterogeneous to such, an account is long overdue of its relationship to dialectics, and why precisely his attempt failed." *Negative Dialektik, Gesammelte Schriften* 6 (Frankfurt am Main: Suhrkamp, 1997), 16. Trans. Dennis Redmond, available online at: http://www.efn.org/~dredmond/ndtrans.html. Adorno's entire project for a negative dialectics can be understood as an attempt to play Hegelian and Kantian motifs against each other.

[3] "What, after all, of the remain(s) [*quoi du reste*] today, for us, here, now, of a Hegel." Derrida, *Glas*, trans. John P. Leavey and Richard Rand (Lincoln: University of Nebraska Press, 1986), 1. If Hegel, as Derrida suggests elsewhere, is the "last philosopher of the book and the first thinker of writing" (*Of Grammatology*, trans. Gayatri Chakravorty Spivak [Baltimore: Johns Hopkins University Press, 1997], 26), this indicates the crucial position he holds within the historical schemata that underlie deconstruction, at least in its early phases, and in this Derrida comes close to Adorno. On Derrida's relation to Hegel, see Stuart Barnett (ed.), *Hegel after Derrida* (London: Routledge, 1998).

[4] In *Identität und Differenz* (Pfullingen: Neske, 1957), 36ff, Heidegger suggests that his relation to Hegel involves three components. 1) *The matter of thinking*, which for Hegel is the absolute concept, and which for Heidegger is the ontological difference. 2) *The guiding principle* of the dialog with the history of philosophy, which for Hegel is to enter into what has been effectively thought, in order to attain a synthetic presentation, and which for Heidegger is to approach the unthought, not in the sense of an absence, but as something that provides space for that which has been thought. 3) *The character of the dialog*, which for Hegel is to surpass the relative one-sidedness of earlier philosophies by including them in an infinite discourse able to express them all, and which for Heidegger is the step back, which makes the finitude of the tradition visible. Heidegger's relation to Hegel is however far from univocal, and if one were to piece together his first references to Hegel—when he, in the habilitation thesis on Duns Scotus, speaks of the need to overcome the difference between history and systematic philosophy—and the later remarks—those in *Being and Time*, the 1929 lecture course on German Idealism and the current state of philosophy (GA 28), the 1930/31 lecture course (GA 32) entirely dedicated to the Phenomenology (which however breaks off at the beginning of the chapter on self-consciousness), the notes on Hegel's *Philosophy of Right* from 1933 (GA 86), and the published and more well-known essays after the war ("Hegels Begriff der Erfahrung," in *Holzwege*, GA 5, and "Hegel und die Griechen" in *Wegmarken*, GA 9)—

perhaps further entrench us in its grip. As Foucault famously notes at the end of his inaugural lecture at the Collège de France in 1970, *L'ordre du discours*, all the anti-Hegelianisms of our time may be nothing but another ruse of history, a kind of detour at the end of which he is still waiting for us, immobile, as the great spider of history that will eventually lure us into his all-encompassing web.[5]

On another note, equally suspicious of the metaphysical and theological dimension of the absolute, but with the view to replacing it with an idea of an embedded and situated concept of reason, some contemporary Anglo-Saxon philosophers, notably Robert Brandom[6] and John McDowell,[7] have reintroduced Hegel in a way that draws him close to pragmatism and to "holistic" theories of meaning, i.e. theories holding that concepts only mean something as part of conceptual networks, but that also contain a commitment to scientific naturalism that may seem surprising for other readers of Hegel. In this interpretation, the problem is not understanding the way in which Hegel's "absolute" consummates classical metaphysics and/or theology, or the extent to which our present moment's seemingly anti-Hegelian claims remain caught up in his system, but how we should understand the situatedness of our conceptual schemes. The "absolute" quality of a conceptual whole would in this sense amount to the absence of an unmediated outside that would serve as an independent reference (thus echoing Sellars's "myth of the given," which is a frequent reference in these readings), and it would not preclude the possibility of there being a plurality

---

the resulting picture would be highly complex and shifting. For more on Heidegger's relation to Hegel, see Susanna Lindberg's contribution below.

[5] Foucault, *L'ordre du discours* (Paris: Gallimard, 1970), 74f. A perception of a generalized anti-Hegelianism similar to Foucault's is put forth for instance in the preface to Deleuze's 1969 thesis *Différence et répétition*, which speaks of a "generalized anti-Hegelianism," where "difference and repetition have taken the place of the identical and the negative, of identity and contradiction." *Difference and Repetition*, trans. Paul Patton (London: Athlone Press, 1994), xix.

[6] See Brandom, *Reason in Philosophy: Animating Ideas* (Cambridge, Mass.: Belknap Press and Harvard University Press, 2009). For a discussion of this somewhat unexpected return of Hegel, see Paul Redding, *Analytic Philosophy and the Return of Hegelian Thought* (Cambridge: Cambridge University Press, 2007). These new frontiers have already generated a considerable discussion; see, for instance, Christoph Halbig, Michael Quante, and Ludwig Siep (eds.), *Hegels Erbe* (Frankfurt am Main: Suhrkamp, 2004), and vol. 3 (2005) of *Internationales Jahrbuch des Deutschen Idealismus*, eds. Karl Ameriks & Jürgen Stolzenberg.

[7] See, for instance, *Mind and World* (Cambridge, Mass.: Harvard University Press, 1994), and *Having the World in View: Essays on Kant, Hegel, and Sellars* (Cambridge, Mass.: Harvard University Press, 2009).

of such absolutes, and would not understand it as a historical termination. (The status of Hegel's absolute is a dealt with in detail in Terry Pinkard's and Susanna Lindberg's contributions, below.)

Others have similarly stressed the social nature of meaning in Hegel, while also foregrounding the motif of conflict and power inherent in intersubjectivity as a structure of "recognition,"[8] which still remains largely tangential in the analytical reading. In the various theories of recognition the stress tends to lie on the social dynamic, and on the open-ended nature of recognition, rather than on conceptual wholes, and the emphasis is more ethical and political than epistemological, although all such theories in the end can be said to question, each in their respective ways, this division. (As both Robert Pippin and Carl-Göran Heidegren point out in their contributions below, the main challenge is to do justice to the transcendental claims while still acknowledging the social sphere.)

In order to overcome, displace, or fundamentally modify the claims to absolute knowledge that Hegel of course makes, one obviously first must grasp what they mean, which is by no means obvious; in fact, the ultimate intent of the Phenomenology has remained mysterious. The great Hegel scholar Otto Pöggeler remarks, in his *Hegels Idee einer Phänomenologie des Geistes*,[9] that his study was presented in order to save Hegel's book from a certain intentionally malevolent use to which it was put by German philosophy departments. If there was an aspiring Ph.D. candidate that the department was reluctant to accept, he would be told: yes, you will be admitted to the program, we just want to you to write a brief essay where you summarize the basic arguments of the Phenomenology. While perhaps apocryphal, the anecdote contains a truth with which most readers of the Phenomenology will be familiar: the labyrinthine quality of the prose, the architectonic complexities of the Hegelian phrase that not only relate to the syntactic structures but also to the very movement and content of his thought, appear to render any attempt at a straightforward summary futile.

---

[8] See most recently Axel Honneth Wellmer, *Kampf um Anerkennung: Zur moralischen Grammatik sozialer Konflikte* (Frankfurt am Main: Suhrkamp, 1992). The theme was first addressed by Jürgen Habermas in his work on the Jena manuscripts (see "Arbeit und Interaktion: Bemerkungen zu Hegels Jenenser 'Philosophie des Geistes,'" in Habermas, *Technik und Wissenschaft als Ideologie* [Frankfurt am Main: Suhrkamp, 1968]), and has since then been explored by many scholars. This theme is developed further in Victoria Fareld's contribution below, where she argues that the idea of recognition presupposes an underlying recognizability.
[9] Pöggeler, *Hegels Idee einer Phänomenologie des Geistes* (Freiburg: Alber, 1973).

And yet the Phenomenology aims to produce precisely such a synoptic overview, to trace the development of sprit from its simplest form to its completion, and to do so in a way that is not merely empirical, but will provide us with a rational story of how consciousness step by step casts off its quality of being a mere love of wisdom, a *philosophia*, and becomes identical to wisdom, a science (*Wissenschaft*).

Maybe there is, as Adorno suggests in the third and final of his *Drei Studien zu Hegel*, "Skoteinos, or How to Read," an essential obscurity in Hegel that should not simply be effaced. Linking together Hegel and the great thinker of difference and identity at the other end of the history of philosophy, Heraclitus—who for Hegel too was an essential reference[10]— Adorno perceives this obscurity as an objective problem pertaining to the matter of Hegel's thought itself. For Hegel, in opposition to the Cartesian clarity of principles, the totality is present in each part and yet goes beyond it, in such a way that "[e]very single sentence in Hegel's philosophy proves itself unsuitable for that philosophy, and the form expresses this in its inability to grasp any content with complete adequacy."[11] As we follow the movement of the constituent parts (the reference here is the Logic, where the problem is further aggravated, although it surely exists in the Phenomenology too), we must always be aware of the system, although it does not form an abstract higher-order concept, but only exists as this immanent movement: "At every moment one needs to keep seemingly incompatible maxims in mind," Adorno notes, "painstaking immersion in detail, and free detachment."[12]

---

[10] See the section on Heraclitus in Hegel, *Vorlesungen über die Geschichte der Philosophie*, Werke, eds. Eva Moldenhauer & Karl Markus Michel (Frankfurt am Main: Suhrkamp, 1986), vol. 18, 319ff, where Hegel claims that "we here can seen land," and "there is no sentence of Heraclitus that I have not taken into my *Logic*" (320). That Heraclitus was "obscure" (*skoteinos*), may, Hegel suggests, have something to do with the quality of his language, as Aristotle also had claimed. But the obscurity of Heraclitus is fundamentally a result of the fact that "profound speculative thought is expressed in this philosophy" (322).
[11] Adorno, *Three Studies on Hegel*, trans. Shierry Weber Nicholsen (Cambridge, Mass.: MIT, 1993), 91.
[12] Ibid., 95.

Towards the system

But how then should we approach this forbidding book? Like all great works, it is marked by its origin, while not being reducible to it: philosophy is not just of its time, Hegel famously notes in the introduction to his *Philosophy of Right*, but is "its own time comprehended in thoughts" (*ihrer Zeit in Gedanken gefasst*).[13] The Phenomenology is located at a crucial juncture in post-Kantian thought, and attempts to continue the movement going beyond the limits set for reason in Kant's critical philosophy, while also respecting and developing the idea of critical reflection on knowledge.[14] But one must also acknowledge the mark of dramatic and momentous shifts in political and social history, leading from the French Revolution and the Terror, of which Hegel provides an incisive analysis in the dialectic of "absolute freedom," to the Napoleonic wars, all of which had a profound impact on German intellectual and political life. And beyond these disruptive events we must also speak of the gradual emergence of the modern state apparatus, with its new bureaucracies and institutions, techniques of power and mechanisms of individualization and subjectification, together with the discourse of political economy as the mode of a new "governmentality," to use the vocabulary of Foucault.[15] From his first texts onwards, Hegel reacts to these transformations, and a reflection on the nature of political modernity, as a quest for the unity of individual subjects and collective orders, traverses all of his works, although it was initially couched in theological language: the individual must be recognized and respected, while still being understood in terms of an overarching order or "spirit" that makes this individuality possible. Fifteen year after the Phenomenology, the *Philosophy of Right* would attempt to solve these problems, but we can already see them germinating in the texts from the Jena period, where Hegel develops a reflection on labor, language, and interaction that can be understood both as a way to conceptualize or

---

[13] Hegel, *Elements of the Philosophy of Right*, trans. H. B. Nisbet (Cambridge: Cambridge University Press, 1991), 21.
[14] That Hegel's arguments can be reconstructed as a critical extension of Kant's transcendental idealism that takes it into the direction of intersubjectivity, is particularly emphasized by Robert Pippin, *Hegel's Idealism: The Satisfactions of Self-Consciousness* (Cambridge; Cambridge University Press, 1989). See also Pippin, *Idealism as Modernism: Hegelian Variations* (New York: Cambridge University Press, 1997).
[15] See for instance Foucault, *Security, Territory, Population: Lectures at the Collège de France, 1977–1978*, trans. Graham Burchell (Basingstoke: Palgrave Macmillan, 2007).

comprehend an emerging social reality as well as a response to the political philosophies of Plato and Aristotle.

On the one hand, it is true that the emphasis on subjectivity situates Hegel within the development of the universal science that was proposed by Descartes as the way for the subject to achieve mastery over the world: it is by carrying out the operations of the *mathesis universalis* that we can at least approach the infinite knowledge of God, and for rationalist philosophy the new mathematical science is the essential tool for achieving this. When we reach Descartes, Hegel says in his lectures on the history of philosophy, we are like sailors who have spent a long time adrift on the open sea, and suddenly can cry out "Land, ho!"[16] This new beginning must be given its rightful due, there is no way back to the cosmic order from which the ego cogito emerged, and in this sense Hegel creates a particularly powerful amalgamation of absolute subjectivity and modernity, understood as the truth of the preceding tradition. Even though his idea of "science" goes far beyond the rationalist version—in fact, Hegel is sharply critical of the overconfidence in mathematics and of any method that proceeds *more geometrico*—the very idea of an all-encompassing science has unmistakable roots in the Cartesian breakthrough.

On the other hand, Hegel stresses that this subject and the operations it carries out in order to objectify and know the world must also be understood as *substance*, i.e., as an intersubjective order embedded in institutions, customs, and practices, or in "objective spirit," as he would later call it. Only in this way can the subject come to know itself in a qualified sense, as the bearer of a rationality that transcends it. If Hegel is a post-Cartesian, this does not mean that he can be taken exclusively as the culmination of a philosophy of subjectivity, as Heidegger often seems to suggest; he is just as much a thinker of intersubjective practices. This is the basic tenet of the contemporary "non-metaphysical" reading favored both in the analytical as well as the hermeneutic tradition, where the notion of "spirit" is reinterpreted in a decidedly non-religious sense that tends towards sociology, as those practices that underwrite and support a certain culture's understanding of itself, and which are absolute in the sense that they have no simple "outside." For others this resolute severing of Hegel's texts from their metaphysical presuppositions, whose structuring role may

---

[16] See *Vorlesungen über die Geschichte der Philosophie*, Werke 20, 120. We can note that the metaphor of the terra firma, first employed with reference to Heraclitus, returns here.

be debated, but whose presence is hard to deny, may not be so much a way to put Hegel back on his feet, as Marx once attempted, as a cutting off of his head; the future will decide the extent to which such readings once and for all manage to separate the "rational core" from the "mystical shell," as Marx claimed to do, or just simply provide a disfigured portrait.[17]

The equation that links subject to substance, and that will produce the idea of the *system* as the necessary mode of existence of truth, also has a decisive historical background in Kant's critical philosophy. Kant too creates a kind of system or "architectonic" that reintegrates the splits and divisions—freedom and necessity, body and soul, reason and nature, etc.—that had been produced by Enlightenment culture. For Kant, all of the earlier theories could be understood as partial truths that, however, lose their legitimacy when they are extended to experience as a totality. The unity of reason that was determined by Descartes on the basis of the *mathesis* consists for Kant in an articulation of levels and domains that must be distinguished as well as united. The unity of reason does not imply that one particular theory should be applied to everything, but calls for a "transcendental reflection" on the relation between spheres of rationality, i.e., on the principles that provide each of them with a particular legislative autonomy while also connecting them on a higher level within a system of ends. The Kantian mind is thus necessarily fractured: it has several positions and functions depending on the telos of its activity, but at the same time it always strives for a unity that in Kant's vocabulary could be called a "regulative idea," or a *focus imaginarius* as he says toward the end of the first Critique (A 644/B 672).[18] In this way, Kant's critical restructuring of reason prefigures the analysis of modernity as a process of rationalization that Max Weber more than a century later would describe in terms of "disenchantment" and bureaucracy, and as the emergence of science and politics as "professions" with their respective

---

[17] Rolf-Peter Horstmann has argued for the inseparability of Hegel's various arguments and specific insights and, on the other hand, such systematic presuppositions, which for him results in a rather pessimistic assessment of the possibility of retrieving Hegel for contemporary purposes: we must swallow him whole or not at all. See Horstmann, "What is Hegel's Legacy and What Should We Do With It?" *European Journal of Philosophy* 7 (2) (1999).

[18] Kant is obviously not referring to the idea of a system in the developed sense of the term, but his claim that the transcendental idea provides the "greatest unity alongside the greatest extension" is precisely what the later system philosophies will attempt to realize.

competences and procedures.¹⁹ Kant can indeed be taken as the first bureaucrat of pure reason, and his invention of a new type of legally and juridically inflected vocabulary—"the tribunal of reason" and the idea of the philosopher as a judge—testifies to this.

After Kant many efforts will be made to rethink this architectural synthesis and indicate a place where a new kind of unity or grounding could be located, and not just in terms of an imaginary focus: reconciliation (*Versöhnung*) must be real, and not just a representation, as Hegel says.²⁰ This is one of the fundamental ways in which history enters philosophy, and to Kant's successors he appeared as naive in simply accepting and systematizing, in an a priori fashion, divisions that in fact had been brought about by the historical process. The responses of Schiller and Hölderlin, and then of Schelling and Hegel, were to introduce the density of the historical process as an essential moment in thought (which can also be understood as a transformation that the concept of history itself underwent in Schelling and Hegel, as is pointed out by Walter Jaeschke in his contribution below). The question of philosophical validity will henceforth be related to the question of historical becoming. Here we pass from a "structural analysis of truth" to an "ontology of actuality," in Foucault's felicitous phrase,²¹ which he applies to Kant's political writings, but which in fact more accurately describes Kant's immediate aftermath. After Kant the historical task will present itself as the overcoming of the distinctions that Kant had made into absolutes, and as the restoration of a unity of reason and world on a higher level, not just as a correlation of ends that we may "reflect" upon, but as a truly substantial and living unity.

The present now appears as a moment of *Entzweiung* and *Zerrissenheit*, a splitting and laceration that results from the Enlightenment and its "philosophy of reflection." This is how the young Hegel paints the present age in his thesis, *Differenz des Fichteschen und Schellingschen Systems der*

---

[19] See for instance the two classic lectures by Weber, "Science as Vocation" (1917) and "Politics as Vocation" (1918), in Max Weber, *The Vocation Lectures*, trans. Rodney Livingstone (Indianapolis: Hackett, 2004).
[20] One case among many would be the introduction to the lectures on aesthetics, where Hegel suggests that Kant brought the "reconciled contradiction" into the space of "representation" (*Vorstellung*), but failed both to develop its concept in a scientific fashion, and to demonstrate it in reality. See *Vorlesungen über die Ästhetik*, Werke 13, 84.
[21] See for instance the sections on Kant and the Enlightenment in Foucault, *Le gouvernement de soi et des autres: Cours au collège de France (1982-1983)*, ed. Frédéric Gros (Paris: Seuil, 2008).

Philosophie of 1801, where the "need for/of philosophy" (*das Bedürfnis der Philosophie*) is at once a subjective and objective genitive: the present needs philosophy to overcome itself just as much as philosophy needs to take a new step to truly become itself. The philosophy of the future, Hegel suggests, must transcend mere reflection in a movement of speculation, i.e. the recognition that we ourselves have in fact produced all the inherited dualisms. Speculation means returning from reflection to a higher identity that acknowledges difference and splitting as part of itself, to the *identity of identity and non-identity*. This move however requires a speculative *leap*, an event in thought and language—and here it is tempting to follow Heidegger and play on the German word *Satz*,[22] which means both "leap" and "sentence"—but it also demands that we remain rational and not succumb to the Romantic temptation to project reconciliation into the sphere of that which transcends reason (for instance into art, as was proposed by Schelling), since this entails the risk that the leap will become a deadly one, a *salto mortale* plunging us into the abyss of non-knowledge.

This is one of the reasons why Hegel always remained critical of all attempts to return to some pre-modern unity, for instance the various versions of ancient Greece that had been proposed in the wake of Winckelmann (although these ideas were in fact based on a misreading of Winckelmann: for him, too, Greece was irretrievably lost, and the invention of art history is a work of mourning).[23] This return is however just as often proposed as a way into the future, as in the case of the anonymous fragment that since its discovery by Franz Rosenzweig has been called "The Oldest System Program of German Idealism," dating from 1796/97 (the handwriting is undoubtedly Hegel's, and he is now generally accepted as its author),[24] which proposes an idea of a future synthesis of art and philosophy that will echo in many subsequent visions of a social-political *Gesamtkunstwerk*, from Wagner and Nietzsche onwards, on both sides of the

---

[22] See Heidegger, *Identität und Differenz*, 20f, *Der Satz vom Grund* (Pfullingen: Neske, 1957), 106f, and the comments on the structure of Hegel's "speculative *Satz*" in the second seminar in Le Thor, in *Seminare, Gesamtausgabe* vol. 15, ed. Curd Ochwadt (Frankfurt am Main: Klostermann, 1986), 325.

[23] For readings of Winckelmann along these lines, see Edouard Pommier, *Winckelmann: Inventeur de l'histoire de l'art* (Paris: Gallimard, 2003), and Elisabeth Decultot, *Johann Joachim Winckelman: Enquête sur la genèse de l'histoire de l'art* (Paris: PUF, 2000).

[24] For discussions of this text, see Christoph Jamme and Helmut Schneider (eds.), *Mythologie der Vernunft: Hegels ältestes Systemprogramm des deutschen Idealismus* (Frankurt am Main: Suhrkamp, 1984).

political spectrum. This new world on the one hand constitutes the fulfillment of the Enlightenment, since it needs to have passed through the moment of sundering and reflection, but it is also a step beyond it. Hegel initially shared something of this Romantic desire to take "the step beyond the Kantian borderline," as Hölderlin calls it in an important letter,[25] and the System Fragment is an obvious case of this, but as we have already remarked, he soon comes to the conclusion that this step or leap must preserve reason and the superior status of philosophy. Absolute knowledge will consist in a conceptual explication of the rational structure of the world, not in any intuitively created work of art or an "intellectual intuition" that lays claim to immediacy. The absolute, Hegel stresses in the preface to the Phenomenology, can neither appear as "shot from out of a pistol," like Fichte's subject, nor can it descend into a "night where all cows are black," like Schelling's absolute qua indifference, but rather can only come at the end, as the result of the totality of conceptual mediations. The Phenomenology, then, will be the project of attaining the absolute beyond the confines of finitude, respecting while also displacing the critical and epistemological claims of Kantianism.

From consciousness to the absolute

The Phenomenology is a sustained and grandiose attempt to lead "natural consciousness" to the completion of absolute knowledge, and to do this by following the movement of consciousness itself. We start off with the most meager of all conceptions of knowledge, "sense-certainty," which claims to have the full richness of the world at its disposal by using words such as "here," "this," and "now," and by trying to hold on to the sensuous particular in its immediacy, either in the form of the object or the subject. This first claim however defeats itself, for as soon as sense-certainty attempts to say what it means, it is forced into the element of universality, which here for Hegel appears as language, the more "truthful" element in the process of *Aufhebung*, the negating yet preserving of the particular. This is the starting point of the dialectic, and it is crucial for Hegel that the movement of

---

[25] Letter to Neuffer, October 10, in Hölderlin, *Sämtliche Werke*, eds. F. Beissner and A. Beck (Stuttgart: Cotta, 1946-85), vol. 6, 137.

negation and preservation not be forced upon consciousness from the outside, by "us," i.e. the narrator and/or reader of the Phenomenology, but that it occur because of the way in which consciousness tests itself by always supposing a standard it subsequently proves unable to live up to. In this way, natural consciousness is driven from station to station, which for it is a painful journey, akin the stations of the cross, an experience of loss and despair that forces it to face up to the power of the negative. For us, who observe this process, the journey means that consciousness attains higher and higher levels of understanding of the necessary intertwining of the world and consciousness, until finally, at the moment of absolute knowing, both come together into a unity which still preserves all the former articulations as an "interiorized" and "remembered" content.

The difficulty with this conception, the implications of which extend beyond Hegel exegesis, is the question whether these two perspectives, the immanence of a finite consciousness that undergoes the experiences and the transcendence of the narrator, who addresses us as the "we" that "knows," can truly be brought together. (There is also the rarely noticed third position of the reader, who knows more than finite consciousness but less than the infinite narrator, and can only be included in the superior narrator called "we" in an insecure and tenuous fashion, which is an experience that most readers can recognize). What type of discourse would be able to bridge the gap between finite and infinite, so as to allow the infinite to emerge out of the finite, while still respecting the strictures of the latter?

This question is further highlighted by the structure of the philosophical system as Hegel sketches it in the preface to the Phenomenology. If the Phenomenology was intended as a "propedeutic" to the true science, and if the latter is identified with the system of categories and absolute determinations of being of which Hegel would subsequently propose a first version in his *Science of Logic* (1812–1816), then this system appears no longer to need, or perhaps even tolerate, a genesis from the point of view of a consciousness that undergoes finite and one-sided experiences. This question whether there can be an "introduction to the *Science of Logic*" was already posed in Hegel's own time, and has been brought up many times since, most recently in the debate sparked by Hans Peter Fulda's *Das Problem einer Einleitung in Hegels Wissenschaft der Logik*, with subsequent responses from

Otto Pöggeler, Werner Marx, and many others.[26] The question at stake can be formulated in different ways, for instance as follows: Does Hegel's Phenomenology already presuppose the structures of the Logic for the movement of dialectics to get started? If this is the case, then the Phenomenology surely cannot be claimed to be a "science" on its own. But what should we then make of the two titles that Hegel puts before the text of the Phenomenology, "Science of the Experience of Consciousness" and "System of Science, Part One: The Phenomenology of Spirit"?

Questions of philology apart—which on the one hand are a result of the confusion concerning titles and subtitles in the Phenomenology, most of which are due to printing errors, and which on the other hand must acknowledge the obvious biographical fact that Hegel's conception had surely evolved between 1807 and 1812, and that his idea of the absolute system was constantly in flux, even at the end—the philosophical problem is to what extent the perspective (which can no longer be a perspective) of absolute knowledge can be harmonized with a situated experience, i.e., how infinity can be reconciled with the finitude of experience. In the preface to the Phenomenology, Hegel speaks of how contemporary consciousness no longer tolerates dogmas and imposed solutions, and that it demands that a "ladder" should be given to it so that it may ascend to the heaven of the concept. But if the ladder is itself part of a science that on the other hand neither needs nor even tolerates it, do we not then see an unbridgeable gulf opening up in the midst of Hegel's system? There would be no way from finitude to infinity, and no way back, once we have passed over to the concept. Modern phenomenological philosophies of finitude, from Husserl to Heidegger, Merleau-Ponty, and onwards, would in this way amount to a return to an immanent perspective: a method that stays within finite consciousness, substitutes the analysis of intentionality, noetic-noematic correlations, and constitution for the false and impossible passage towards infinity promised by Hegel, and rejects the split vision of his system as contradictory and dogmatic metaphysics.

---

[26] See Hans Peter Fulda, *Das Problem einer Einleitung in Hegels Wissenschaft der Logik* (Frankfurt am Main: Klostermann, 1965) and "Zur Logik der 'Phänomenologie' von 1806," in Fulda and Dieter Henrich (eds.), *Materialien zu Hegels "Phänomenologie des Geistes"* (Frankfurt am Main: Suhrkamp, 1979), Otto Pöggeler, "Die Komposition der 'Phänomenologie des Geistes,'" *ibid.*, and Werner Marx, *Hegel's Phenomenology of Spirit*, trans. Peter Heath (Chicago: University of Chicago Press, 1988).

Something similar would also apply to the concept of spirit: For Hegel, at least as he is read traditionally, spirit would be a going beyond of all finite perspectives toward an absolute subject that finds itself in its otherness and returns to itself in the circularity of the ab-solute as that which is ab-solved from external reality. In rejecting the onto-theological structure of the speculative method, modern philosophies of finitude would then be led to view a concept like *Geist* with the utmost suspicion, as the remnant of a theological discourse that can have little or no credibility today. *Geist* in this view is not so much a Cartesian ghost in the machine as the name for an impossible and untenable third-person objectivity of the subject-object correlation, which has to be abandoned if we are to adhere to a strict analytic of finitude, whether this be in the Husserlian or Heideggerian version.[27] Against this, other readings have, as we noted, stressed the pragmatic and social dimension of the term, which too, although from a different perspective, amounts to reading it in the sense of cultural and conceptual finitude. In this sense, Hegel's "spirit" is a concept that either must be rejected, or understood in a way that departs from several of Hegel's own metaphysical and theological presuppositions.

These structural complexities, and the question of whether Hegel consummates something called the "metaphysical" tradition, belong to the systematic horizon against which the Phenomenology as a whole in the final analysis is to be measured. But it must also be stressed that the text as it stands remains an almost infinite resource of philosophical ideas, no matter how we judge its ultimate position inside some Hegelian system, the very existence of which is in fact highly tenuous: if the *Science of Logic* in its first version already testifies to a different view of the system than the one announced in the preface to the Phenomenology, this also shows that the question of the first book's compatibility with the rest of the system must in several respects remain conjectural. Regardless of how we judge the book's

---

[27] Against this "official" version of phenomenology, it has been claimed that the discourse on *Geist* is by no means absent from Husserl and Heidegger, but in fact often surfaces in critical places, as Derrida claims; see *De l'esprit: Heidegger et la question* (Paris: Galilée, 1987). This is particularly connected to the way in which both Husserl and Heidegger conceptualize Occidental history and philosophy, fusing them into a unity where the history of philosophy and the philosophy of history become one gradual unfolding of a singular structure, regardless of whether this is understood as a teleology of reason that has to be saved from the danger of an irresponsible technicism and a forgetfulness of the constitutive role of transcendental subjectivity, as in Husserl's *Krisis*, or as a progressive oblivion of being, where Husserl's recourse to a constituting subjectivity is part of the problem rather than part of the solution, as in Heidegger.

ultimate claim, we still need to traverse the text of the Phenomenology itself, on a path that will take us through a series of "shapes of consciousness" (*Gestalten des Bewusstseins*), and on this long and laborious journey we encounter many figures that after Hegel have become detached from the movement of the Phenomenology as such, and have entered into a general philosophical vocabulary. We move through the dialectic of master and slave, which links together death, desire, and work (perhaps the most famous figure, which through the highly original reading proposed by Kojève in the 1930s became the matrix for a long tradition of philosophies of desire, from Sartre and Bataille to Lacan and Deleuze);[28] unhappy consciousness, which was first emphasized and read as an autonomous problem by Jean Wahl in the 1920s;[29] Antigone and Creon, who in Hegel's reading both believe they are doing the right thing and in this will tear asunder the harmonious fabric of Greek ethical life; the "lacerated language" of *Rameau's Nephew*, which completes the movement of *Bildung* in a vertiginous re-evaluation of all values, and at the end of *l'ancien régime* already proposes something that comes close to Nietzsche's analysis of nihilism; the French revolution and the subsequent terror that, in its affirmation of absolute freedom, unleashes the "fury of destruction"; and the beautiful soul who retreats into himself and his moral certitude, and wants to find peace by always forgiving the crimes of the other. Without here attempting to produce an exhaustive list, we can see the extent to which Hegel's text brings together analyses of philosophical theories and political events, artworks and religious experiences, virtually all the facets of existence in a narrative that claims to be both historical and logical, or, more precisely, includes and transcends both of these categories.

---

[28] For a discussion of this line of interpretation, see Judith Butler, *Subjects of Desire: Hegelian Reflections in Twentieth-Century France* (New York: Columbia University Press, 1987). It must be emphasized that the story of French readings of Hegel does not in fact begin with Kojève. The reception in the 1920s and '30s—where we, apart from Kojève, find Jean Wahl's important *Le malheur de la conscience dans la philosophie de Hegel* (1929), but also works, little known today, by Alain, Victor Basch, and Victor Delbos—attempts to limit the validity of the dialectic to human history and praxis, and forms reaction against earlier readings, even less known today, which presented a panlogicist Hegel whose interpretation of the sciences was highlighted. For a discussion of the first phases of this reception, see Bruce Baugh, *French Hegel: From Surrealism to Postmodernism* (New York: Routledge, 2003), chap. 1.

[29] See the previous note. The influence of Wahl's book on subsequent existential phenomenology is shown by Baugh, *French Hegel*.

Since the publication of the book, the debate has raged as to whether all, or some, or perhaps none of its chapters can be read as a reflection on empirical history. While there is an undeniable presence of historical narration in the book (specifically in the chapters on spirit and religion), and many of the factual events that are obliquely alluded to in the text seem to have a much more important structuring role than that of mere illustrations (this theme is treated in Sven-Olov Wallenstein's contribution below, with particular reference to art) the question remains as to how this squares with the attempt to provide an epistemological and not simply historical explanation of the succession of figures. It has been proposed that the text is in fact is a "palimpsest," resulting from the fact that Hegel changed his outlook in the process of writing or even "lost control" of it,[30] and which should lead us to distinguish between a true and a merely apparent phenomenology. Others have proposed that this structural confusion, especially in the latter half of the book, simply results from a failed because insufficiently thought-through attempt to combine perspectives that in fact are irreconcilable.

Yet many readers perceive Hegel's later and perhaps more coherent versions of the system, as they develop from the first edition of the *Encyclopedia of the Philosophical Sciences* (1817) onwards, as much more sterile and artificially constructed than the dramatic writing of the Phenomenology, precisely because of its violent tensions, enigmatic transitions, and often insane complexity. The contorted architectonic of Hegel's phraseology somehow suggests there was a need for a language of laceration, one that could only be turned into a system at the expense of its violence and labyrinthine beauty. Perhaps this is what Hegel himself discovered toward the end of life, when he planned to revise the text for a new edition—almost immediately after having begun he broke off and noted: "Curious early work, not to be rewritten" ("Eigenthümliche frühere Arbeit, nicht Umarbeiten").[31]

---

[30] See Pöggeler, *Hegels Idee einer Phänomenologie*, 350.
[31] See Hegel's note in Wolfgang Bonsiepen's edition of the Phenomenology in the *Gesammelte Werke*, vol. 9 (Hamburg: Meiner, 1980), 448.

INTRODUCTION

Translating Hegel into the present

The initial question that provided the impetus for this collection was whether it is possible, indeed even desirable, to "translate" Hegel into a contemporary philosophical idiom—be it phenomenology, deconstruction, critical theory, analytical philosophy, or something else entirely. The seeming advantage of a translation in this sense is that it makes Hegel easier to comprehend, and eliminates many of his idiosyncrasies, or at least translates these idiosyncrasies into our own. In creating a context for his thought that would appear to allow it to be assimilated into our present concerns, it sets up a framework that allows us to discern "what is living and what is dead in Hegel," to use Croce's famous formulation.[32] Yet which idiom, or idioms, would be most appropriate to this act of translating? Which type of philosophy is the proper "heir" to Hegelianism? What type of vocabulary would be able to transcribe, in the most faithful way, the language of idealism?

For a long time, enmity towards Hegel was endemic within analytical philosophy (according to Russell, the expulsion of the Hegelian ghost was one of those acts that allowed the analytical tradition to come into its own), whereas in German philosophical culture, he has always been central, at least up to the later phases of the Frankfurt School; since Kojève's lectures in the 1930s, he has been a major influence on French thought, in particular because the creation of a compound "phenomenology" based on the Hegel-Husserl-Heidegger triad provided his texts with an immediate relevance to the present situation. The antagonism in the Hegel reception may have become weaker today, as a "post-analytical" philosophy, drawing on pragmatism, but on other sources as well, begins to look to Hegel for inspiration, although resistance to Hegel has by no means disappeared.

On the other hand, one must also be aware of the risks attending the above sort of "translation." It is not impossible that the "post-metaphysical" Hegel often presented today in fact amounts to a flattening of historical depth, a foreshortening of perspective that deprives his thought of its productive distance and difference with respect to the present. There may be something essentially Hegelian, and not just in the sense of a "historically true" Hegel (for instance his systematic intention, which, if taken at face

---

[32] Benedetto Croce, *Ciò che è vivo e ciò che è morto della filosofia di Hegel* (Bari: Laterza, 1907); *What is living and what is dead of the philosophy of Hegel*, trans. Douglas Ainslie (Kitchener, Ont.: Batoche, 2001).

value, would prohibit a reading that develops some of his ideas while leaving others aside), but in the sense of something that might act as an illuminating counterpoint, or even as a challenge, to the present, that gets lost in this translation.

The question is whether "translating" could mean something other than a mere transposition of one vocabulary into another, for example: might it allow for a kind of transformation of both the present and the past? Is there something like a "hermeneutic situation" (as the concept is developed by Heidegger) that should guide our relation to Hegel today? And if this "situation" were to be determined as the end of metaphysics—versions of which, in addition to the Heideggerian, have indeed proliferated in modernity: the overturning of Platonism, the death of God, the impossibility of a philosophical system, the dissolution of philosophy into the sciences, and for that matter the idea of a "postmetaphysical" philosophy—what would this imply for our reading of Hegel, who was the first to proclaim the end of metaphysics (albeit in terms of its completion and fulfillment)?

Finally, and at a more straightforward level, there is the question of the extent to which the above bears upon the practice of the translator of Hegel. (A question addressed in the contributions of Delaney and Lefebvre.) Hegel's German, especially in the Phenomenology, was a very unusual German—a violent stretching and bending of the limits of syntax according to the logic of the "speculative proposition" delineated in the preface: a "conflict between the form of a proposition per se and the unity of the concept which destroys that form," producing a discourse that "destroys the distinction between subject and predicate" to such an extent that it is "only the kind of philosophical exposition which rigorously excludes the ordinary relations among the parts of a proposition which would be able to achieve the goal of plasticity."[33] The general questions posed above of the appropriate contemporary "idiom" for Hegelianism bear on the choices of the translator, and, of course, the translator's choices affect the contemporary reception of Hegel.

---

[33] Translation from Terry Pinkard's still unpublished translation (2008), currently (2011-07-27) available online at: http://web.mac.com/titpaul/Site/Phenomenology_of_Spirit_page.html.

INTRODUCTION

The contributions in this volume

The first contribution, Robert Pippin's "On Hegel's Claim that Self-Consciousness is 'Desire in General' ('Begierde überhaupt')" takes its point of departure in the chapter on self-consciousness. This claim about self-consciousness, Pippin suggests, is embedded in a complex and highly counterintuitive general position on self-consciousness. That position is: from the minimal sense of being aware of being determinately conscious at all (apperception), to complex avowals of who I am, of my own identity and deep commitments, Hegel develops a notion of self-consciousness as a practical achievement of some sort. It must be understood as the result of an attempt, and never, as it certainly seems to be, as an immediate presence, and it often requires some sort of struggle. And furthermore, he sees such an attempt and achievement as necessarily involving a relation to other people, as inherently social. The crucial turning point in his argument is the claim that self-consciousness should be understood as "desire in general."

Pippin begins by highlighting the importance of Kantian apperception in the first four chapters of the Phenomenology. This helps us see not simply how the self-consciousness chapter is rooted in fundamentally Kantian philosophical concerns, but, more importantly, is also much more continuous with the previous three chapters of the Phenomenology. To be sure, others have argued for the continuity of the first four chapters. McDowell, for example, contends that the topics of "desire" and "life" in chapter four are simply different ways of talking about the relation between a subject and object, their mutual dependence and independence—in other words, it is a continuation and attempt to finish off the problems remaining at the end of chapter three. For Pippin the issue is more focused on the nature of apperception—just what it is for a being to be not simply a recorder of the world's impact on one's senses, but to be for itself in its engagements with objects—and how Hegel believes this must become a question of our practical engagement with the world, with others.

Like Pippin, Walter Jaeschke begins with the relevance of Hegel's predecessors, with a focus specifically on Schelling and Fichte. On the basis of transcendental-philosophical conceptions of a "history of self-consciousness," Hegel's Phenomenology is reinterpreted—in light of the conditions of its genesis as a "*genealogy* of consciousness"—as a "genealogy of *spirit*," which for the first time displays the constitutive significance of the historical formation of knowledge for knowledge itself. Jaeschke traces the historical background of this new project, including the important but still obscure details of how and when Hegel conceived the idea that the history of self-consciousness falls within time.

Because the historical path of the experience of self-consciousness is, finally, the path of becoming science, the Phenomenology takes on the function of an introduction to Hegel's System of Science. Beyond the questions for Hegel scholars about the role of the Phenomenology in the rest of Hegel's system, there is also the matter of transforming the problems posed by the Phenomenology into, or seeing them as applicable to, present problems and methods in philosophy. After all, the question of the relation of continually unfolding spheres of objective spirit to one another, and to absolute spirit, has by no means been solved, nor perhaps even adequately posed.

If there is anything associated with Hegel, rightly or wrongly, it's the notion of the historical nature of truth. Nonetheless, Hegel by no means wants to give up the role of philosophy as the contemplation of eternal truths. Terry Pinkard argues in his contribution that the final chapter of the Phenomenology, "Absolute Knowledge," is about precisely the harmonization of these two seemingly mutually contradictory aspects: that philosophy is the contemplation of eternal truths, and that philosophy is its own time grasped in thoughts.

The final chapter, "Absolute Knowledge," has often been claimed to be the most difficult chapter in an already excruciatingly difficult work. Hegel attempts not just to summarize the entire path traversed by consciousnesses, but also to explain absolute knowledge. Part of what we learn in the Phenomenology is that a concept cannot be understood, or even exist, apart from its being put into practice. The concept of sense-certainty qua absolute judgment, for example, means nothing until we try to "realize" it, at which point we grasp it, and also see its limits. How is absolute knowledge realized? Knowing, Hegel tells us in the penultimate paragraph of the book, finally sees itself as historically contingent, its grasp of itself is like seeing a "gallery of pictures": grasping the particularities of our historical development is the contingent; whereas grasping *that* spirit is historical is the timeless.

The last chapter of the Phenomenology is also the point of departure for Susanna Lindberg's contribution. "Absolute Knowledge," which presents the ultimate *Aufhebung* of the book—the passage from finitude to infinity, from representation to concept—is examined from the point of view of

Heidegger's critique of Hegel. Heidegger holds that Hegel suppresses time, ends history, and destroys the possibility of finite thinking.

Lindberg argues that, on the contrary, the concept actually produces time; it is liberated in the form of nature and the past, instead of being enslaved. Indeed, Heidegger's selective readings of Hegel have acted as a provocation, which has lead many scholars to show how Hegelian thinking could actually be a thinking of a finite, contingent, natural, and figurative reality. Lindberg presents an interpretation of spirit in a similar vein: spirit is not a separate absolute cogito, but pure activity, a force of figuration and defiguration. Such a spirit is not the opposite of finite reality: it is infinite existence and a thinking of the finite.

Carl-Göran Heidegren is the first to have published a book-length commentary on the Phenomenology in a Scandinavian language (*Hegels Fenomenologi: En analys och kommentar*, 1995). Here, he addresses a number of fundamental structural matters involved in interpreting the Phenomenology. These include the problem of the two titles, and the two separate tables of content.

Rather than choosing between the two tables of content, Heidegren grounds an interpretation in the dynamic internal to consciousness described by Hegel in the introduction, that consciousness develops via a comparison between its object and the "in itself"—what it takes to be the measure of the truth of its object. From this he develops a unique ordering of the experience of consciousness into different "spheres," from the experience of "something other than itself" at the beginning of the book, through the experience of itself as "absolute in the form of picture-thinking" directly before Absolute Knowledge.

Staffan Carlshamre's contribution, "Hegel's Anomalous Functionalism," also comments on some structural questions posed by the book's bewildering table of contents, arguing that reason is both the third of a first triad (C in one numbering), and the first of a second triad (AA in the next triad of reason-spirit-religion): subject and object are united in reason after the self-consciousness chapter, but this also makes reason able to play the objective role in which spirit represents the subjective pole.

Carlshamre's primary interest here is, however, "observing reason." The pattern of triads recurs at many levels in the Phenomenology, and observing reason is the first of three parts of the reason chapter. Observing reason itself has three main sections—the observation of physical nature, the observation of the psyche, and the observation of the psycho-physical relation between the body and the mind. Carlshamre points out the contemporary relevance of Hegel's discussion by highlighting his anti-reductionism, a position Hegel maintains for conceptual rather than metaphysical reasons. Biological categories cannot be reduced to the categories of physics and chemistry; indeed, Hegel argues that there can be no scientific laws connecting the two domains—as hinted in the title of this article, his argument to that effect bears a certain resemblance to Donald Davidson's argument for the anomalousness of the mental.

Victoria Fareld's contribution explores the ways in which Hegel's philosophy could be made into a key element in a political philosophy which begins not with reason, sociality, or autonomy, but rather with exposure, vulnerability, and dependence. She thus translates Hegel into our time less by focusing on the historical context of his philosophy than by seeking new, contemporary contexts for his ideas.

Fareld understands the dependence that is manifest in the struggle for recognition as a state of being *exposed*. Understanding this dependence as exposure makes possible a shift of focus from recognition to recognizability. This, in turn, involves a shift from the relation between self and other to the social space and the practices governing it. The emphasis on the larger social process of recognizability raises a number of questions: Under what conditions, under what social norms, is an individual recognizable as a unique individual? What are the mechanisms that make some people unrecognizable? Finally, she offers an argument for the contemporary relevance of a certain way of thinking dialectically, by exploring the condition of what she refers to as being made "dialectically redundant"—a situation where some people appear as non-recognizable, by being dialectically abandoned.

Sven-Olov Wallenstein investigates the dual role played by artworks and aesthetic artifacts in Hegel's writing. In Hegel's many varying statements on art, beginning with the earliest texts, moving through the Phenomenology and up through the last lectures on aesthetics, art is present in two senses. On the one hand, it is an object of analysis, and its role is circumscribed within the logic of a historical narrative that treats it in terms of its capacity to provide us with an adequate presentation of the movement of the concept. In the Phenomenology, art thus gradually emerges from out of its intertwinement with religion and finally reaches the state of "absolute art"—and this is where it ends, in Greek comedy and a momentary state of happiness, both unprecedented and without sequel, where man feels completely at home in the world, but at the price of his own substance. In this, the Phenomenology can be taken already to prefigure the later theses on art that hold it to be a "thing of the past," something that must be superseded by philosophy as an adequate way of grasping the concept in the medium of thought itself.

On the other hand, artworks often seem to function as what could be called "operators." In this respect, they operate as models for thought that appear at strategically located junctures in the text, halfway between conceptual articulations, which as such would be indispensable, and illustrations, which would be merely sensuous and particular representations of properly conceptual structures. This use of art as a philosophical tool doesn't simply contradict the theses on art as a thing of the past with respect to its "highest aim," but in fact draws Hegel close to some of Schelling's ideas about art as an "organon," and opens up the possibility of a different type of exchange between art and philosophy that constitutes one of the most vital aspects of the Hegelian heritage in contemporary philosophy of art

Pirmin Stekeler-Weithofer argues that questions of translations and interpretation of a philosophical author cannot be separated from questions concerning the main topics and aims, the overall structure and the path of the argument(s). With respect to the Phenomenology, this seems even more true than with most other texts in the history of philosophy. Stekeler-Weithofer proposes a reading of the text as a work of conceptual clarification: it is a series of deconstructions of our ideas about ourselves, our knowledge of and practical reference to things and to ourselves, and a contribution to an analysis of the institutional status of understanding, reason, intelligence, and spirit.

As an example of this, he undertakes a close reading of the opening part of the chapter on self-consciousness (which addresses many of the themes treated in Robert Pippin's text), suggesting that we here encounter a fundamental analysis of sociality that does not yet presuppose persons that are able to act intentionally, but understands them as already conditioned by social institutions.

The final two contributions deal with the act of translating the text of the Phenomenology itself. Brian Manning Delaney, who, with Sven-Olov Wallenstein, translated the Phenomenology into Swedish, compares the challenges of translating Hegel into Swedish with the challenges of translating Hegel into another Germanic language, English. He begins by pointing out how the mere fact of the difficulty of Hegel's German makes translating him into any language extremely challenging. He shows how aspects of the multiple meanings of German words can be more naturally captured in Swedish, while the relative flexibility of English grammar, along with its vast vocabulary, makes possible more precise translation choices.

Although German and English are, historically, more closely related than German and Swedish, German and Swedish are both "original" languages, in Vico's sense, and this makes the literal senses of the words more palpable. Yet this means that when the roots of a Swedish word are different from those of the German word it translates— which, because of the historical distance between German and Swedish, they often are—the "valence" of Hegel's text will seem very different to reader of Swedish; for example, Geist ("a furious wind" to a German, like a ghost almost) might be, as *ande* in Swedish, softer and more "airy"; an object (*Gegenstand*) doesn't so much resist ("stand against") as provide an objective, or goal (*föremål* in Swedish- "the goal before one"). This different feel might not necessarily be an inaccuracy, but is perhaps rather an enrichment in our understanding of Hegel, a new perspective on a thinker who is bound to remain enigmatic. Given the difficulty of understanding Hegel, the enrichment provided by a translation into a new language, with a distinct history, or even by new translations into languages into which Hegel has already been translated, likely exceeds any unavoidable loss in fidelity.

Jean-Pierre Lefebvre, who translated the Phenomenology into French in 1991, presents an analysis of the challenges of translating Hegel into French. One important factor at play in his own translation that is absent in the work of the Swedish translator of Hegel is a long tradition of translation of philosophical texts from German to French. This itself has changed the nature of translation, and even the nature of French philosophizing. Whatever the existing storehouse of accepted—or partly accepted— translation choices may make available, the historical distance of French from German creates a particular challenge for the French translator.

On a more technical level, Lefebvre discusses the idea of *parasitage*, the relation that a word, in its own language, exhibits in relation to its semantic and thus cultural periphery, which prohibits a word-to-word translation, and calls for an attentive understanding of the way in which language has an economy, and limits the use of a purely technical vocabulary. Everyday language, in this sense, is what philosophy must draw upon, but philosophy also transforms it in an act of constant creation.

INTRODUCTION

* * *

This collection of texts has its origin in a symposium dedicated to Hegel's Phenomenology, held at the Goethe Institute in Stockholm (September 5–7, 2008), on the occasion of the first Swedish translation of the text. In this sense, the general rubric, "Translating Hegel," took its cues from the particularity of this occasion—which itself was a philosophical event, since the Phenomenology had to wait more than 200 years to be translated into Swedish—but also attempts to span a whole set of general philosophical problems.

We would like to thank the Goethe Institute for hosting the event as well as supporting it financially, the Department of Culture and Communication and the Publications Committee at Södertörn University, and the Foundation for Baltic and East European Studies, whose generous support was essential both in organizing and in producing this book.

Stockholm, May 2012

Brian Manning Delaney
Sven-Olov Wallenstein

On Hegel's Claim that Self-Consciousness is "Desire Itself" *(Begierde überhaupt)*

ROBERT B. PIPPIN

I

Kant held that what distinguishes an object in our experience from the mere subjective play of representations is rule-governed unity. His famous definition of an object is just "that in the concept of which a manifold is united." (B137) This means that consciousness itself must be understood as a discriminating, unifying activity, paradigmatically as judging, and not as the passive recorder of sensory impressions. Such a claim opens up a vast territory of possibilities and questions since Kant does not mean that our awake attentiveness is to be understood as something we intentionally *do*, in the standard sense, even if it is not also a mere event that happens to us, as if we happen to be triggered into a determinate mental state, or as if sensory stimuli just activate an active mental machinery.

Kant also clearly does not mean to suggest by his claim that "the form of consciousness is a judgmental form" that consciousness consists of thousands of very rapid judgmental claims being deliberately made, thousands of "S is P's" or "If A then B's" taking place. The world is taken to be such and such without such takings being isolatable, intentional actions. What Kant *does* mean by understanding consciousness as "synthetic" is quite a formidable, independent topic in itself.[1]

Now Kant's main interest in the argument of the deduction was to show first that the rules governing such activities (whatever the right way to describe such activities) cannot be wholly empirical rules, all derived from

---

[1] I present an interpretation of the point in "What is Conceptual Activity?" forthcoming in *The Myth of the Mental?*, ed. J. Shear.

experience, that there must be rules for the derivation of such rules that cannot themselves be derived, or that there must be pure concepts of the understanding; and secondly that these non-derived rules have genuine "objective validity," are not subjective impositions on an independently received manifold, that, as he puts it, the a priori prescribed "synthetic unity of consciousness" "[…] is not merely a condition that I myself require in knowing an object, but is a condition under which any intuition must stand in order to become an object for me." (B138) Kant seems to realize that he gives the impression that for him consciousness is a two-step process; the mere reception of sensory data, and then the conceptualization of such data, but he works hard in the pursuit of the second desideratum to disabuse his readers of that impression.

Aside from some Kant scholars, there are not many philosophers who still believe that Kant proved in this argument that we possess synthetic a priori knowledge, although there is wide admiration for the power of Kant's arguments about, at least, causality and substance. But there remains a great deal of interest in his basic picture of the nature of conscious mindedness. For the central component of his account, judgment, is, as already noted, not a mental event that merely happens, as if causally triggered into its synthetic activity by sensory stimuli. Judging, while not a practical action initiated by a decision, is an *activity* sustained and resolved, sometimes in conditions of uncertainty, *by* a subject and that means that it is normatively structured. The rules of judgment governing such activity are rules about what ought to be judged, how our experience ought to be organized (we distinguish, judge, for example, successive perceptions of a stable object as really simultaneous in time, and not actually representing something successive). Such rules are not rules describing how we do judge, are not psychological laws of thought. And, to come to the point of contact with Hegel that is the subject of the following, this all means that consciousness must be inherently *reflective or apperceptive*. (I cannot be *sustaining an activity*, implicitly trying to get, say, the objective temporal order right in making up my mind, without in some sense knowing I am so taking the world to be such, or without apperceptively taking it so. I am taking or construing rather than merely recording *because* I am also in such taking holding open the possibility that I may be taking falsely.) So all consciousness is inherently, though rarely explicitly, self-conscious. It is incorrect to think of a conscious state as just filled with the rich details of a house-perception, as if consciousness merely registers its presence; I take or judge the presence of a house, not a barn or gas station; or in Kant's famous formula: "the '*I think*' must be able to accompany all my representations." But what could be meant by "inherently," or "*in some sense* knowing I am taking or judging it to be such and such"? In *what* sense am I in *a relation to myself* in any conscious relation to an object? That is, the claim is that all consciousness involves a kind of self-consciousness, taking S to be P and thus taking myself to be taking S is P. But in a self-relation like this the self in question cannot be just another object of intentional awareness. If it were, then there would obviously be a regress problem. By parity of whatever reasoning established that the self must be able to *observe* itself as an object in taking anything to be anything, one would have to also argue that the *observing* self must also be observable, and so one. The self-relation, whatever it is, cannot be a two-place intentional relation.²

II

Hegel's own most famous discussion of these issues is found in the first four chapters of his 1807 *Phenomenology of Spirit* (PhG hereafter). The first three chapters of that book are grouped together under the heading "Consciousness" and the fourth chapter is called simply "Self-Consciousness." (This fourth chapter has only one sub-section, called "The Truth of Self-Certainty" and that will be the focus of the following discussion.³) Accordingly, especially given the extraordinarily sweeping claims Hegel makes about his indebtedness to the Kantian doctrine of apperception,⁴ one

---

² The post-Kantian philosopher who first made a great deal out of this point was Fichte, and the modern commentator who has done the most to work out the philosophical implications of the point has been Dieter Henrich, starting with *Fichtes ursprüngliche Einsicht* (Frankfurt am Main: Klostermann, 1967).
³ This is quite a typical Hegelian title, and can be misleading. By "The Truth of Self-Certainty" (Die Wahrheit der Gewißheit seiner selbst), Hegel does *not* mean, as he seems to, the truth *about* the self's certainty of itself. He actually means, as we shall see, that the *truth* of self-certainty is not a matter of self-certainty at all, just as sense-certainty was not certain. This relation between subjective certainty and its realization in truth is a basic structure of the PhG. Its most basic form is something like: the truth of the inner is the outer, rather than anything suggested by the title (as in: how to explain the fact of such self-certainty).
⁴ "It is one of the profoundest and truest insights to be found in the *Critique of Pure Reason* that the unity which constitutes the unity of the *Begriff* is recognized as the original synthetic unity of apperception, as the unity of the I think, or of self-consciousness." *Wissenschaft der Logik*, Bd. 12 in *Gesammelte Werke*, ed. Rheinisch-

would expect that these sections have something to do with the Kantian points noted above, and so with the issue of the self-conscious character of experience and the conditions for the possibility of experience so understood. But there has been a lot of understandable controversy about the relation between the first three chapters and the fourth. Since the fourth chapter discusses desire, life, a struggle to the death for recognition between opposed subjects, and a resulting Lord-Bondsman social structure, it has not been easy to see how the discussion of sense-certainty, perception and the understanding is being *continued*. Some very influential commentators, like Alexandre Kojève, pay almost no attention to the first three chapters. They write as if we should isolate the chapter on Self-Consciousness as a free-standing philosophical anthropology, a theory of the inherently violent and class-riven nature of human sociality. (There are never simply human beings in Kojève's account. Until the final bloody revolution ushers in a classless society, there are only Masters and Slaves.) Others argue that in chapter four, Hegel simply changes the subject to the problem of sociality. We can see why it might be natural for him to change the subject at this point, but it is a different subject. (Having introduced the necessary role of self-consciousness in consciousness, Hegel understandably changes the topic to very broad and different questions like: what, in general, *is* self-consciousness? What is a self? What is it to be a being "for which" things can be, to use Brandom's language, who offers his own version of the change-of-subject interpretation.)[5] More recently, some commentators, like John McDowell and Pirmin Stekeler-Weithofer, have argued that there is actually neither a new beginning nor a shift in topics in chapter four. In McDowell's treatment the problem is an extension and development of the

---

Westfälischen Akademie der Wissenschaften (Hamburg: Felix Meiner, 1968 -), 221; *Science of Logic*, trans. A. V. Miller (Amherst: Humanity Books, 1969), 584.

[5] There are other interpretations which tend to isolate the argument in chapter four in other ways, construing it as a kind of "transcendental argument" that aims to prove that the "consciousness of one's self requires the recognition of another self." Axel Honneth, "From Desire to Recognition: Hegel's Account of Human Sociality" (ms forthcoming). On *that* issue itself ("*from* desire *to* recognition") and on the one and a half pages of argument in Hegel that seek to establish this, Honneth has a number of valuable things to say. But, as I will be arguing, no convincing interpretation of the chapter is possible that does not explain the underlying structure of the "Consciousness-Self-Consciousness" argument in the book as a whole. And I don't believe that Honneth's very brief remarks about understanding ourselves as "creators of true claims" or "the rational individual [...] aware of its constitutive, world-creating cognitive acts" presents that structure accurately.

one that emerged in the first three chapters but still basically concerns that issue: how to understand the right "equipoise" between independence and dependence in the relations between subjects and objects. What appear to be the orectic and social issues of chapter four are for McDowell "figures" or analogies for what remains the problem of the mind's passive dependence on objects and active independence of them in our experience of the world, in just the sense sketched above in the summary of Kant (i.e. neither independent subjective imposition, nor merely passive receptive dependence). What we have is a picture of our active, spontaneous self in a kind of mythic confrontation and struggle with its own passive empirical self, struggling at first, futilely for radical independence, and then an initial but doomed relation of dominance (as if the soul tries to make of its own corporeal nature a *Knecht* or mere servant). So for McDowell, by "desire" Hegel does not mean to introduce the topic of desire as a necessary element in the understanding of *consciousness* itself (as the text, however counterintuitively, would seem to imply). Rather, says McDowell, "'Desire überhaupt' functions as a figure for the general idea of negating otherness, by appropriating or consuming, incorporating into oneself what at first figures as merely other, something that happens in perception, say."[6] And "life," the next topic in the chapter, is said to exemplify the structure of *der Begriff*; let us say: the basic logical structure of all possible intelligibility, all sense-making.[7] The struggle to the death for recognition is said to be a rich and colorful "allegory" of the possible relations of the independent and dependent sides within one consciousness. And so McDowell asserts that chapter four does not yet directly introduce the issue of sociality at all, despite the famous phrase there about the new presence of an "I that is a We and a We that is an I."

This interpretation has the very great virtue of preserving a connection with the first three chapters, but, I will argue, while the general issue of the logic of the relation between independence and dependence is certainly applicable to the relation between spontaneous apperception and the passive empirical self, McDowell's interpretation, however rich in itself, fails

---

[6] John McDowell, "The Apperceptive I and the Emprical Self: Towards a Heterodox Reading of 'Lordship and Bondage' in Hegel's *Phenomenology*," in *Hegel: New Directions,* ed. Katerina Deligiorgi (Chesham: Acumen, 2007), 38.

[7] Especially the relation between universal and particular. And there is a good deal of truth in that characterization. The experiencing subject inevitably becomes aware of itself as a living being of a kind, something it shares with all other such beings, and itself as a singular subject, whose own life is not "life" in general or its species-life.

to do justice to the radicality of what Hegel actually proposes. I want to argue that Hegel means what he says when he says that self-consciousness *is* "desire überhaupt,"[8] if it is to be relevant to the question of the apperceptive nature of consciousness itself, and that this *thereby* provides the basis for the claim that self-consciousness attains its satisfaction only in another self-consciousness.[9]

So here stated all at once is the thesis I would like to attribute to Hegel. (That is, in chapter four. As noted, the entire book is a meditation on self-consciousness, on the becoming self-consciousness of *Geist*.) I think that Hegel's position is that we misunderstand all dimensions of self-consciousness, from apperception in consciousness itself, to simple, explicit reflection on myself, to practical self-knowledge of my own so-called "identity," by considering any form of it as in any way observational or inferential or immediate or any sort of two-place intentional relation. However we come to know anything about ourselves (or whatever self-relation is implicit in attending to the world), it is not by observing an object, nor by conceptualizing an inner intuition, nor by any immediate self-certainty or direct presence of the self to itself. From the minimal sense of being aware of being determinately conscious at all (of judging), to complex avowals of who I am, of my own identity and deep commitments, Hegel, I want to say, treats self-consciousness as (i) a practical *achievement*

---

[8] Hegel's developmental procedure here requires a general cautionary note. The identification of self-consciousness with desire occurs at a very early stage, as Hegel begins to assemble the various dimensions and elements he thinks we will need in order to understand the self-conscious dimension of consciousness. Initially Hegel is only saying: we have *at least* to understand that self-consciousness must be understood as mere desire (another sensible translation of "Begierde überhaupt"). It will prove impossible to consider such self-consciousness *as merely desire* and nothing else, and that impossibility is the rest of the story of the chapter. But this procedure means that from now on self-consciousness must be still understood as inherently orectic, whatever else it is.

[9] Brandom also thinks of the PhG as an allegory; in his case an allegory of various dimensions of the issue of conceptual content. Robert Brandom, "The Structure of Desire and Recognition: Self-Consciousness and Self-Constitution," *Philosophy and Social Criticism*, 33 (2007), (hereafter SDR). For example, he thinks of Hegel's treatment of the struggle to the death as a "metonymy" for the issue of commitment (of "really" being committed). But it is only that, one of many exemplifications of what it means in fact to have the commitment that one avows. Being willing to lose one's job, for example, could be another exemplification. Here and throughout, I want to resist such allegorical or figurative interpretations in both Brandom's and McDowell's accounts.

of some sort.¹⁰ Such a relation must be understood as the *result of an attempt*, never, as it certainly seems to be, as an immediate presence of the self to itself, and it often requires some sort of striving, even struggle (and all of this even in accounting for the self-conscious dimension of ordinary perceptual experience.) It, in all its forms, is some mode of mindedness that we must achieve, and that must mean: can ultimately fail to achieve fully and once having achieved can lose. It is nothing like turning the mind's eye inward to inspect itself. Admittedly, it seems *very* hard to understand why anyone would think that my awareness, say, not just of the lecture I am giving, but whatever kind of awareness I have that I am in the process of giving a lecture, am actually following the appropriate rules, should involve any such practical activity. It seems so effortless to be so self-aware; there is no felt desire or striving or struggle involved, and as a report of what seems to me to be the case, it even appears incorrigible. But Hegel wants to claim that as soon as we properly see the error of holding that the self in any self-awareness is immediately present to an inspecting mind, his own interpretation is just thereby implied. If the self's relation to itself *cannot* be immediate or direct, but if some self-relation is a condition of intentional awareness, the conclusion that it is some sort of *to-be-achieved* follows for him straightforwardly.¹¹ Even a minimal form of self-conscious taking opens up the possibility of taking falsely or in a way inconsistent with other (or all) such takings and so sets a certain sort of task. More on this in a minute; this is the central motive for his version of the claim that consciousness is apperceptive.¹²

---

¹⁰ This is contrary to the interpretation by Fred Neuhouser, "Desire, Recognition, and the Relation between Bondsman and Lord, in *The Blackwell Guide to Hegel's Phenomenology*, ed. K. Westphal (Oxford: Wiley-Blackwell, 2009), 37-54, who argues that Hegel in effect changes the subject from apperception to a practical self-conception and self-evaluation. I think Hegel's presentation is motivated by the internal inadequacies of the Kantian notion of apperception. Without that issue in view, we won't have a sense of *why* the problem of self-consciousness's unity with itself should emerge here, which such a unity "must become essential to it" and the discussion of a single self-conscious being certain of its own radical and complete independence (*Selbstständigkeit*) will have to appear unmotivated, simply a new theme. Cf. 42.
¹¹ So self-consciousness, while not "thetic," to use the Sartrean word, or intentional or positional, is *sort of* or *vaguely* positional, caught at the corner of our eye, or glimpsed on the horizon. It is not intentional at all.
¹² John McDowell has suggested (in a response to a presentation of an earlier version of this lecture at the Kokonas Symposium at Colgate University in November 2008) that the notion of "achievement" is a misleading term here, that whatever achievement is involved in being able to judge apperceptively should be understood along the model of

Another way of putting this point, one that ties in with almost every aspect of Hegel's philosophical approach, would be to point out that if self-consciousness or any form of taking oneself to be or be committed to anything is not introspective or observational then it must always be *provisional*. Such a self-regard requires some confirmation or realization out in the world and for others for it to count as what it is taken to be. The clearest examples of this occur in Hegel's theory of agency where one cannot be said to actually have the intention or commitment one avows, even sincerely avows, until one actually realizes that intention and the action counts as that action in the social world within which it is enacted. (And of course, people can come to find out that their actual intentions, as manifested in what they actually are willing to do, can be very different from those they avow, even sincerely avow.)[13]

And (ii) he sees such an attempt and achievement as necessarily involving a relation to other people, as inherently social. This last issue about the role of actualization begins to introduce such a dependence, but it is hard to see at the outset why other people need be involved in the intimacy and privacy that seems to characterize my relation to myself.

---

learning a language, of being initiated into a linguistic community, something that involves no notion of struggle or practical achievement in the usual sense. It just happens. But (a) Hegel is here describing just the minimal conditions for such a capacity to be in effect and it is only as he explores the implications of the realization of this capacity that he introduces the orectic and social issues that follow and (b) what Hegel is describing is like the acquisition of a linguistic capacity as long as we admit that such an acquisition finally has to involve much more than acquiring rules of grammatical correctness. To be initiated into a linguistic community is to be initiated into all the pragmatic dimensions of appropriateness, authority, who gets to say what, when and why. One is not a "speaker" as such until one has learned such matters of linguistic usage and Hegel wants to treat such norms in terms of their historical conditions, primarily in this chapter the social conditions and social conflict "behind" any such norms. See also his "On Pippin's Postscript," in *Having the World in View* (Cambridge: Harvard University Press, 2009). Cf. Habermas's account of what a full pragmatics of language has to take in, how full initiation into a linguistic community means that speakers "no longer relate *straightaway* to something in the objective, social, or subjective worlds; instead they relativize their utterances against the possibility that their validity will be contested by other actors." Jürgen Habermas, *The Theory of Communicative Action*, trans. Thomas McCarthy (Boston: Beacon Press, 1984) Vol. I, 98-99. In Hegel's account, the standards for this unique kind of challenge to a speaker or agent cannot be made out transcendentally or "quasi-transcendentally," as Habermas sometimes says, but will require the unusual reconstructive phenomenology under consideration here.

[13] This issue is the central one and is explored at length in my *Hegel's Practical Philosophy: Rational Agency as Ethical Life* (Cambridge: Cambridge University Press, 2008).

His case for looking at things this way has three main parts. In a way that is typical of his procedure, he tries to begin with the most theoretically thin or simple form of the required self-relation and so considers the mere sentiment of self that a living being has in *keeping itself alive*, where *keeping itself alive* reflects this minimal reflective attentiveness to self. Such a minimal form of self-relatedness is shown not to establish the sort of self-relatedness (normative self-determination) required as the desideratum in the first three chapters. He then asks what alters when the object of the desires relevant to maintaining life turns out not to be just another object or obstacle but another subject and, in effect, he argues that everything changes when our desires are not just thwarted or impeded, but challenged and refused. And he then explores how the presence of such an other subject, in altering what could be a possible self-relation, sets a new agenda for the rest of the *Phenomenology*, for both the problems of sapience and agency.

III

The central passage where the putative "practical turn" in all this takes place is the following.

> But this opposition between its appearance and its truth has only the truth for its essence, namely, the unity of self-consciousness with itself. This unity must become essential to self-consciousness, which is to say, self-consciousness is *desire* itself. (§167) ("*Begierde überhaupt*," which could also be translated as "desire in general," or "desire, generally" or "mere desire." I am following here Terry Pinkard's translation.)[14]

The passage presupposes the larger issue we have been discussing—the way Hegel has come to discuss the double nature of consciousness (consciousness of an object, a this-such, and the non-positional consciousness or implicit awareness of my taking it to be this-such)[15] and so the opposition, or, as he says, the "negativity" this introduces within consciousness, the fact

---

[14] Pinkard's translation is a valuable facing-page translation and is available at http://web.me.com/titpaul/Site/Phenomenology_of_Spirit_page.html. The paragraph numbers in the text refer to his translation as well.

[15] "As self-consciousness, consciousness henceforth has a doubled object: The first, the immediate object, the object of sense-certainty and perception, which, however, is marked *for it* with the *character of the negative*; the second, namely, *itself*, which is the true *essence* and which at the outset is on hand merely in opposition to the first." (§167)

that consciousness is not simply absorbed into ("identified with") its contents, but has also, let us say, taken up a position toward what it thinks.[16] To understand this, we need the following passage from the Introduction.

> However, consciousness is for itself its concept, and as a result it immediately goes beyond the restriction, and, since this restriction belongs to itself, it goes beyond itself too. (§80)[17]

He is actually making two claims here. The first is the premise of his inference: that "consciousness is for itself its concept." The inference seems to run: If we understand *this* properly, we will understand why he feels entitled to the "and as a result," the claim that consciousness is thereby immediately "beyond" any such restriction or concept that it sets "for itself." (I want to claim that this all amounts to a defense of the claim that consciousness must be understood as apperceptive.) He means to say that normative standards and proprieties at play in human consciousness are "consciousness's own," that is, are *followed* by a subject, are not psychological laws of thought. This is his version of the Kantian principle that persons are subject to no law or norm other than ones they have subjected themselves to.[18] (This is what is packed into the "for itself" here.) This does not mean either in Kant or in Hegel that there are episodes of self-subjection or explicit acts of allegiance or anything as ridiculous as all that;

---

[16] His formulation later in the *Berlin Phenomenology* is especially clear: "There can be no consciousness without self-consciousness. I know something, and that about which I know something I have in the certainty of myself ["das wovon ich weiss habe ich in der Gewissheit meiner selbst"] otherwise I would know nothing of it; the object is my object, it is other and at the same time mine, and in this latter respect I am self-relating." G. W. F. Hegel: *The Berlin Phenomenology*, trans. M. Petry (Dordrecht: Riedel, 1981), (hereafter, BPhG), 55.

[17] He also introduces here a claim that will recur much more prominently in this account of the difference between animal and human desire. "However, to knowledge, the goal is as necessarily fixed as the series of the progression. The goal lies at that point where knowledge no longer has the need to go beyond itself, that is, where knowledge works itself out, and where the concept corresponds to the object and the object to the concept. Progress towards this goal is thus also unrelenting, and satisfaction [n.b. the introduction of *Befriedigung*] is not to be found at any prior station on the way. What is limited to a natural life is not on its own capable of going beyond its immediate existence. However, it is driven out of itself by something other than itself, and this being torn out of itself is its death." (§80).

[18] This principle is of course primarily at home in Kant's practical philosophy, but it is also at work in the theoretical philosophy, particularly where Kant wants to distinguish his own account of experiential mindedness from Locke's or Hume's.

just that norms governing what we think and do can be said to govern thought and action only in so far as subjects, however implicitly or habitually or unreflectively (or as a matter of "second nature"), accept such constraints and sustain allegiance; they follow the rules, are not governed by them. (As all the post-Wittgensteinean discussion of rule-following has shown, there cannot be any rules for the following of these rules, so one can be said to be following such rules in carrying out what is required without any explicit calculation of how to do so.) How the allegiance gets instituted and how it can lose its grip are matters Hegel is very interested in, but it has nothing to do with individuals "deciding" about allegiances at moments of time.) Or, to invoke Kant again, knowers and doers are not explicable as beings subject to laws of nature (although as also ordinary objects, they *are* so subject), but by appeal to their representation of laws and self-subjection to them.

And he means this to apply in ordinary cases of perceptual knowledge too. I know what would count as good perceptual reasons for an empirical claim on the basis of whatever "shape of spirit" or possible model of experience is under consideration at whatever stage in the PhG. That is, Hegel considers empirical rules of discrimination, unification, essence/appearance distinctions, conceptions of explanation, etc., as normative principles, and he construes any some set of these as a possible determinate whole, as all being simply manifestations of the overriding requirements of a "shape of spirit" considered in this idealized isolation of capacities that makes up Chapters I-V, and he cites possible illustrations of such a shape and such internal contradictions (determinate illustrative actual cases like trying to say "this here now," or trying to distinguish the thing which bears properties from those properties).The concepts involved in organizing our visual field are also norms prescribing how the visual field ought to be organized and so they do not function like fixed physiological dispositions. We are responsive to a perceivable environment in norm-attentive ways. Finally, since the principles involved guide my behavior or conclusions only in so far as they are accepted and followed, they can prove themselves inadequate, and lose their grip. This is what Hegel means in the conclusion of his inference by saying that consciousness "immediately goes beyond this restriction." It is always "beyond" any norm in the sense that it is not, let us say, stuck with such a restriction as a matter of psychological fact; consciousness is always in a position to alter norms for correct perception, inferring, law-making or right action. Perception of course involves physiological processes that are species-identical across centuries and cultures, but perceptual knowledge also involves norms for attentiveness, discrimination, unification, exclusion and conceptual organization that do not function like physiological laws. And so (as Hegel says, "as a result") we should be said to stand always by them and yet also "beyond them." (This can all still seem to introduce far too much normative variability into a process, perception, that seems all much more a matter of physiological fact. But while Hegel certainly accepts that the physiological components of perception are *distinguishable* from the norm-following or interpretive elements, he also insists that they are *inseparable* in perception itself. As in Heidegger's phenomenology, there are not two stages to perception; as if a perception of a white rectangular solid which is then "interpreted as" a refrigerator. What we *see* is a refrigerator.)

The second dimension of this claim from §80 concerns how such consciousness is "beyond itself" in another way. Besides the claim that consciousness, as he says, "negates" what it is presented with, does not merely take in but determines what is the case, the claim is also that ordinary, everyday consciousness is *always* "going beyond itself," never *wholly* absorbed in what it is attending to, never simply or only *in* a perceptual state, but always resolving its own conceptual activity; and this in a way that means it can be said both to be self-affirming, possibly issuing in judgments and imperatives, but also potentially "self-negating," aware that what it resolves or takes to be the case might not be the case. It somehow "stands above" what it also affirms, to use an image that Hegel sometimes invokes. It adds to the interpretive problems to cite his canonical formulation of this point, but it might help us see how important it is for his whole position and why he is using language like "negativity" for *consciousness itself*. (Such terminology is the key *explicans* for his eventual claim that self-conscious consciousness is desire.) This is from the "Phenomenology" section of the last version of his *Encyclopedia* (The "Berlin Phenomenology" again).

> The I is now this subjectivity, this infinite relation to itself, but therein, namely in this subjectivity, lies its negative relation to itself, diremption, differentiation, judgment. *The I judges, and this constitutes it as consciousness;* it repels itself from itself; this is a logical determination.[19]

---

[19] BPhG, 2, my emphasis.

So the large question to which Hegel thinks we have been brought by his account of consciousness in the first three chapters is: just *what is it* for a being to be not just a recorder of the world's impact on one's sense, but to be *for itself* in its engagements with objects? What is it in general *for a being to be for itself*, for "itself to be at issue for it in its relation with what is not it"? (This is the problem that arose with the "Kantian" revelation in the Understanding chapter of the PhG that, in trying to get to the real nature of the essence of appearances, "understanding experiences only itself," which, he says, raises the problem: "the cognition of *what consciousness knows in knowing itself* requires a still more complex movement." (§167, m.e.) This is the fundamental issue being explored in chapter four. That the basic structure of the Kantian account is preserved until this point is clear from:

> With that first moment, self-consciousness exists as *consciousness*, and the whole breadth of the sensuous world is preserved for it, but at the same time only as related to the second moment, the unity of self-consciousness with itself. (§167)[20]

This passage and indeed all of §167 indicate that Hegel does have in mind a response to the problem of a self-conscious consciousness (of the whole breadth of the sensible world) developed in the first three chapters (what *is* the relation to itself inherent in any possible relation to objects?), and that he insists on a common sense acknowledgement that whatever account we give of a self-determining self-consciousness, it is not a *wholly* autonomous or independent self-relating; the "sensuous world" must be preserved.

But it is at this point that he then suddenly makes a much more controversial, pretty much unprepared for, and not a all recognizably Kantian, claim.

> But this opposition between its appearance and its truth has only the truth for its essence, namely, the unity of self-consciousness with itself. This unity must become essential to self-consciousness, which is to say, self-consciousness is *desire* itself. (§167)

---

[20] Cf. again the Berlin Phenomenology: "In consciousness I am also self-conscious, but *only also*, since the object has a side in itself which is not mine." (BPhG, 56).

Hegel is talking about an "opposition" between appearance and truth here because he has, in his own words, just summarized the issue of consciousness's "negative" relation to the world and itself this way.

> Otherness thereby exists for it *as a being*, that is, as a *distinguished moment*, but, for it, it is also the unity of itself with this distinction as a *second distinguished* moment. (§167)

That is, consciousness may be said to affirm implicitly a construal of some intentional content, but since it has thereby (by its own "taking") negated any putative immediate certainty, since it is also always "beyond itself," its eventual "unity with itself," its satisfaction that what *it* takes to be the case *is* the case and can be integrated with everything else it takes to be case, requires the *achievement* of a "unity with itself," not any immediate certainty or self-regard. (This is his echo of the Kantian point that the unity of apperception must be achieved; contents must be, as Kant says, "brought" to the unity of apperception.)

But still, at this point, the gloss he gives on the claim that "self-consciousness is desire" is not much help. The gloss is, as if an appositive, "This [the unity of self consciousness with itself] "must become essential to self-consciousness, which is to say, etc." The first hint of a practical turn emerges just here when Hegel implies that we need to understand self-consciousness as *a unity to be achieved*, that there is some "opposition" between self-consciousness and itself, a kind of self-estrangement, which, he seems to be suggesting, we are moved to overcome. The unity of self-consciousness with itself "muß ihm wesentlich werden," must become essential to the experiencing subject, a practical turn of phrase that in effect almost unnoticed serves as the pivot around which the discussion turns suddenly and deeply practical. (As we shall see, it eventually does much more clearly "become essential" as a result of a putative encounter with another and opposing self-conscious being. And it is clearly practical in the sense in which we might say to someone, "You're wasting chances for advancement; your career must *become* essential to you.")

Since the self-conscious aspect of ordinary empirical consciousness is much more like a self-determination, or one could say a resolve or a committing oneself (what Fichte called a self-positing) than a simple self-observation or direct awareness, he begins again to discuss consciousness as a "negation" of the world's independence and otherness. We are overcoming the indeterminacy, opacity, foreignness, potential confusion and disconnectedness of what we are presented with by resolving what belongs together with what, tracking objects through changes and so forth.[21] Hegel then makes another unexpected move when he suggests that we consider the most uncomplicated and straightforward experience of just this striving or orectic for-itself-ness, what he calls life.

> By way of this reflective turn into itself, the object has become *life*. What self-consciousness distinguishes from itself *as existing* also has in it, insofar as it is posited as existing, not merely the modes of sense-certainty and perception. It is being which is reflected into itself, and the object of immediate desire is something *living*.... (§168)

This is the most basic experience[22] of what it is to be at issue for oneself as one engages the world. As Hegel says, we begin with what we know we now need, a "being reflected into itself," and our question, how should we properly describe the self of the self-relation necessary for conscious intentionality and ultimately agency, is given the broadest possible referent, its own mere life. We have something like a sentiment of self as living and, as we shall see, needing to act purposively in order to live. Other objects too are not now merely external existents, "*not merely the modes of sense-certainty and perception*" (although they are *also* that) but now also (in order to move beyond the empty formality of "I am the I who is thinking these thoughts") they are considered as *objects for the living subject*, as threats to, means to, or indifferent to such life-sustaining. This brute or simple *for-itself* quality of living consciousness (which form of self-relation we share with animals) will not remain the focus of Hegel's interest for long, but, if it is becoming plausible that Hegel is indeed trying to extend the issue raised in the Consciousness section (and neither changing the subject, nor repeating the problem and desideratum in a figurative way) it already indicates what was just suggested: that he is moving quickly away from

---

[21] Cf. "The 'I' is as it were the crucible and fire which consumes the loose plurality of sense and reduces it to unity... the tendency of all man's endeavors is to understand the world, to appropriate and subdue it to himself; and to this end the positive reality of the world must be as it were crushed and pounded, in other words, idealized." *Enzyklopädie der philosophischen Wissenschaften, Erster Teil. Die Wissenschaft der Logik*, in *Werke* (Frankfurt: Suhrkamp, 1969-79), Bd. 8, 118; *Hegel's Logic, Being Part One of the Encyclopedia of the Philosophical Sciences*, trans. W. Wallace (Oxford: Clarendon Press, 1982), 69.

[22] That is, the one that presupposes the least.

Kant's transcendental-formal account of the apperceptive nature of consciousness. The I is "for itself" in consciousness for Kant only in the sense that the I (whoever or whatever it is) must be able to accompany all my representations. The world is experienced as categorically ordered because I in some sense order it (I *think* it as such and such) and that activity is not merely triggered into operation by the sense contents of experience. It is undertaken, but I do so only in the broad formal sense of temporally unifying, having a take on, the contents of consciousness, bringing everything under the unity of a formally conceived apperceptive I. (This simply means that every content must be such that *one continuous I can think it*.) The "I" *is* just the unity effected. The subject's relation to objects is a self-relation only in this sense, and Hegel has introduced what seems like a different and at first arbitrary shift in topics to my sustaining my own life as the basic or first or most primary model of this self-relation, not merely sustaining the distinction between, say, successions of representations and a representation of succession.[23]

---

[23] The section on life, essentially §168 to §174 is among the most opaque of any passages in Hegel (which is saying something). What I need here is Hegel's basic framework, in which he starts with the claim that with our "reflective turn" ("durch diese Reflexion in sich selbst") consciousness is related to "life." Self-relation as mere sentiment of oneself as living and as having to maintain life though does not establish my taking up and leading my determinate life as an individual. I am just an exemplar of the species requirements of my species, playing them out within the infinite "totality" of life itself as genus. Just by living I am nothing but a moment in the universal process of life, a kind of Schellingean universal (who talked this way about life). But throughout, the framework is: the first *object* of self-consciousness is life. That is, Hegel does not suddenly decide to talk about life, just qua life. As he says several times, he wants to understand life as the immediate object of desire (itself the most immediate form of self-relation), a sentiment of self that opens a gap, something negative to be filled (requires the negation of barriers to life and the negation of stasis, in the face of the need to lead a life). That is, I take a main point to be that introduced in §168: in this self-relation, there is an "estrangement" (*Entzweiung*), "between self-consciousness and life," as he says. All through the phenomenology of "life as the infinite universal substance as the object of desire," the problem Hegel keeps pointing to is how, under what conditions, the self-relating can be said to become a relating to self that is me, a distinction within the universal genus, life. I seem rather just to submit myself to the imperatives or demands of life for my species. Rather than being the subject of my desire, I am subject to my desire. The first three chapters have already established the need to understand some sort of normative autonomy and this first actuality of self-relatedness, life and leading a life, conflicts with this requirement unless such a subject can establish its independence of life. What is important to my account here is the course of this "becoming determinate" account until it begins to break into its conclusion, toward the end of §172, until "this estrangement of the undifferentiated fluidity is *the very positing of individuality*" ("dies Entzweien der unterschiedlosen Flüssigkeit ist eben das Setzen der Individualität"). Such a self-deter-

It is not arbitrary because Hegel has objected, and will continue to object throughout his career, to any view of the "I" in "I think" as such a merely formal indicator of the "the I or he or it" which thinks. In Hegel's contrasting view, while we can make a general point about the necessity for unity in experience by abstracting from any determination of such a subject and go on to explore the conditions of such unity, we will not get very far in specifying such conditions without, let us say, more determination already in the notion of the subject of experience. This criticism is tied to what was by far the most widespread dissatisfaction with Kant's first *Critique* (which Hegel shared) and which remains today its greatest weakness: the arbitrariness of Kant's Table of Categories, the fact that he has no way of deducing from "the 'I think' must be able to accompany all my representations" *what* the I *must* necessarily think, what forms it must employ, in thinking its representations. The emptiness of Kant's "I" is directly linked for Hegel to the ungroundedness and arbitrariness of his Table of Categories.[24]

However, understanding this charge would take us deep into Hegel's criticisms of Kantian formality. What we need now is a clearer sense of what Hegel is proposing, not so much what he is rejecting. Let me first complete a brief summary of the themes in chapter four (once we begin reading it this way) and then see where we are.

IV

As we have seen, if a self-conscious consciousness is to be understood as striving in some way then the most immediate embodiment of such a striving would be a self's attention to itself as a living being.[25] That is how it

---

mined individual must be established and that requires especially a different, non-natural relation with another subject who must realize the same self-relatedness. What Hegel struggles to say after this is why, without the inner mediation by the outer, i.e. without a self-relation in relation to another self, this fails, a typically Hegelian coming a cropper. See the different account in Neuhouser, *op.cit.*, 43.

[24] Hegel's formulation of this point is given in §197 in his own inimitable style. "*To think* does not mean to think as an *abstract I*, but as an I which at the same time signifies being-*in-itself*, that is, it has the meaning of being an object in its own eyes, or of conducting itself vis-à-vis the objective essence in such a way that its meaning is that of the *being-for-itself* of that consciousness for which it is."

[25] It may help establish the plausibility of this reading to note how much this practical conception of normativity and intentionality was in the air at the time. I have already

is immediately for itself in relation to other objects. Living beings, like animals, do not live in the way non-living beings (like rocks or telephones) merely exist; they must strive to stay alive, and so we have our first example of the desideratum, a self-relation in relation to objects. Life must be led, sustained, and this gap between my present life and what I must do to sustain it in the future is what is meant by calling consciousness *desire* as lack or gap, and so a negation of objects as impediments.[26] If consciousness and desire can be linked as closely as Hegel wants to (that is, identified) then consciousness is not an isolatable registering and responding capacity of the living being that is conscious. And if this all can be established then we will at this step have moved far away from considering a self-conscious consciousness as a kind of self-aware spectator of the passing show and moved closer to considering it as an engaged, practical being, whose practical satisfaction of desire is essential to understanding the way the world originally makes sense to it (the way it makes sense of the world), or is intelligible at all. Hegel's claim is that consciousness *is* desire, not merely that it is accompanied by desire. (Obviously this claim has some deep similarities with the way Heidegger insists that *Dasein*'s unique mode of being-in-the-world is *Sorge*, or care and with Heidegger's constant insistence that this has nothing to do with a subject projecting its pragmatic concerns onto a putatively neutral, directly apprehended content.)

At points Hegel tries to move away from very general and abstract points about living beings and desire and to specify the distinctive character of desire that counts as "self-consciousness," as was claimed in his identification. He wants, that is, to distinguish actions that are merely the natural expression of desire (and a being that is merely subject to its desires), and a corresponding form of self-consciousness that is a mere

---

indicated how indebted this chapter is to Fichte. Ludwig Siep has clearly established how much Hegel borrowed from Fichte for the later sections on recognition and his practical philosophy in general. See his *Anerkennung als Prinzip der praktischen Philosophie* (Alber: Freiburg/Munich, 1979) and in many of the important essays in *Praktische Philosophie im Deutschen Idealismus* (Suhrkamp: Frankfurt am Main, 1992).

[26] Readers of Peirce will recognize here his category of "Secondness." As in "you have a sense of resistance and at the same time a sense of effort. [...]. They are only two ways of describing the same experience. It is a double consciousness. We become aware of ourself [sic] by becoming aware of the not-self." C.S. Peirce, *Collected Papers of Charles Sanders Peirce*, eds. Charles Hartshorne and Paul Weiss (Cambridge: Harvard University Press, 1931-5), vol. I, 324. An excellent exploration of the links between pragmatism and Hegel is Richard Bernstein, *Praxis and Action* (Philadelphia, PA: University of Pennsylvania Press, 1971).

sentiment of self, from actions undertaken in order to satisfy a desire, the actions of a being that does not just embody its self-sentiment but can be said to act on such a self-conception. He wants to distinguish between natural or animal desire and human desire and so tries to distinguish a cycle of desires and satisfactions that continually arise and subside in animals from beings *for whom* their desires can be objects of attention, issues at stake, ultimately *reasons* to be acted on or not. This occurs in a very rapid series of transitions in §175 where Hegel starts distinguishing the cycle of the urges and satisfactions of mere desire from a satisfaction that can confirm the genuinely self-relating quality of consciousness, rather than its mere self-sentiment.

That is, we have already seen a crucial aspect of the structure of Hegel's account: that any self-relating is always also in a way provisional and a projecting outward, beyond the near immediacy of any mere self-taking. Conscious takings of any sort are defeasible, held open as possibilities and so must be tested; and avowed commitments must be realized in action for there to be any realization of the avowed intention (and so revelation of that the subject was in fact committed to doing). The projected self-sentiment of a merely living self is *realized* by the "negation" of the object of desire necessary for life, part of an endless cycle of being subject to one's desires and satisfying them. This all begins to change at the end of the paragraph (§175), as Hegel contemplates a distinct kind of object which, in a sense *"negates back,"* and not merely in the manner of a prey that resists a predator, but which can also, as he says "effect this negation in itself"; or, come to be in the self-relation required by our desiring self-consciousness. That is, Hegel introduces into the conditions of the "satisfaction" of any self-relating another self-consciousness, an object that cannot merely be destroyed or negated in the furtherance of life without the original self-consciousness losing its confirming or satisfying moment. He then identifies a further condition for this distinction that is perhaps the most famous claim in the Phenomenology.

It is this one. "Self-consciousness attains its satisfaction only in another self-consciousness." (§175). He specifies this in an equally famous passage from §178. "Self-consciousness exists *in* and *for itself* because and by way of its existing in and for itself for an other; i.e., it exists only as recognized."

So Hegel wants to introduce a fundamental complication in any account of the self-relation he is trying to show is constitutive for intentional consciousness and purposive deeds. As we have seen, consciousness is said to be "beyond itself" because its self-relating self-determining is always defeasible (or challengeable in the case of action) and so its being in its very self-relation in some way "held open" to such a possibility is considered a constitutive condition. In the broadest sense this means that such takings and doings are supported by reasons, even if mostly in deeply implicit and rarely challenged ways. (Conscious takings can always "rise" to the level of explicit judgments and defenses of judgments; habitual actions can be defended if necessary.) Hegel now introduces the possibility—unavoidable given the way he has set things up—that all such considerations are uniquely open to challenge by other conscious, acting beings. Such challenges could initially be considered as merely more natural obstacles in the way of desire-satisfaction in all the various forms now at issue in Hegel's account. But by considering imaginatively the possibility of a challenge that forces the issue to the extreme, a "struggle to the death," Hegel tries to show how the unique nature of such a challenge from another like-minded being forces the issue of the normative (or not just naturally explicable) character of one's takings and practical commitments, and any possible response, to the forefront. To be norm-sensitive at all is then shown to be not just *open* to these unique sorts of challenges, but to be finally *dependent* on some resolution of them. It is on the basis of this account, how we can be shown to open ourselves to such challenges and such dependence just as a result of a "phenomenological" consideration of the implications of the apperception thesis, that Hegel begins his attempt to establish one of the most ambitious claims of the Phenomenology of Spirit: the sociality of consciousness and action.

V

So where does all this leave us? In general we have a picture of a self or subject of experience and action estranged from, or divided within itself (without, as he put it, a "unity" that "must become essential to it") but conceived now in a way very different from Plato's divided soul, divided among distinct "parts" in competition for rule of the soul as a whole, and in a way very different both from other forms of metaphysical dualism, and from what would become familiar as the Freudian mind, split between the conscious and the distinct unconscious mind, or most explicitly for Hegel (and for Schiller) in distinction from the Kantian conception of noumenal and phenomenal selves. In a way somewhat similar to and in an unacknowledged way, in debt to Rousseau, Hegel treats this division *as a result*, not in any factual historical sense but as a disruption of natural orectic unity that must always already have resulted, can only be rightly understood as effected. This division functions in Hegel as it does in some others as the source of the incessant desire not for rule or successful repression but for the wholeness so often the subject of broader philosophical reflections on human life. Hegel does not accept the Platonic or Cartesian or Kantian account of a fixed dualism and so entertains this aspiration for a genuine reconciliation of sorts within such divisions. This is so in Hegel because he does not treat this division as a matter of metaphysical fact. The problem of unity emerges not because of any discovery of a matter-of-fact divided soul, but in the light of the realization that what counts as an aspect of my agency and what an impediment to it or what is a constraint on freedom, is a different issue under different conditions. In this light, under the conditions Hegel entertains in this chapter, the natural cycle of desire and satisfaction is interrupted in a way for which there is not an immediate or natural solution, and one's status as subject, judger, agent, is now said to emerge, in varying degrees, imagined under a variety of those possible conditions, as a result of this putative unavoidable conflict. The premise for this account is the one we saw much earlier. Hegel's way of putting it was that consciousness must always be thought to be "beyond itself"; more expansively put: that we have to understand a human self-relation as always also a projection outward as much as a turn inward. Once we understand such a self-relation as a normative self-determination, such a self is open, opens itself to, counter-claim, contestation, refusal, a different form of negation that forces a different sort of response, what Hegel will describe as initially a struggle for recognition.

This is a lot to get by reflection on Kant's central idea, that "The 'I think' must be able to accompany all my representations," but that is, I have argued, Hegel's source. It is this reflection on Kantian spontaneity, understood by Hegel as also a self-dividing or self-alienating, that grounds the hope for an effected or resultant form of reconciliation of self with other, and thereby self with self.

VI

Let me conclude with a return to Kant, now in a broader way. I have argued that for Hegel self-consciousness is not the awareness of an object, at least not any observed object, and that it is a dynamic process, a doing in a way and a thinking in a way, not any momentary, second-order awareness. Somewhat surprisingly, he called that whole process "desire" and I suggested that this was because, looking at things this way, such a way of knowing oneself in knowing or doing anything, not being momentary or punctuated in time, must involve some projection over time, a way of constantly and implicitly being attentive to, or at least open to the possibility of, whether one had it right, either about what one believed to be true, or about what one was doing or whether one had the reasons one took oneself to have. This is, I think, the most important *aperçus* in what we call German Idealism and it receives its fullest expression in Hegel's thought. (The formulation just used was closer to the way Fichte would put the point in his discussion not of *Begierde* or desire but of *Streben* or striving in his account of self-consciousness, or what he called a *Tathandlung*, a deed-activity.) I can put the same point another way, and at a very high altitude, by noting something unusual about Kant.

In what is known as the First Introduction to his last *Critique*, *The Critique of Judgment*, Kant presented a very ambitious summary of his understanding of the basic human capacities involved in our knowing, doing, or feeling anything. He divided these capacities up into three components, listing first what he called the basic "faculties of the mind," and then to each basic faculty, he assigned what he called a "higher cognitive faculty," something like the higher expression of such a faculty. So, to the basic "cognitive faculty," he assigned "understanding" as the higher faculty; to the basic capacity to feel pleasure and pain he assigned as its higher counterpart the faculty of judgment (as in aesthetic pleasure and aesthetic judgment). And then, in a move somewhat at odds with the standard picture of Kant's philosophy, he listed as our third basic capacity "desire" (*Begehrungsvermögen*) and assigned to it as the expression of *its* higher cognitive faculty, "reason."[27]

---

[27] He also assigned to each "a priori principles." These were, respectively, "lawfulness, purposiveness, and obligation,'" and to each he assigned a "product," respectively: "nature, art and morality." *Kritik der Urteilskraft*, in *Gesammelte Schriften*, ed.

Why would he make such a connection? I want to say that it is because for Kant reason is not a mere calculative faculty, as if a tool to be applied in the realization of ends. Rather, in the simplest sense, to be a creature with rational responsiveness is to be a creature that expects, demands, wants, struggles for justification, warrant, a righteousness both intellectual and moral; or, put another way, it is to feel a lack when such a justification is lacking. In his most familiar formulation of the point, to be a creature of reason is to be *unable* to rest content with knowledge of the mere "conditioned," but to seek to ascend always to knowledge of the "unconditioned." (Kant noted that even the demonstration by his critical philosophy that such knowledge was impossible would have no effect on such yearning and the continuation of such quests. Indeed even the resolutely prosaic Kant was inspired to use a variation of an erotic image: "We shall always return to metaphysics as to a beloved one with whom we have had a quarrel." (A850/B878)) Reason, he put it in another context, must be said to have *its own "interests,"* its own teleological structure clearly evident when we act and know that we are acting in one way rather than another, inspiring in all such cases the need for justification, especially to others (for Kant, to all others). It was this structure that would provide the basis for Kantian morality. One could put the point in the Hegelian terms framed earlier: to be such a reason-responsive creature is to be self-related in this erotic way in relation to all objects to be known and actions to be carried out, to be, as Hegel said in his peculiar way, "beyond oneself." And what else is this sort of self-relation, so described—a striving, inability to rest content, all in a uniquely reason-sensitive way—but "desire"?

This way of looking at things is the source of his most beautiful image for this aspect of his project, an image that (typically) resonates both with Christian and pagan undertones. (The image could be said to embody the last moment of romantic optimism in German philosophy, although it had a final materialist echo in Marx's project.) Later in the PhG (§669), Hegel describes human existence itself as a "wound" ("Wunde"), but one which, he says, has been self-inflicted and which (one infers, which *therefore*) can be healed, even "without scars" ("ohne Narben").

Königlich-Preussische Akademie der Wissenschaften (Berlin: de Gruyter, 1922), vol. V, 198.

The Self-Consciousness of Consciousness

WALTER JAESCHKE

The "history of *self-consciousness*" is the "*history* of self-consciousness." This sounds like a tautology, and from a formal point of view, it is one—that is, if we abstract from the content and assume that "history of self-consciousness" always means the same thing. In my view, however, we need to note the difference between these two histories and to consider the grounds for passing over from the first history to the second, and to understand the second not only as a different form, but as the real and effective history of self-consciousness. The history of self-consciousness in the first sense can only refer to the form it took in the transcendental philosophy of Fichte, and subsequently in the different version formulated by Schelling; in the second sense—this should be no surprise, given the aim of this lecture—it is carried out in Hegel's *Phenomenology of Spirit*, on the basis of a different self-consciousness, with a different method and a different systematic function. First, I would like briefly to review this background and sketch the difference between these two versions; then, in the second part of my talk, I will explicate the new form that the process that leads from consciousness to self-consciousness has taken in the Phenomenology, with respect to its intellectual preconditions and its systematic function; and finally, in the third part, I will pose the question of how we should assess this concept of a "history of self-consciousness" beyond its role in Hegel's System of Science.

I. The transcendental-philosophical "history of self-consciousness"

The great, abiding achievement of transcendental philosophy is that it is has pushed the I—or "self-consciousness," as it has primarily been called since

Schelling—to the center of philosophical questioning; not as a substance that is, on its own, finished and without structure, but as a subject that is activity, and is constituted through activity. The I to which we ascribe knowledge and actions is based on actions—necessary yet unconscious actions, which constitute consciousness in the first place. In his *Grundlagen der gesammten Wissenschaftslehre* (*Foundations of the Entire Science of Knowledge*)[1] Fichte presents the "system" of these necessary actions. Since this system forms the foundation of consciousness, it is not necessarily, and not even primarily, contained in consciousness. But it can be made conscious, raised into the sphere of "representation"—not of course via introspection, but through transcendental-philosophical reflection. The action that raises the complete system of necessary actions into consciousness is however itself not a necessary action, but a free action—namely the one that through an act of reflection presents these actions, in the Doctrine of Science, in a systematically ordered fashion and raises them up to the form of knowledge. This is however not an individual act, occurring at a particular point in time, carried out by the singular individual, Fichte. For him, the whole history of philosophy is rather nothing other than a sequence of progressive attempts to raise that which lies at the foundation of all consciousness, always and unchangingly, to consciousness, and to do this in a free manner. These attempts have been increasingly successful: human spirit "first begins to dawn via a blind groping about, and only out of this does it pass over into daylight." All philosophers "have sought to separate out, through reflection, the necessary mode of action of human spirit from its contingent conditions; and all of them have in fact, only with more or less purity, and more or less completely, separated them out; on the whole, the philosophizing power of judgment has however constantly progressed and come closer to its goal."[2]

In the vocabulary of the *Critique of Pure Reason*, this historically progressing clarification of the mode of action of human spirit can be called a "history of pure reason" (B 880)—that is, if one does not prefer to reserve this provocative expression which joins "reason" and "history" for a more particular version of the relation between reason and history than the one we find in Fichte. The Doctrine of Science presents the "system of human

---

[1] Where the author speaks of Fichte's *Wissenschaftslehre*, we will use "Doctrine of Science." Trans.
[2] Fichte, *Gesamtausgabe der Bayerischen Akademie der Wissenschaften*, ed. Reinhard Lauth (Stuttgart: Frommann, 1962–2012), vol. I/2, 140–143, 146. Henceforth: GA.

knowledge," although this system precedes the Doctrine in the necessary actions of spirit; the Doctrine must accordingly correspond to this presupposition. The philosophers that propose this system are in this respect "not the lawgivers of human spirit, but its historiographers; certainly not journalists, but rather pragmatic writers of history" (GA I/2, 147). Their task is not to invent the system of human spirit, but to find and describe it. Thus two different histories can be told here: on the one hand, the history of the descriptions of knowledge made by these pragmatic writers of history, on the other hand, the history of knowledge itself, the writing of the very history of that which is described.

However, that which is presupposed by the historiographers of human spirit is not something actually given; it first needs to be raised to the level of consciousness—indeed, by consciousness itself. For this, no mere description of something simply found will do, but rather a systematic explication is required. The pragmatic writing of the history of human spirit thus takes the form of a transcendental-philosophic reconstruction of the necessary actions of consciousness. Here, the concept of history and the concept of science coincide, concepts which until the end of the eighteenth century and even in Kant[3] were directly opposed: The history of human spirit *is* its science, and this science assumes the character of a history of human spirit—where history is however not to be understood in a previous sense, as a report on an object that did not necessarily have a temporal structure. The acts, always free, that describe the outlines of this system, are located in the broader context of a history of reason which spans all of time—but they also, every one of them, sketch a non-temporal history of reason—or a history of self-consciousness, as Schelling, six years later, would succinctly formulate it in the *System of Transcendental Idealism*.

In the context of this system, the history of self-consciousness acquires a role that is central, although not clearly demarcated. Indeed, Schelling understands the task of this *System* in the following sentence: "The whole object of our inquiry is nothing but the explication of self-consciousness."[4] And this explication of self-consciousness is, for Schelling as well, not the explication of a fixed substantial object from an external point of view; it is

---

[3] Immanuel Kant, *Akademieausgabe* (Berlin: Deutsche Akademie der Wissenschaften zu Berlin, 1900f), vol. XX, 340–343.

[4] Schelling, *System des transzendentalen Idealismus*, in *Historisch-kritische Ausgabe, Werke*, ed. Harald Korten & Paul Ziche (Stuttgart: Frommann-Holzboog, 2005), I, vol. 9/1, 152. Henceforth: AA.

the description of a trend towards an "infinity of actions" of self-consciousness and in this way it is a history of self-consciousness. However, because an infinite history of self-consciousness would be necessary in order to describe all these actions, Schelling is compelled to create an abbreviated version of this history: "Philosophy can thus only enumerate those actions which, in the history of self-consciousness, have constituted epochs, and present them in their interrelation. [...] Philosophy is thus a history of self-consciousness which has different epochs, and by which this One absolute synthesis is successively composed." (AA I / 9, 91)

The history of self-consciousness, which Schelling retells, is, to be sure, the story of "actions"—but not of "deeds" or even, "experiences (*Erlebnisse*) of self-consciousness." It is the transcendental-philosophical history of the genesis of self-consciousness, that is, the conditions under which the I first comes to intuit itself: it is indeed the history of the progression of the self-intuition of the I, but as a systematically complete enumeration of "hierarchical series of intuitions" [...] through which the I raises itself to consciousness to the highest potency" (AA I / 9, 25). Even in this very pithy phrase, there is a decisive characteristic that does find expression: This hierarchical series does not itself have a historical structure, but it is an architectonically conceived, static order that is presented in the form of a sequence only by the narrator. Schelling still uses the word "history" in the traditionally subjective sense of "report," "account," not in the objective sense of a development that occurs in time, which was not used so much at that time. The "history" (*Geschichte*) being told by Schelling is not a temporal sequence, but the "story" (*Historie*) of a hierarchically layered order and of a functional coherence of the system of self-consciousness. There is yet an additional aspect here: Even if "the whole of philosophy" is, for Schelling, a "progressive history of self-consciousness," as it were, supported by monuments and documents (AA I / 9, 25), such "monuments and documents" have no historical character. Therefore, Schelling also calls this "history" an explanation of the "mechanism of the I"—without saying anything else with this phrase than "history of self-consciousness." To the extent that Schelling's history of self-consciousness unfolds in the three "epochs," it is an explanation of the "mechanism of the I," though dressed up in the vocabulary of a current of thought, that began to take hold towards the end of the eighteenth century, against the previously dominant rationalist current of thought and its concept of science.

On the other hand, the development from consciousness to self-consciousness, and from reason to spirit, which Hegel outlines in his *Phenomenology of Spirit*, is neither a hierarchical sequence of potencies, nor a mechanism of the I, but a veritable history of self-consciousness—even though he does not refer to it as such, presumably in order not to blur the distinction between it and the transcendental-philosophical conception, which, at the time, was occupied by talk of a history of self-consciousness. This development is no longer a "science of the actions of the I," but rather a "science of the experience of consciousness," and it is only *that* consciousness which undergoes experiences whose constitution occurs behind its back, and is to be reconstructed in a transcendental-philosophical fashion. The writing of the history of human spirit, and also the pragmatic aspect of the writing of its history, only begin where the transcendental-philosophical frameworks have been superseded and human spirit is subjected to a history in the temporal sense—or rather: where its development, which occurs according to its own immanent laws, constitutes history *as* history constituted. "The history of *self-consciousness* is the *history* of self-consciousness"—this now means: The effective [*wirkliche*] "history of self-consciousness" is not the "mechanisms" of its necessary actions that can be reconstructed in a transcendental-philosophical way, but rather falls within temporal history, or more precisely: it makes the temporal development into a plurality of *histories*—to a history of self-consciousness in the narrow sense as well as to the histories of reason and of spirit, which only in their totality comprise all aspects of a history of consciousness. What "spirit" is cannot be grasped without history—without history in the new, succinct understanding of the word!—and this applies just as well to reason, and in a rudimentary way, even to self-consciousness.

More important for Hegel than the transcendental-philosophical reconstruction of the necessary actions of human spirit is the understanding of the historical development of knowledge, the development of consciousness into self-consciousness, and finally, the self-knowing of spirit. The shift in point of view that he hereby enacts, also implies a criticism of the orientation of the program that antedates this new approach: without the reconstruction of the historical development of spirit, the transcendental-philosophical work remains but a torso. For—to turn Kant's famous phrase against his own program—the historical development itself is part of the conditions of possibility of knowledge as well as of the conditions of the possibility for the objects of knowledge. If the insight that Hegel's "phenomenology" rests upon is formulated in this way, then his program can unproblematically become part of the program of a transcendental-philosophical history of self-consciousness. And yet: Hegel's insight does not affect the core of the transcendental-philosophical program, yet it gives it up, or at least downplays its importance, and instead it establishes a successor program on a new terrain in a new form and with a new method. The central point of dissent, the difference, although not between the Fichte-Schellingean system, and the Hegelian, but the difference between the Fichte-Schellingean transcendental philosophy and Hegelian phenomenology lies precisely in this question: Does the history of self-consciousness limit itself to the history of its invariant structure and the successive synthesis of its functions, or is that which occurs a development of self-consciousness which is historical in an emphatic sense? If we affirm the latter, and have reason to assume not only a variation in knowledge of the thing that is external and indifferent to it, but a historical development in which, before anything else, all the series of necessary conditions of self-awareness are traversed completely, then, this development concerns necessarily also the conditions of possibility for knowledge and also the objects of this knowledge—be it in the form of a moderate modification, or in the form of a far-reaching, as it were, "substantial" displacements.

II. The Phenomenology as history of self-consciousness

The question presented in the first part of my talk cannot of course be decided by choosing between Fichte and Schelling, on the one hand, and Hegel, on the other. Today it is no less an explosive question, and the answers given are no less momentous today than they were then—on the contrary. Here, I will not yet be addressing these general issues, but will remain with the *Phenomenology of Spirit*. Neither will I attempt to find an answer to the question posed. In this second part, I would instead like to sketch the outline of the program that follows from Hegel's historical insight. But, initially in the form of a small excursus, I would like throw out the question of the genesis of this insight: When and how does Hegel come to this insight that the history of self-consciousness—or generally: of spirit—falls within time?

First a few words about "when"—in particular because this question about the "when" will prove itself relevant with respect to content. The history of the genesis of the *Phenomenology of Spirit* is shrouded in mystery—so much so that in order to clarify the history, one would be inclined to call upon the apocalyptic *topos* of the hidden book that only will be revealed at the end of days. In fact, this obscurity is deepened rather than cleared up by Hegel's biographer Karl Rosenkranz. Rosenkranz does indeed tell us that Hegel developed "the concept of experience which consciousness makes of itself," in his introductions to the *Logic* and *Metaphysics*, and that "starting in 1804, the basis for the phenomenology" emerged from this. Since the key manuscripts have been lost, these claims can no longer be assessed, and, moreover, it is well known that Rosenkranz is never weaker than in his chronology of Hegel's writings. We have no direct statements from Hegel or any third party. It is true that in a letter written in the early summer of 1805, Hegel announces—obviously, somewhat optimistically—that his *system of philosophy* was to appear as soon as the fall of that year—but this does not provide any clues to the conception of a "phenomenology." In the announcement for his lectures for the summer semester 1806, he has still not mentioned it; he only announces that his book *System of Science* will soon appear and that he will use this as the basis of lectures on speculative philosophy or logic. There is no mention of a "phenomenology"—and this, at a time when the typesetting of the introduction had begun, and Hegel distributed the first galley proofs to his students. It is only in the summer of 1806, in his lecture announcements for the winter semester 1806/07, when substantial parts of the book already had been typeset, that Hegel for the first and only time mentions "Phaenomenologia mentis"—but here too he does not announce it is a separate publication, but as something that would precede the first part of the "system of science." Even in the summer of 1806, he has still not grasped that instead of his "system," it would be only the "before" that would appear. During this very summer 1806, this "before," however, assumes such enormous proportions that Hegel finally finds it advisable to indicate on the title page that it is the first part of the system—which previously hadn't been under consideration.

It comes as no surprise that this highly complicated situation surrounding the genesis of the book has produced, in the last century, a great number of interpretations based on the history of the book itself. Here, I will not go into such questions, but only the conditions under which Hegel reached his insight—which is decisive for the conception of the Phenomenology—into the constitutive significance of the historical dimension of knowledge. Since the sources remain doggedly silent, the question of the "how" cannot be solved by reference to them. All we can do is attempt a post factum reconstruction of his motives—and for that reason, I must step back and limit myself to two such motives, which, given the way they are related to each other, are entirely applicable for the clarification of the emergence of the new conception.

Reflections on this problem must start from what we know about Hegel's concept at the time of an introduction to a "system of the sciences"—and what we know is not much. From all the years in Jena we only possess a single, very fragmentary and sketchy introduction: the first sketch for a system from the winter 1801/1802.[5] It does not however provide us with a possible paradigm for the later Jena conception of an introduction. It ascribes this introductory function to a Logic still separated from the Metaphysics, whereas at the time of the Phenomenology, Logic and Metaphysics, understood as speculative philosophy, form the first, and proper, part of the system. What is common to the earliest introduction and the one that Hegel planned in 1806 is probably that he did not understand them as a didactic guide, but as a "scientific introduction," i.e., as a justification from the point of view of the system. This is why he counters the accusation, if not implausible then at least somewhat mean-spirited, of skepticism, and that it would be impossible to ascend to the absolute of the Philosophy of Identity on the ladder of earthly things,[6] with the explicit assertion that the individual rightly demands of science that it should "at least offer him the ladder with which to reach this standpoint" (GW 9, 23)—and this is not just a didactic ladder. Yet, to offer him this ladder also means to demand of him that he should climb up on it and raise himself above his natural consciousness. From the point of view of the genesis of the work, this systematic task of the introduction, to offer the ladder to the individual, no doubt has priority over the conception of a "phenomenology of spirit," and the question then becomes what prompted Hegel to present this ladder in the form of a "phenomenology."

For there is in fact a further piece of evidence that takes us closer to the answer. Rosenkranz indeed says that Hegel had developed "the concept of the experience that consciousness has of itself," out of which "the seeds of

---

[5] Hegel, *Gesammelte Werke* (Hamburg: Meiner, 1998), vol. 5, 257–265. Henceforth: GW.
[6] Gottlob Ernst Schulze, *Aphorismen über das Absolute*, in *Philosophisch-literarische Streitsachen*, ed. Walter Jaeschke (Hamburg: Meiner, 1993), vol. 2/1, 337–355, citation on 350.

the Phenomenology" had developed.[7] "Science of the experience of consciousness"—this is indeed the original intermediary title, subsequently removed on Hegel's instruction, which at the beginning of the book separates the introduction from the first part of the system, which as a whole in turn has the function of an introduction to the system. A "science of the experience of consciousness" can however be adequate to the task of introducing us to the "system of science" only if the thematic experience that consciousness undergoes and has of itself leads to the threshold of the system: only if the path of the experience of consciousness at the same time is the path of becoming of science. The experience of consciousness must then comprise nothing less than "the whole of its system, or the entire realm of the truth of spirit" (GW 9, 61). But how should we more precisely understand this "truth of spirit," of which the introduction speaks? The preface, which was written at a later stage, explains this more exactly: in order to "lead the individual from his uneducated standpoint to knowledge" we must "look at the general individual, the world spirit, in its formation" (GW 9, 24). This later claim presupposes the insight that Hegel had gained in the meantime, relating to the historical development of self-consciousness: the insight that this history is not just the history of the different ways self-consciousness can be described, but the history of its formation—its own history. In order to reach a state of completion, a history of self-consciousness must transcend the description of the mechanism of the individual human spirit and look at world spirit in its formation—which means: in its historical formation. To once more use the earlier plastic image: a ladder, to be sure merely made up the rungs of transcendental philosophy and only reaching as far as this philosophy, would not be tall enough to take us all the way up to the self-consciousness of spirit. It would at least need a historical extension, or better: it would need to be replaced by a ladder that reaches much higher, and which is constructed on the basis of a history of consciousness—this term however now taken in a wholly new sense. Climbing this ladder would, for the individual, then amount to, in a Heraclitean fashion, both a path of despair and a path of elevation.

The conception of the Phenomenology, and precisely of its later and shapeless parts, depends on this insight into the significance of the history

---

[7] Karl Rosenkranz, *Georg Wilhelm Friedrich Hegels Leben* (Berlin: Duncker & Humblot, 1844), 202, 214.

of knowledge for knowledge itself, and into the significance of the historical path of spirit, which Hegel understood in the summer of 1806. But is this really an insight, or is it a grandiose mistake, which was to foster the subsequent relativistic historicisms, to claim that the history of knowledge not only has an additive or illustrative function, but is constitutive for knowledge, and that it transforms and founds knowledge? Hegel's intention is not only to provide "a general philosophical history of human spirit or of reason,"[8] as his opponent Fries at the time accurately claimed. In such a history, the various philosophical images that describe knowledge could parade before us without changing anything in knowledge itself. And just as little does Hegel want, in the manner of Fichte, to bring together in a grand plan the various successive attempts to identify the invariant "true system" of those actions that constitute the I, and that lies at the basis of all of history. What he claims is rather that such a general philosophical history of human spirit is itself a necessary precondition for the system of science, since knowledge is itself historically formed—and this not in the sense of a mere addition, a growth of knowledge, but as a qualitative transformation. Given this assumption of a historically unfolding system of knowledge, the differences between the previous attempts to gain knowledge of this system can be easily explained: it is not a question of merely varying, more or less successful, perhaps even progressing, and yet always failed presentations of an invariant system, but of historically differing presentations of a system which itself develops historically.

For Hegel the constitutive significance of the history of knowledge for the shaping of knowledge depends on the specific structure of spirit, or better: on the relation between individual and universal spirit, which is specific to spirit as such. His insight into the historical development of knowledge is founded on the premise of a philosophy of spirit. In the general spirit, past knowledge of past existence has been sublated and reduced to a moment; the individual participates in this "general spirit," or in Hegel's words: "Past existence is an already acquired property of general spirit, which constitutes the substance of the individual, or his inorganic nature," a nature of which the individual then in the process of his formation takes possession and consumes—a process of formation through which the "general spirit or substance gives itself its self-consciousness"

---

[8] Walter Jaeschke, *Hegel-Handbuch: Leben—Werk—Schule* (Stuttgart: Metzler, 2003), col. 177b.

(GW 9, 25). We can translate this from a language that has become foreign to us—and first into Hegel's own later vocabulary: Hegel is here trying to articulate ideas that he later, in his lectures on the history of philosophy—and perhaps not even later, but even simultaneously—formulates as the idea of "historicity." The movement that spirit traverses on the way to its self-consciousness *is* a historical movement. In this movement, that which the individual self-consciousness holds to be true is transformed, and since self-consciousness participates in this spirit and its movement, and takes possession of its content as its heritage, both its knowledge of objects as well as its knowledge of itself is marked by this history. "What we are," he will later say, "we are at the same time historically," for the "common and everlasting" in the history of thought (or in the language of the Phenomenology: the "substantial which belongs to the universal spirit") is "inseparably intertwined with the fact that we are historical."[9] As I have noted, Hegel's language can be translated into another language, where it can be understood as the discovery of a particular quality of human cognition, which makes processes of cultural learning possible.

Before coming back to this point, I would however like to pinpoint more precisely the conditions of genesis, and the systematic place, of these ideas. In Hegel's philosophical milieu at the time, this idea is nowhere to be found: we have to go all the way back to Herder to find something similar. Nor can this insight into the historical movement of the substantiality of spirit be found in Hegel's own earlier work. And as far as we know, it does not stem from the sphere of the problems relating to the introduction to the system—they have at first no place there. It is rather due to Hegel's elaboration of his program for a philosophy of spirit from the middle of his Jena period. Above all, we must take note of the fact that Hegel during that precise semester which preceded his formulation of the new insight, for the first time lectured on the history of philosophy. Even if we, apart from a few fragmentary phrases, posses neither reliable sources nor second-hand accounts, there can no doubt about the intertwining of these two domains. We can still find traces of the language of the preface to the Phenomenology in the manuscripts to Hegel's lectures on the history of philosophy from 1823. Therefore it is not too hazardous to claim that the insight that lies at the basis of the particular form of the introductory function ascribed to the

---

[9] Hegel, *Vorlesungen über die Geschichte der Philosophie*, eds. Pierre Garniron & Walter Jaeschke (Hamburg: Meiner, 1994), I, 6.

Phenomenology is due to Hegel's study of the history of philosophy in the winter of 1805 and 1806; in close connection with this, we should also situate those parts of the philosophy of spirit from this semester, which deal with the history of religion. All that was required to proceed from a "science of the experience of consciousness" to a "science of the phenomenology of spirit," was the step from an insight into the particular nature of spirit, which he had elaborated in his work on the history of philosophy, to a general insight into the particular nature of spiritual processes—where the concept of "appearing knowledge," so frequent already in the earliest parts of the work, in the introduction, formed an outstanding bridge.

With respect to the chronological coincidence of Hegel's work on a new conception of the introduction and on the philosophy of spirit, and especially on the history of philosophy, the idea imposes itself that such an introduction must provide a retrospective view of the historical elevation of spirit. But perhaps this idea, in the very moment of its flashing forth, had too much suggestive force. Can the task of providing an "introduction" to the system—in the sense of a scientific justification—be said to be solved with the retrospective view of "appearing knowledge," or must this retrospection take place under the guidance of well-defined precepts given by "science"? Mere history would not be science in the emphatic sense, and Hegel does not claim that the Phenomenology is a history, but a science—albeit not a science in the same sense as the disciplines that follow it in the "System of Science." And yet: its scientific quality resides precisely in that it presents this "path of natural consciousness, that pushes forth towards true knowledge" (GW 9, 55) in an adequate way, and that it resolutely holds this knowledge up to the eyes of a natural consciousness that wants to refuse it. The becoming of knowledge is a necessary becoming, although not in the sense of blind necessity, but of an immanent necessity of spirit. The necessity required by the claim to science of the Phenomenology exclusively lies in the adequate reconstruction of the inner lawfulness of the process of knowledge that is presented. The negation of natural knowledge as well as of the historical shapes of consciousness fall within this process: its "negative" side, according to which it is a "path of despair," as well as its "positive" side, that it constitutes "the complete series of shapes" of spirit (GW 9, 56f). The starting point and the ending point, as well as the dynamics of this process of appearing knowledge, are purely determined through the inner structure of knowledge. Its justification lies only in its showing the historical movement to truly be the movement towards science, and to culminate in "absolute knowledge."[10] There is no external evidence that reason guides this process. No other proof can be given; natural consciousness cannot be persuaded by arguments of a science that it has rejected, but only by being shown the untruth of appearing knowledge, and thereby the historical process of its own sublation.

III. A new epistemology

Hegel thus conceives the introduction to the System of Science—at least in the later and more substantial parts—in the form of a genealogy. The *Phenomenology of Spirit* is a genealogy of spirit, broken up into the histories of self-consciousness, of reason, and of spirit. It displays the development of appearing spirit; it is a "monstration," but is not a "demonstration." To come back to the image of the ladder, which I have already used several times: the ladder that the Phenomenology offers to natural knowledge, so that it may ascend to absolute knowledge as the gateway to the system, is just as much historical as it is scientific—and this is not coincidental, but depends on the fact that history is nothing but the necessary path of the development of spirit, the knowledge of which on the other hand is the object of science. This is not meant to deny the constructive features of above all this particular book. But what it contains of construction should only serve the reconstruction of the historical unfolding of spirit itself.

Through this conception—which undoubtedly is in motion and not a unity, but grew during the writing process and probably only emerged during this process—Hegel gave a new solution to the problem of an introduction to his philosophy, which was surprising when compared to his firsts attempts, but also convincing, and not only when one looks back to the earlier ones. The unity that is the basis of this solution was never rejected by Hegel. It is not dependent on the introductory function, just as this function is not dependent on the unity. If Hegel's insight is correct, that the spiritual world has a specific processual structure, through which spirit can attain self-consciousness, and that consequently can be described as a history of self-consciousness—namely as a history of the progressive unfolding and substantial adaptation of knowledge and its formation, and

---

[10] Walter Jaeschke, "Das absolute Wissen," in Andreas Arndt & Ernst Müller (eds.), *Hegels "Phänomenologie des Geistes" heute* (Berlin: Oldenbourg Akademieverlag, 2004), 194–214.

that knowledge is raised to the level of self-knowing—*if* this insight is correct, then an introduction to a system of philosophy *must*, strictly speaking, have this form given to it by Hegel. This would appear in a different light if, for instance, the already mentioned model that we find in Fichte's Doctrine of Science were correct, and the philosophical programs would be related to each other like different descriptions of the always identical system of actions of human spirit. In this case, an introduction to a system in the form of a history of consciousness would only be a kaleidoscopic mix without philosophical relevance. Here I will not decide in favor of one of these—or even a third—model, but only stick to this: these questions, which are not marginal, have only been discussed in philosophy, and not only in philosophy, since Hegel's program. Earlier conceptions like Kant's triad of dogmatism, skepticism, and criticism have on the other hand only had marginal significance.

This is why the question of whether a history of consciousness is able to function as an introduction to philosophy is only one way to approach the problem. The other approach goes far beyond this context and beyond Hegel's idea of the system. With his new solution to the problem of an introduction Hegel unwittingly posed a general problem, one that is revolutionary and new, and has gigantic dimensions—a problem that can also be pursued at a greater distance from Hegel's systematic options and ambitions, in fact can and ought to be pursued without any reference to Hegel—and a problem that unfortunately even today is far from being solved. In the third and concluding part of my talk I would like to address, at least partially, this approach to the history of self-consciousness, which abstracts from Hegel's system—even if I can only briefly point to a few tasks, without claiming to be exhaustive or to present a systematic view.

If—and I say this with emphasis—the historical changes in knowledge are not only to be described as a constant change of the objects of knowledge, or as a quantitative expansion through inclusion of new content, but also as a qualitative unfolding that transforms knowledge itself and retrospectively also its constitution, then this must also have effects on an epistemology that corresponds to the structure of a historically developing knowledge: an epistemology that grasps the historical development of knowledge. Given the conditions mentioned above, this is no mere question of philosophical taste, but a compelling claim. Whoever is unwilling to be subjected to this claim must reject this hypothesis as irrelevant. But also in this context it must be tested again.

In his far-reaching history of self-consciousness, there is one domain that Hegel does not include—the domain that transcendental philosophy places under the same rubric. This could be seen as in indication of the fact that Hegel does not see the domain of necessary actions of spirit, the mechanism of spirit, as subjected to history—just as, later, Hegel does not present the forms of subjective spirit in the form of a history. The history of consciousness does, as it were in a first act, contain a preceding history of the genesis of individual consciousness, and then of its historical adventures, but only the history that it traverses. But already the shaping of forms of knowledge—intuition, understanding, reason—appears as a historical sequence, in a process of the cultural development of cognition. Here I will only refer to the capacity for making generalizations and abstractions, of which there is good reason to assume that they do not develop independently of spiritual and cultural conditions and achievements. Ludwig Feuerbach, who incidentally was also a passionate reader of the Phenomenology, once pointed out that sensory intuition, even though it appears to be the most simple and primitive form of knowledge, is the latest one historically speaking—the latest one, since it presupposes that we have achieved the high level of abstraction required to see a thing as a thing. And Hegel indeed devotes a detailed chapter in his Phenomenology to this domain of the thing. And yet it seems as if there would be more work to do on the level of phylogenesis, whereas this has already been carried out with respect to the analysis of analogous ontogenetic processes.

All questions relating to a categorical development of our interpretation of the world are located in the same context. If that which Jacobi previously had said is true, something that is today confirmed by cognitive science,[11] i.e. that the causal interpretation of the processes of nature is not dependent on our theoretical intuition of a connection between cause and effect, but is mediated through our experience of our own actions, then we can ask how much bearing this insight has on our causal, and in particular teleological patterns of our understanding of the world—and furthermore, what this means for a history of self-consciousness. But this is only one example out of many—and it only relates to a first and basic domain. I need not emphasize that comparable problems appear in the practical sphere, with regard to the formation of our moral and legal ideas.

---

[11] Michael Tomasell, *Die kulturelle Entwicklung des menschlichen Denkens: Zur Evolution der Kognition* (Frankfurt am Main: Suhrkamp, 2006).

As a second and far more complex domain, I would like to mention the inner connection of the forms of objective and absolute spirit, to speak like Hegel. This of course requires no laborious demonstrations, since we are dealing with domains that are historically formed and continue to unfold in history. And even if one concedes that this development in each case has an immanent logic, they must still all be included in the history of self-consciousness, or more precisely: the history of self-consciousness itself is essentially the history of the objectification of self-consciousness in these forms, even though they at the same time have substantial character for the individual consciousness. In his Phenomenology, which in a surprising way unifies so many processes that appear to be different, and in this produces a convincing quality, Hegel has still isolated these processes and treated them in succession—a decision that may be regrettable, but given that his presentation is sufficiently complex as it is, was also a happy one. This however does not change the fact that there is an unresolved problem for future research hidden here. No one would claim that the partial histories of these domains—language, law, science, art, religion, and finally philosophy—have nothing in common. How they are connected, in our own or other traditions; how they are related to an overarching history of consciousness, whether and how they dovetail with one another, whether and to what extent they presuppose one another and relate to other forms of that society to whose life-world they belong—all of these are questions posed by Hegel's *Phenomenology of Spirit* in the context of the problem of an introduction, and which it also has attempted to answer partially, undoubtedly with often insufficient means. They are surely not false questions, and not questions that are only posed in the context of Hegel's philosophy, but questions that he brought up because they concern central aspects of our understanding of our world and of ourselves—and yet we cannot even say that two hundred years after the publication of the Phenomenology an adequate framework of questioning for the revival of these themes exists. Perhaps we could take the two hundred year jubilee of the Phenomenology as the occasion to take up once more the problems it posed.

Translated by Brian Manning Delaney and Sven-Olov Wallenstein.

Absolute Knowledge
Why Philosophy is its Own Time Grasped in Thought

TERRY PINKARD

Hegel says both that his philosophy is the contemplation of eternal truths and that all philosophy "is its own time grasped in thought." Needless to say, how one harmonizes those two claims has been the subject of much, and mutually exclusionary, commentary. What I want to argue here is that this harmonization is the central thesis of the concluding chapter of the 1807 *Phenomenology* titled "Absolute Knowledge" (at least in most of the important ways), and that this tells us something important both about this chapter in particular and about Hegel's thought in general.

Like the introduction, the "Absolute Knowledge" chapter is very short, unlike most of the chapters in the rest of the book. Almost immediately after introducing that section, Hegel tells us that what is at stake here is the "infinite judgment" (what he had earlier just as obscurely called the "speculative proposition"). Such a judgment would be one about what Kant had called the "unconditioned," which, as we know from the very first sentence of the first *Critique*, is the kind of subject matter with which human reason is burdened and about which it is forever doomed to raise "questions which, as prescribed by the very nature of reason itself, it is not able to ignore, but which, as transcending all its powers, it is also not able to answer."[1] Now, up until the last chapter, it has been precisely this "unconditioned" which has been the "object" that is being examined at each stage of the Phenomenology. For example, as any reader knows, the Phenomenology begins with an examination of "sense-certainty" and quickly finds, just as Kant said it would, that when it goes beyond the otherwise unproblematic experience of sense-certainty and asserts an un-

---

[1] Kant, *Critique of Pure Reason* (London: Macmillan, 1929), A vii.

conditioned status for it (that is, asserts it as a fully self-sufficient status), it finds itself embroiled in various contradictions, and since reason cannot rest in a contradictory state, in order to avoid the contradiction, reason finds it has thereby landed itself in the position of asserting something very different than what it first thought it was asserting. The first "infinite judgment" was that sense-certainty has no conditions outside of itself—that sense-certainty is, in the language Schelling and Hegel chose to adopt, the "absolute." However, that "infinite judgment" proved itself to be—as an *infinite* judgment—false. All the other objects that are investigated in the Phenomenology are other candidates for being the "absolute," and each of them is supposedly generated by some kind of logic that propels one from the failure of one of them to achieve that status to the assertion of the next one.

Thus, just as, by Hegel's lights, Kant had genuinely shown that reason is led to the assertion of antinomies when it goes beyond experience and makes judgments about the unconditioned, so too Hegel wants to argue that when we take some finite, limited sphere of experience to be the unconditioned (to be, to use the language of Kant that Hegel adopted for his own use, "the in-itself"), then we too end up in something like the Kantian antinomies. Only the "in-itself" would be the true, that is, would be free from the kinds of contradictory burdens that weigh on all conditioned attempts at reaching the unconditioned. Because of this, so Hegel argues, the logic of these kind of failures at first provokes us into asserting that the "object" of our investigations is, *as* something taken to be the unconditioned, something like an "absolute essence," something which lies behind appearance and which manifests itself to us only in a partial way, and our grasp of which is therefore itself also only partial and faulty. (The terms, "absolute essence," first appears in the introduction and the "Consciousness" section of the book.) However, the phrase "absolute essence" does not appear in "Absolute Knowledge." Why?

The first thing to note about all the objects under study in the Phenomenology (prior to the last chapter) is that they exhibit contradictions only when a kind of *reflection* enters the picture, that is, only when, to cite Kant's lines once again, reason raises "questions which [...] it is not able to ignore, but which [...] it is also not able to answer." What the investigations of these initial objects of examination—from sense-certainty to the various forms of spirit and religion—*seem* to show us are reason's *limits*, that is, they seem to show us the points at which reason runs out and something else seems the most likely candidate to enter the picture. The *limit* of something is, of course, the point at which something ceases to be what it is and becomes something else, or the point at which something runs out, and one moves from it to another thing.[2] Hegel's useful term for this is "negativity": The negative of something is its limit, what demarcates it from something else, that is, the point where it ceases to be what it is or where it ceases to exercise the authority it otherwise has.[3] Indeed, we could say with Hegel that it is the negativity of the initial objects themselves in the (at first) naïve assertion of their status as the unconditioned that pushes us to such self-undermining reflection in the first place.[4]

Novalis, as is well known, ironically quipped that whereas we everywhere seek the unconditioned, *das Unbedingte*, all we find are things (*Dinge*). As a quip, that fairly well sums up a big chunk of the first part of the Phenomenology. By the time we have been pushed to take, variously, not just "things" but maybe "reason" itself—as a Kantian might insist, in its "transcendental employment"—or where we take even more generally "spirit" in one of its historical shapes, or even "religion" in one of its historical shapes as the "unconditioned," we are left at the end schematically with two different "infinite judgments." The first is that "the *being of the I is a thing*"[5] Especially given the success of the sciences in the modern world, this perhaps needs no further motivation; if we apply reason to the study of "things," we will find that more and more, the naturalist stance—very roughly, that all explanation is causal, and that the natural sciences are the best suited vehicles for producing such causal explanations—looks like the most promising attitude to take. The quick objection that this ignores the normativity at work in such naturalist explanations is of course itself quickly parried by extending naturalism to the social sciences; there may

---

[2] Thus, if Kant was correct about the limits of reason, then it would indeed have made sense for him to have said that in showing reason's limits, he had made room for faith (or, to put it in the Schellingian idiom, to have made room for intellectual intuition.)
[3] This rather quick characterization of negativity conflates, as I think was Hegel's intention, two different senses of negativity, a descriptive sense and a normative sense; it is part of Hegel's complex claim that the descriptive sense depends on the normative sense, even if that is not immediately apparent. That is a topic for a longer discussion.
[4] This is ultimately to push us into a concept of *self-relating negativity*, that is, the kind of *normative* self-distinction that subjects carry out and which is the presupposition of marking out all the other kinds of negativity. Part of Hegel's enterprise is to show us that the kind of negativity involved in, as it were, *descriptively* distinguishing things from each other impels us to acknowledge a kind of *normative* negativity at work in that first activity.
[5] §790. References to the *Phenomenology of Spirit* are to my own translation, available at http://web.me.com/titpaul/Site/Phenomenology_of_Spirit_page.html.

indeed be science, but there is also "science studies" where we learn just how contingent any of the procedures and methods of practicing scientists have been (and still are). Generalized to an even greater degree, the social science thesis can be put in this form: Any "shape of consciousness" can be grasped as a "thing," that is, as something obeying merely positive, socially established rules.[6] Pushed to its conclusion, this form of infinite judgment finally ends up in more or less sophisticated versions of psychologism or "sociologism" of some sort, something that the post-Hegelian nineteenth century saw proliferate. However, this defeats itself as a statement of the unconditioned, since it basically says that the unconditioned is itself conditioned; no matter how sophisticated it gets, it still runs up against the really rudimentary objection that its own truth claims are themselves merely the product of following positive rules and yet also carry within themselves the sense that they are more than that. Both Frege's and Husserl's loud protests against the psychologism of their day were in effect protests against such a view, namely, that the "infinite judgment" really could be that "the *being of the I is a thing.*"[7]

In the very next paragraph after introducing that particular candidate for the "infinite judgment," Hegel gives us a statement of something close to subjective idealism, namely, the opposing infinite judgment to the effect that "the thing is the I."[8] If all we encounter in our search for the unconditioned is "things," then it seems that the unconditioned must itself be a statement of what "reason" ultimately requires, which is itself a requirement imposed by us *on* things. This amounts to the claim that whatever normative force things turn out to have itself ultimately has to do with their relation to humans. On this view, nature as the object of "observing reason" becomes disenchanted, and that amounts to saying that nature ("things") has no meaning except in relation to humans, to "subjects" (that is, to the "I"). It would not be too much of a stretch to see this rather anachronistically as Hegel's own statement of a kind of crude pragmatism—or as the parody of pragmatism that likes to say that truth is simply what "works" *for us.* Hegel does indeed have his own stand-in for that kind crude pragma-

---

[6] See ibid.
[7] Frege would of course howl even more loudly about being associated with any philosophy that took the "I" as playing some kind of pivotal role in normative accounts. Frege was far more impressed with the idea of the normative being beyond the realm of the merely psychological.
[8] §791.

tism—what in the Phenomenology he calls "utility," namely, the view that whatever meaning things have for us is to be determined by their utility *for us*, such that even the value of truth in science is supposedly only a utility "for us." On that view, "we" set the standards, and we compel things to live up to them.[9] On the terms of that "infinite judgment," what things are depends on how "we" cut the world up, and that depends ultimately on "our" interests.

In these closing sections, it is clear that that Hegel thinks that neither of the two mutually exclusive "infinite judgments" is on its own true, and it is also equally clear that one cannot simply combine both. However, each represents a distinct line of thought to which one is led when one reflects on what it is to claim to know something or to be committed to something; each represents, that is, another specific turn in the dialectic, that is, in the attempt to grasp the "unconditioned." To escape from the "either/or" of these two "infinite judgments," Hegel proposes what he calls a "reconciliation" of spirit with itself, although it is at first at least a little unclear as to just what this reconciliation is supposed to be—whether it really is something that carries the full theological overtones of *Versöhnung* or whether it is merely another metaphysical or logical move in the system.

In this respect, Hegel notes in the next paragraph[10] that *action* is the first division of what he calls the "simplicity of the concept." (This is surely not merely a nod to Goethe's well known statement in *Faust* that in the beginning, there was not the word but the deed[11]; it most likely nods even more deeply to Hölderlin's claim that the original act is that of a primordial division of subject and object.) From out of that original division, he notes, a "return"—apparently, to a unity that replicates in some form the so-called simplicity of the concept—is supposed to be staged.

To make this point and explicate it, Hegel refers back to the way he has staged the final confrontation of the "Spirit" chapter as two "beautiful souls" confronting each other. The confrontation is between two agents who have each reached the point where each takes for granted that the only grasp reason has of "the unconditioned" consists in the demands of *practical*

---

[9] Or, as Kant so typically put it, philosophers have "learned that reason has insight only into that which it produces after a plan of its own, and that it must not allow itself to be kept, as it were, in nature's leading-strings, but must itself show the way with principles of judgment based upon fixed laws, constraining nature to give answer to questions of reason's own determining." Kant, *Critique of Pure Reason*, B xiii.
[10] §793.
[11] "Im Anfang war die Tat."

reason to be bound by the unconditional duty to act in terms of an unconditional moral command. This requires on the part of each agent an attempt at an inner purity—a willingness to submit all one's maxims to the unyielding demands of something like the categorical imperative—which is potentially at odds with the other contingent features of one's life (one's needs, desires, personal commitments and the contingency of the world in which such actions are realized). The problem confronting them is then itself framed in terms of the kind of self-consciousness in which during and after the eighteenth century "we" found ourselves enmeshed, namely, that "we" are now acutely aware of the finitude, or contingency, of our standards—one thinks in particular of Hume's challenge to the traditional views on the matter—and of the equal necessity of justification of those standards. Put more generally: The philosophical confrontation between Kant and Hume—put even more generally: whether there are any categorical imperatives or only hypothetical imperatives—was itself anchored in a social and existential worry about whether there was in fact any grasp of the "unconditioned" at all—a worry which played itself out in very concrete religious and moral disputes. If, to put it in terms of Kant's response to Hume, the only "unconditioned" of which we can get any grasp is that which practical reason offers us in the form of pure duty, and if therefore the only true justification we can have is either that of transcendental philosophy—i.e., Kant and/or Fichte—in the theoretical realm and that of adherence to pure duty in the practical realm, then the issue is how agents who take this to be the unconditioned are entitled to deal with each other.

This confrontation is thus an exhibition—a *Darstellung*, as Hegel would have it—of Hegel's more general and ambitious thesis about the nature of conceptual content: The meaning of a concept cannot be fully (or "concretely") determined until one sees how it is put into practice or "realized" over time.[12] Hegel rejects the idea that concepts can have a determinate meaning that can be specified independently of their use in practices, and this thesis is itself part of Hegel's transformation of the Aristotelian metaphysics of the actualization of a substance's potentialities into a philosophy of a different sort—a dialectical social and historical theory of meanings as historically and socially realized in the practices in

---

[12] Hegel respectively calls this the "Ausführung" and the "Verwirklichung" (sometimes "Realisierung") in the Phenomenology.

which they find their homes. In turn, this means that understanding concepts cannot be a matter of specifying the meaning of concepts and then looking for the applications of the meaning; on the Hegelian account, the way in which the general concept is particularized makes a difference to the content of the general concept itself. In the Phenomenology, this thesis is not, as it were, independently argued; instead, Hegel constructs the various accounts in that book as *exhibitions* of this thesis about conceptual content. As one moves from putative grasps of the "unconditioned" which, as Kant claimed, display contradictoriness in themselves—from the object of sense-certainty as failing to exhibit itself as an adequate account of the unconditioned in light of its contradictory character, all the way to other such accounts, such as the contradictions implicit in taking "the thing that matters," *die Sache selbst* as "the unconditioned"—one comes to *see* that there simply is no practice-independent, or "realization-independent," grasp of conceptual meaning.[13] As it were, meaning cannot be established apart from use, but meaning is not reducible to use.

The confrontation between the two beautiful souls is thus the existential *enactment* of a more general *theory* of conceptual content that has been in the process of development throughout the entire Phenomenology. Each agent experiences the tension between his own individual desires and commitments. Each sees that his only grasp of the unconditioned is, as it were, his purity of heart, his own unconditional assent to submit all of his maxims to the test of the moral law. Each thus finds himself in the same position as the other, as each of the two beautiful souls is in effect the authority-conferring self—or, in a less orthodox Kantian mode, is the self who submits himself to the unconditional authority of reason—but who is equally as well a contingent, situated self who seeks to establish just what that authority requires. Each is, moreover, convinced that, since it is the authority of reason itself to which one is submitting, each has within himself all the resources necessary for determining just what it is that impersonal reason requires. Given that setting, the enactment quickly splits into two different understandings of what unconditional duty requires, a

---

[13] This thesis about conceptual content does become more and more a feature of explicit argumentation as Hegel develops his thoughts in his later works and lectures. The Phenomenology is, in his own words, simply the "ladder" one climbs to attain the kind of high-altitude vantage point at which the thesis begins to appear. The Encyclopedia is Hegel's more explicit set of arguments for this thesis; it remains a matter of dispute, however, whether the Phenomenology's manner of Darstellung is more persuasive than the more systematic arguments of the Encyclopedia.

split which itself stems from two different understandings of what moral *judgment* requires in the conditions of the acceptance of unconditional duty. Each makes a judgment as to what it required of him; one agent sees the purity of his motive as preserved in his actions despite the contingency of their realization (that is, he sees that irrespective of how his deeds might appear to others or what shape they might take in the world of contingency, the purity of his motive remains intact); the other agent sees the purity of his motive as lying solely in his capacity for moral *judgment* itself and not in action at all. One thus acts and takes this to preserve the beauty of his soul, provided he adopt something like an ironic stance toward his actions (or, more likely, to the consequences of those actions, matters of which he is not fully in control); the other does not act and takes the beauty of his soul to be evidenced by his refusal to sully himself with the impurity of the world.

Ultimately, each comes to *see* himself in the other as each comes to admit that in Kant's terms, he is radically evil, that is, each comes to understand that he cannot easily pry apart the contingency of his own situated perspective (and thus his own individuality, or "self-love") and his demand for a unconditional justification of his actions. Without this acknowledgement on the part of each that both have reason to suspect the other of dissembling, of hypocrisy, or of saying and doing what he does out of merely strategic considerations, and without this acknowledgement becoming mutual, this kind of push toward moralism becomes unlivable since it imposes demands for purity that cannot be acknowledged by the other. This awareness of the identity of each within a larger whole in turn leads each of them to forgive the other, since neither was, as it were, without sin (i.e., without Kantian radical evil); it is in that way that the dialectic of beautiful souls is the existential *enactment* of the conceptual dialectic between the unconditional demands of reason and our contingent situatedness. Such an enactment *precedes* the conceptual grasp of what has been enacted. (The owl of Minerva, we also know, only flies at dusk.)

As Hegel phrases it, "this unification has *in itself* already come to pass" and that what is still lacking is only "the simple unity of the concept," the conceptual comprehension of just what it is to which our form of life has already given voice.[14] At first, as he puts it, this is expressed in religious terms, as the reconciliation "in God" that is carried out through the acts of mutual forgiveness. However, this is only a resolution in what Hegel

[14] §795.

diagnoses as a case of "representational thought"; we "picture" an entity which both stands outside of us and within us and which serves as the whole within which we hold together what seems like an insurmountable contradiction (between our intended ascent to a timeless realm of reasons—the concept in "its eternal *essence*"—and our existence in a conditioned, contingent historical world—"the concept which *exists there*, that is, which acts").[15]

Once that has been grasped as the problem, then, as Hegel says, our "sole contribution here is in part to *gather together* the individual moments" into a statement of how to combine a focus on the *history* of spirit, of our own mindedness, while at the same time managing "to cling to the concept in the form of the concept."[16] It is this which requires us to look at the last contingent shape of knowledge, namely, "absolute knowledge."

What is that shape? Hegel's initial statement of it cannot help but be puzzling. "Spirit is," he says, "science."[17] Perplexing as that may look at first, it is an integral part of Hegel's claim which has to do with how the development to absolute knowledge is itself the result of the logic of modernity's inward turn in *life*—of spirit as an *in-sich-gehen*—which has for its penultimate *philosophical* expression Kant's switching the topic from reason's knowledge of objects (metaphysics) to reason's knowledge of itself (the critical philosophy). It is this which Hegel explains in noting that it is the modern world *itself* that is thus conceived in the spirit of "science." *Science*, as the rigorous, theoretical pursuit of knowledge becomes the new watchword—that is, the mark of a world of "experts" instead of the world of "noblemen" it has replaced—and this is the spirit which "knows what it is."[18] (Indeed, it is Hegel's all too trusting faith in the experts and the bureaucracy they inhabit which made him an legitimate object of suspicion for later people such as Adorno). This form of life thus is in the process of becoming a "knowing substance" as it is put into practice in the developing institutions of modern life (such as modern families, careers open to talent, constitutional states, universities organized around the union of teaching and research, and so forth), and it is the development of those institutions and *practices* which have preceded its own self-conscious realization within

---

[15] §796: "der aber sein ewiges Wesen aufgibt, da ist, oder handelt."
[16] §797.
[17] §799.
[18] §800.

modern *philosophy* that this is indeed exactly what it is.[19] (To put it another way: The revolutions of modernity—scientific and political, among others—have preceded its philosophical grasp of itself.[20]) Thus, time itself becomes the "intuited concept"; we affirm the temporality of concepts (that is, their historicity) without at the same time giving up on the necessity to give them a rational, "scientific" justification and development.[21]

For philosophy to grasp its own time, it must therefore have grasped the idea that "that nothing is *known* that is not in *experience*, or, as it can be otherwise expressed, nothing is *known* that is not available as *felt truth*."[22] That is, it grasps its substance (i.e., its form of life in terms of what unconditionally counts for it and which enters into it as a set of dispositions, a "second nature") as historically developing and temporally situated. For that form of life, out of what looked like sheer contingency (the chaos of history) or out of what looked like something determined by some set of natural laws (which we cannot ever get quite right) there turns out to have been, *retrospectively seen*, a purpose, which was never intended at any step along the way. History has a direction that exhibits Kant's conception of purposiveness without a purpose; the purpose emerges only after the fact, after we have found out in *practice* what it was that we had *meant* all along. This purpose, as we might say, itself develops out of the practice of giving and asking for reasons, which itself points us in the direction of truth-seeking; the practice of giving and asking for reasons itself involves an implicit self-consciousness, a stance from which one can criticize the norms of the practice, and when one begins to work out that form of self-consciousness, one finds oneself taking a reflective, inward turn. One finds that what one meant is that the "I think" *can* accompany all my representations, that is, that I can see all my conceptions, no matter how

---

[19] §801.
[20] Hegel makes the further claim (§801) that in its initial development, this modern substance is such that it invites a kind of "sense-certainty" reading of itself (as understanding itself as part of "science"). Modern skepticism, we might say, is the "positive" moment of this movement. (§801).
[21] §801. This is to take to its logical conclusion—at least in Hegel's Logic—Kant's admonition that we fall into error when we seek to go beyond the bounds of possible experience; it merely takes Kant's claim one step further into making our own situatedness and contingency itself a condition of possible experience, something Kant had already implicitly formulated in his conception of "radical evil," that as moral agents, we are also situated individuals who strive to attain the unconditioned standpoint of pure duty but who can never be sure that they have succeeded.
[22] §802.

entrenched they may be, as possibly only *my own*—and therefore possibly not *true*—conceptions.

That this begins to come to its culmination in a "scientific world" whose logic impels itself to reflect about itself and increasingly to make that kind of reflection integral to its own picture of itself means that this development ceases to be an exclusively European movement and must instead happen as the development of the *world* spirit, that is, of "universal humanity" (a conception that Hegel, at least in the Phenomenology, claims originates first with the Greeks).[23] It is thus not merely the expression of a particular "spirit of a time" or even what is nowadays rather emptily called "a culture"; it is the expression of a spirit, the scientific spirit, which properly is possible for all and which genuinely belongs to all. It also follows—although Hegel himself is, shall we say, more than merely reluctant to draw this conclusion—that this new spirit must understand its very own historical situatedness and realize that it too is in something similar to the situation in which the two beautiful souls had landed themselves. The French Revolution had already given one voice to this by eschewing talk of traditional rights and instead proclaiming the rights of man, and even though religion (i.e., Christianity) has long proclaimed that God loves all equally, spirit had until 1789 not yet fully reached the point where it had fully grasped that this is the result of putting certain concepts into practice; up until "absolute knowledge," spirit was thus only a collection of "national spirits" and not yet the "world spirit."[24] However, now—that is, somewhere around the last half of the chapter on absolute knowledge—we have a spirit which, although in the process of grasping itself in its universality, is still alienated from itself, and which, if it is to fully grasp itself, that is, to become fully self-conscious, must come to terms with its own alienation.

This type of reflection is identified by Hegel by a paragraph later as "absolute negativity," a term first introduced in the Phenomenology virtually in passing in the "Self-Consciousness" chapter.[25] The negative of something is, as we noted, its limit, the point at which it ceases to be what it is or where a norm has the limits to its authority. In this Hegelian jargon, "things" in the most general sense have their "negativity" in something else;

---

[23] §727.
[24] §802. This nicely mirrors Goethe's remark to Eckermann that the age of "world literature" is now upon us and that it is incumbent on us, now that we have grasped that, to hasten its arrival.
[25] §803.

what something is will be a function of what it is not. Originally, in the "Self-Consciousness" chapter, Hegel argued that initially the confrontation between the two agents who are each seeking recognition resulted in a relation of mastery and servitude, which it at first treated simply as a social *fact*—to the effect that the limits of the servant's authority over his life are set externally to him, by the master—but which, as emerging from of the common point of view generated by these relations, becomes something that is no so much merely *factual* (and thus based on relations of power and interest) and instead more *normative*, and which offers the prospect of a kind of *freedom* that would itself be a *self*-limitation, not a factual limitation by an other—ultimately a self-limitation compatible with limitation by an other. This would be not merely "finite" but *absolute* negativity as a type of self-limitation. From the kind of self-reflection captured in Fichte's deliberately provocative slogan of "I = I," the agent who in reflecting on himself as a contingent individual, a product of his time, is now called upon to grasp itself as the "absolute distinction." This is, as Hegel puts it, originally the "immediate *unity* of *thought* and *being*" as the *thought of* "thought's relation to what is the case."[26] The point is that this kind of hyper-reflection, so characteristic of modernity, is itself both the expression of and is made possible by certain types of institutions and practices within modern life; it is thus "contingent" on that world coming into being, on what Hegel calls the "*actual history*" of spirit's development.[27]

The enacted failures of attempts at self-limitation, both individually and collectively, have led to the impasse between the two putative "infinite judgments" with which the chapter begins. That impasse is set aside when the genuine "infinite judgment" about the way in which the period of the book's genesis understands itself as a historical period that attempts to grasps itself timelessly *as a* contingent historical period; in doing so, it "becomes historical." Hegel thus concludes that in doing so, in creating such a "scientific world," spirit has "won" for itself its concept, that is, has brought to a close its movement insofar as that movement is seen as culminating in the world of a "scientific" form of life. What remains to be shown is the *logic* of this movement, which up to this point has been *exhibited* but not yet constructed on its own.[28]

---

[26] §803.
[27] That this whole section amounts to establishing the normatively self-limiting nature of freedom is made apparent, I would argue, in ibid., §§788, 799.
[28] §804.

Thus, in the second from the last paragraph, Hegel says that "science contains within itself the necessity to empty itself of the form of the pure concept and to make the transition from the concept into *consciousness*," which amounts, as he notes, to the idea that "knowing is acquainted not merely with itself, but also with the negative of itself, that is, its limit."[29] This is the genuine "infinite judgment," itself a more determinate statement of the idea that the content of the "universal" is itself not independent of how it is actualized, put into practice. To say that this "knowledge is of its own limit" is also another way of stating that its philosophy can be nothing other than its own time grasped in thoughts.

In the final paragraph, Hegel notes that this grasp of itself as contingent, as the result of an "actual history" that now understands itself *as historical*, is something like a "gallery of pictures," and its activity can only be that of a kind of "recollection" of where it has been.[30] This new "scientific" world is thus, once again, a form of life that starts over again as if it had no past, or as if its unprecedented life had nothing to learn from its recollection of where it had come from; its view of its own history is that of a "gallery of pictures," merely of what has come before but now is no more. However, *our* grasp of it—"our grasp" as that of those who have just finished reading the book—is not itself merely a piece of historical knowledge but is something new, namely, philosophical history, the "*science* of *phenomenal knowledge,*" that is, "*begriffne Geschichte,*" history comprehended in terms of what has been *meant*. This in turn means that Hegel's conception of absolute knowledge and of philosophical history is not, as it has almost always been taken to be, a *teleological* view of history at all (at least strictly speaking). Instead, history turns out to be a case of, as we noted, purposiveness without a purpose, the kind of purposiveness Kant restricted to organisms and to the experience of beauty. For something to be explained teleologically in the strict sense, the explanation must explain some activity in terms of the end at which the activity was aimed. Individual actions and even some collective actions thus are paradigm cases where such teleological explanation is at home. However, the history of spirit exhibits no such teleology in that sense; spirit *had no purpose in mind* as it worked itself out. Instead of there being such a direct teleology at work, there is instead a kind of *logic* that impels itself from one position to another

---

[29] §806.
[30] §808; the image of the gallery is not new to Hegel; Novalis, for example, noted that "anecdotal history" could be seen as a "gallery of actions."

and which eventually exhausts its possibilities in the comprehension of itself as "absolute knowing." This logic has both a direction and an end-point, but it is not making its moves *in order to* reach that end-point. Nonetheless, having reached it, it now sees where its culmination lies, namely, in the logic of a form of life that takes freedom as self-direction to be its "infinite," that is, where the conceptual is "unbounded." This in turn means that it must understand itself, to use Robert Pippin's term, as "unending modernity," the continual dissatisfaction of a life that continually submits everything to criticism, although, as the pragmatists like to put it, not the whole all at once.[31]

Hegel speaks of a goal (*Ziel*) here, but that goal is, oddly enough, the timeless grasp of our own contingency.[32] Both Robert Pippin and John McCumber have each noted the oddity of Hegel's ending with misquoted lines from Schiller instead of his own words.[33] Without the "*comprehended* history," (the *begriffne Geschichte*) of the Phenomenology, the figure of "absolute knowledge" would, Hegel says, be "lifeless and alone." Philosophy, as grasping its own time in thought, would be empty and relatively meaningless if it were to divorce itself from its history or from art and religion (which is not to say that philosophy without religion is not possible, merely that philosophy must comprehend what it was that religion was always inadequately trying to say). At best, philosophy without its history would be only a formal enterprise rearranging the pieces of the "infinite judgments" of its own time into something like more perspicuous structures and bringing out the oppositions inherent in them (as in fact much academic philosophy does). What motivates and empowers the standpoint of absolute knowledge is its sublation of these other modes of seeking the unconditioned, and it exists

---

[31] Robert Pippin, *Modernism as a Philosophical Problem: On the Dissatisfactions of European High Culture* (Cambridge, Mass.: Blackwell, 1991). That Hegel's own views of modernity as continually up for grabs, although not all at once, is similar to the stance attributed to American Pragmatism is not itself accidental.

[32] §808: "This revelation is thereby the sublation of its depth, that is, its *extension*, the negativity of this I existing-within-itself, which is its self-emptying, that is, its substance—and is its *time*."

[33] Robert Pippin, paper given at Eastern APA, 2008; John McCumber, "Writing Down (Up) the Truth: Hegel and Schiller at the End of the Phenomenology of Spirit," in R. A. Block & P. D. Fenves (eds.), *The Spirit of Poesy: Essays on Jewish and German Literature and Thought in Honor of Géza Von Molnar* (Evanston, Ill.: Northwestern University Press, 2000).

only as the "recollection" and "inwardizing" of those modes.[34] Without that grasp of itself as contingent and yet demanding justification of itself—a task which has now become not national but global, that is, a demand of the "world spirit," not of nations—it would indeed be "lifeless and alone,"[35] a piece of philosophy cut off from the practical roots which sustain its thought of itself, and would thus be a merely formal enterprise (lifeless) having no real link to the rest of the form of life of which it is a part (alone). But, thanks to the Phenomenology's logic, it is supposedly not lifeless; instead, in the final metaphor it finds its own "infinity," that is, its true infinite judgment "foaming" up to it as its continual self-critique makes it continually dissatisfied with where it has been.

---

[34] The way in which this kind of philosophical, conceptual grasp of things depends on its preserving the earlier results of art and religion is admirably treated in Benjamin Rutter, *Hegel on the Modern Arts* (Cambridge: Cambridge University Press, 2011).
[35] §808.

From Finite Thinking to Infinite Spirit
How to Encounter Hegel after Heidegger's Translation

SUSANNA LINDBERG

The *Phenomenology of Spirit* ends with a description of "absolute knowledge," or "knowing," *das absolute Wissen*. The wording is impressive: *what* is absolute knowledge, "spirit knowing itself in the shape of spirit" or "comprehending conceptual knowledge"?[1]

In our day it is uncommon to make the claim that knowledge should be *absolute—truth and certainty of all of reality*. But the claim was disconcerting in Hegel's time, too: at that time, the German Idealists' demand for absoluteness appeared as a defiant transgression of the limits of healthy reason defined by Kant. Hegel's reason is more than "reasonable." It thinks that knowledge is not worthy of its concept if it is not absolute, and that a human being is not worthy of his determination (*Bestimmung*) if he does not believe that he is worthy of the absolute. Not that the absolute would be the *object* of the human being's meditation. On the contrary, knowledge is the *absolute's own knowledge*, and what we're really asking is how the human being could participate in it. The *Phenomenology of Spirit* is an answer to this key question of the age: it is a propaedeutics in which human consciousness is gradually brought up to the measure of the absolute.

Each of the previous chapters of the Phenomenology described aspects of this formation (*Bildung*) of self-consciousness. In the last chapter, called "Absolute Knowledge," self-consciousness has to exceed itself one more

---

[1] "[...] das absolute Wissen; es ist der sich in Geistesgestalt wissende Geist oder das *begreifende Wissen*." *Phänomenologie des Geistes*, in Hegel, *Werke*, eds. Eva Moldenhauer & Karl Markus Michel (Frankfurt am Main: Suhrkamp, 1970), vol. 3, 582. *Phenomenology of Spirit*, trans. Terry Pinkard §798. Henceforth quoted in the text as PhG. This and other quotations from the Phenomenology are from Pinkard's translation (quoted in the text as Pinkard, with paragraph number), available online at http://web.mac.com/titpaul/Site/Phenomenology_of_Spirit_page.html.

time—it has to overcome the very character of its being self-consciousness—and understand that it really is absolute spirit.

All the previous figures (*Gestalt, Gestaltung*) of spirit have been particular; their unilaterality, finitude, and historiality account for their contradictions and negativity. This is precisely why they have been analyzed as *figures* and *representations* (*Gestalt* and *Vorstellung*) and not as pure *concepts* (*Begriff*). Even the penultimate chapter, "Revealed Religion," is characterized by particularity. Hegel says that the *contents* of the "revealed religion," that is to say of Christianity, are already the absolute spirit, but the *form* is still one of simple representation (*Vorstellung*). This form of representation still has to be sublated (*aufgehoben*) if absolute knowledge is to reach conformity with its concept, that is to say, if it is to be truly *conceptual*. In other words, absolute knowledge must overcome the finitude and the historiality of all of its previous formations, and reach a knowledge that is absolute, in the sense that it is also infinite and eternal. From the point of view of the *presentation*, this means a transition from figure and representation to concept.

The transition from representation to concept remains difficult in the Phenomenology, too. It is the *Aufhebung par excellence*, in which absolute knowledge overcomes finitude—and conserves it; it shows the *truth of finitude*, its *eternity*.[2] Such an idea of the absolute is difficult and actually ambiguous. Some have deduced that the infinity of absolute knowledge means its detachment from the contingencies of finite, historical reality, and its condensation in a pure conceptual construction described in the *Science of Logic*, where it is also called "God's thought before creation."[3] Others, on the contrary, believe that absolute knowledge is the infinite thinking of *finite* reality, thinking that maintains and endures the negativity of nature, history, and human life. Absolute knowledge is the *reason* of reality, not its *rationalization*. In principle, "absolute knowledge" demands that we maintain both aspects of reason. But how deep in reality can spirit really push its roots?

The strength of Heidegger's radical and partly scandalous interpretation of Hegel lies in its capacity to show and to test the ambiguity of the "infinite thought of the finite." This is why I will now examine precisely Heidegger's interpretation of the absolute knowledge chapter.

---

[2] See *Wissenschaft der Logik*, Werke 5, 163–164; trans. A. V. Miller, *Hegel's Science of Logic* (New York: Humanities Press, 1969), 147–149.

[3] *Wissenschaft der Logik*, Werke 5, 44; *Science of Logic*, 50.

In his long career, Heidegger gave around fifteen lecture courses on Hegel; he published one book and three important articles on Hegel, and discussed him in several other books and conferences; notes of his lecture courses on Hegel continue to appear posthumously.[4] Heidegger's interpretations have provided an important provocative impulse to Hegel scholarship particularly when it comes to questions of time, history, and the appearing of being. Heidegger's example has also encouraged philosophers to try to locate the human being in Hegel's system—although Heidegger himself never interpreted the Hegelian subjectivity as a human being, but only as the subject of absolute knowledge. Heidegger's interpretations of Hegel have been almost as influential as his interpretations of Nietzsche and Hölderlin. He clearly knew Hegel well and took him seriously. But he recognized in Hegel an *adversary* (no doubt this accounts for the reserved attitude towards Heidegger shown by certain Hegel scholars). For Heidegger, Hegel stands for the "completion of metaphysics,"[5] and in this regard, he is precisely what Heidegger wanted to overcome, or at least clearly separate himself from, in his own "thinking of being."

The primary focus of Heidegger's interpretations of Hegel is the *Phenomenology of Spirit*. He appreciates this book greatly and takes it to be an "event in the history of being,"[6] and its "rushed, bridled, almost insane"[7] difficulty shows how the event of the Phenomenology surpassed even Hegel's own forces. Heidegger admires the book. Nevertheless, it seems to me that it was difficult for him to follow its rhythm and to grasp it. In his lecture courses he seems to *start* the book over and over again ("Hegel's Concept of Experience" analyzes the introduction and, *Hegel's Phenomenology of Spirit*, the consciousness chapter, and he hardly ever goes as far as

---

[4] In particular, the book *Hegels Phänomenologie des Geistes* (winter semester 1930–1931), GA 32, the opuscule *Identität und Differenz* (Pfullingen: Neske, 1957), and the articles "Hegels Begriff der Erfahrung," in *Holzwege* (Frankfurt am Main: Vittorio Klostermann, 1980), and "Hegel und die Griechen," in *Wegmarken* (Frankfurt am Main: Vittorio Klostermann, 1958). One should also note the conferences and the discussions in "Hegel und das Problem der Metaphysik" (1930), in *La fête de la pensée, hommage à François Fédier*, eds. H. France-Lanord & F. Midal (Paris: Lettrage, 2001), and "Vier Seminare (Le Thor, 1968)," in *Seminare*, GA 15. Among the posthumous lecture courses one should note at least the volumes GA 28 *Die deutsche Idealismus*, GA 68 *Hegel*, GA 36/37 *Sein und Wahrheit*, and GA 86 *Seminare: Hegel - Schelling*.
[5] "Überwindung der Metaphysik," in Heidegger, *Vorträge und Aufsätze* (Stuttgart: Neske, 1994), 72; trans. Joan Stambaugh, "Overcoming Metaphysics," in *The End of Philosophy* (Chicago: University of Chicago Press, 2003), 89.
[6] Martin Heidegger, *Hegel (1938–1942)*, GA 68, 73.
[7] Heidegger, *Der deutsche Idealismus*, GA 28, 214.

the self-consciousness chapter—although he once said that it is only with that chapter that the book actually begins.[8]

Heidegger reads these texts from the point of view of the absolute, which is the perspective of the end of the book. His key question is: Why does Hegel think that knowledge must be absolute? What does absoluteness mean? Heidegger's answer is as follows: "[for Hegel] the *fundamentum absolutum* is thought as the absolute itself. For Hegel, the absolute is spirit: that which is present to itself in the certainty of unconditional self-knowing ["das in der Gewissheit der unbedingten Sichwissens bei sich selbst Anwesende"]."[9] Heidegger does not approach the mystery of the absolute by analyzing a "saying of the absolute" (*Spruch*) that Hegel would advance, as he usually does in his commentaries on previous philosophers. One could even say mordaciously that the heart of his interpretation of the Phenomenology is the chapter on absolute knowledge—the precise interpretation of which has been omitted (or at least not published) by him. What Heidegger does, instead, is *translate* Hegel's *word* "absolute" into a language commensurate with Heidegger's own thinking. "Absolut" is "Absolvenz"; the *absolute* is *absolution*, which is a religious term for exculpation, remission, and accomplishment.[10] By this Heidegger means an emancipation from immediate objectivity so that things shall only be observed from the point of view of representation[11]—and contrary to Hegel, Heidegger makes no distinction between concept and representation. This makes clear Hegel's distance from Heidegger's own thought—for Heidegger seeks to destroy representational thinking, to penetrate through it into being itself. Actually, this schematic opposition does not take us very far, but in any event I will not develop it further here, since Heidegger's argument with Hegel is not my focus today.[12] My aim is simply to show how Heidegger's scant remarks point to essential moments in the absolute knowledge chapter.

---

[8] Heidegger, *Die Metaphysik des deutschen Idealismus (Schelling)*, GA 49, 176.
[9] Heidegger, "Hegels Begriff der Erfahrung," *Holzwege*, 125; trans. Julian Young and Kenneth Haynes, "Hegel's Concept of Experience," in Heidegger, *Off the Beaten Track* (Cambridge, Cambridge University Press, 2002), 97.
[10] "Hegels Begriff der Erfahrung,"132; "Hegel's Concept of Experience," 102; *Hegel (1938–1942)*, 83.
[11] "Hegels Begriff der Erfahrung," 140 et seq.; "Hegel's Concept of Experience," 108 et seq.
[12] I treat the subject extensively in my *Heidegger contre Hegel: Les irréconciliables* (Paris: L'Harmattan, 2010).

Two quotations from "Absolute Knowledge" are at the heart of his entire interpretation of Hegel.

According to the first one, time is the concept itself that exists there [*Begriff der da ist*], and when spirit grasps its concept, it annuls / erases / effaces / obliterates time [*tilgt die Zeit*]. Here is the entire passage:

> Time is the concept itself that exists there [*Die Zeit der Begriff selbst der da ist*] and is represented to consciousness as empty intuition. Consequently, spirit necessarily appears in time, and it appears in time as long as it does not grasp its pure concept, which is to say, as long as it does not annul time [*nicht die Zeit tilgt*]. Time is the pure self externally intuited by the self but not grasped by the self; time is the merely intuited concept. Since this concept grasps itself, it sublates its temporal form, comprehends the act of intuiting, and is intuition which has been conceptually grasped and is itself intuition which is comprehending.— Time thus appears as the destiny and necessity of the spirit that is not yet consummated within itself. (PhG, 584; Pinkard §803)

Heidegger leans on this passage in 1927, in *Being and Time*'s famous critique of the Hegelian conception of time, the conclusion of which is that time is for Hegel only a provisional otherness, exteriority, and alienation.[13] Heidegger repeats the same judgment in 1957, in "Die onto-theologische Verfassung der Metaphysik." Spirit *falls* into time, and in the movement of comprehension, time is *destroyed* and *effaced*.[14] In his analysis, Heidegger actually relates Hegel to Aristotle.[15] According to Heidegger, Hegel's time is simply the time of nature, the eternal succession of nows; and Hegel's concept is so much like the eternal self-movement of Aristotle's god that you cannot tell them apart.

Heidegger knows, however, that absolute knowledge is not an idea detached from nature: it is the *mediation* of idea and existence. For Hegel, the Greek reference is not sufficient for the understanding of this mediation, but Christianity provides him with a good model of mediation in its description of the incarnation of the idea as a finite man and its resurrection into God's infinity. This is why Heidegger's second key expression from the absolute knowledge chapter is: "the comprehended

---

[13] Heidegger, *Sein und Zeit* (Tübingen: Max Niemeyer Verlag 1984), §82, 434–435.
[14] Heidegger, *Identität und Differenz*, 33–36.
[15] *Sein und Zeit*, §82, 432–433, cf. Jacques Derrida, "Ousia et grammè," in Derrida, *Marges de la philosophie* (Paris: Minuit, 1972).

history is the 'Golgotha of absolute spirit.'" The expression comes from the very last lines of the Phenomenology:

> *The goal*, absolute knowledge, that is, spirit knowing itself as spirit, has the recollection of spirits as they are in themselves and as they achieve the organization of their realm. Their preservation in terms of their freestanding existence appearing in the form of contingency is history, but in terms of their conceptually grasped organization, it is the *science of phenomenal knowledge*. Both together are conceptually grasped history; they form the recollection and the Golgotha of absolute spirit, the actuality, the truth, the certainty of its throne, without which it would be lifeless and alone; only –
>
> *Out of the chalice of this realm of spirits*
> *Foams forth to him his infinity.*
> (PhG, 591; Pinkard §808.)

Here, the "comprehended history" is the "Golgotha of absolute spirit" (and not only the "altar on which the happiness of nations, the wisdom of states, and the virtue of individuals is slaughtered," like in the later lectures on the philosophy of history, which follow the scheme of tragedy.[16] As "Golgotha," history is identified with Christ's suffering and death, and spirit with life after resurrection. The idea of the Christ as the determinate historical existence (*Dasein*) of the absolute was the principal content of the previous chapter, "Revealed Religion," and "Absolute Knowledge" was supposed to have the same contents as "Revealed Religion," differing only in form. The logic of Christianity explains how the idea *touches* finite reality—only to leave it immediately behind. Finitude is simply something into which the idea *falls*, and that it overcomes in its *resurrection*. The properly finite aspect of finitude—its contingency, negativity, contradictions and death— are left over like mortal remains that spirit will not touch.[17]

---

[16] *Vorlesungen über die Philosophie der Geschichte*, Werke 12, 35; trans H. B. Nisbet, *Lectures on the Philosophy of World History: Introduction; Reason in History* (Cambridge: Cambridge University Press, 1975), 69.

[17] Drawing on Bataille's work, Derrida examines in *Glas* everything that the spirit cannot "digest" and which therefore "remains": the illegitimate child, the desiring woman, all kinds of waste and uselessness. On the contrary, certain newer interpretations have sought to prove that Hegel gives an essential position to such elements that escape spiritual determinations: they belong to the category of contingency. See Bernard Mabille, *Hegel, l'épreuve de la contingence* (Paris: Aubier, 1999), and Jean-Marie Lardic,

Heidegger juxtaposes the "Golgotha of absolute spirit" with the "speculative Good Friday" described on the last lines of the opuscule *Glauben und Wissen* (1802). Here, too, spirit rises from the terror of the death of God to resurrection, from the most painful conceptlessness to the freest figure of the concept.[18] Thinking of these passages, Heidegger interprets the absolute spirit essentially as the Parousia of spirit.[19] *Parousia* is a theological term meaning the Christ's second coming at the End of Days. Applied to the Phenomenology, it means that it is in absolute knowledge that spirit appears entirely and definitively. Of course spirit is always already "with us," *bei uns*; but it has to endure the slow and painful process of the formation of self-consciousness in order to present this being-close-to-us *as such*, not only *at* the light of the absolute but *as* the light of the absolute.[20] The Parousia of the absolute is like God's perfect presence to us. According to Heidegger, Hegel's absolute is "onto-theological": it is God turned into *logos*; on the one hand, it is detached from history (it is not the particular god of a historical people), on the other hand, it remains theological (that is to say, it is a theory of the Supreme Being, *causa sui*). This is how Heidegger interprets Hegel as a theological thinker, although hardly as a Christian thinker.[21]

The idea of the Parousia of the absolute sketches a kind of "end of history." The Parousia of the absolute does not end history with any particular event. (As Hegel says, the Christ's historical existence is far behind us and it has not stopped history;[22] and of course Hegel says nothing about a "world spirit on a horseback" in the chapter on "absolute knowledge.")[23] On

---

"La contingence chez Hegel," in Lardic, *Hegel: Comment le sens commun comprend la philosophie* (Arles: Actes sud, 1989).

[18] *Glauben und Wissen*, Werke 2, 432–433.

[19] "Hegels Begriff der Erfahrung," 198; "Hegel's Concept of Experience," 153.

[20] Ibid., 137; ibid., 106.

[21] *Identität und Differenz*, 64.

[22] Cf. *Vorlesungen über die Geschichte der Philosophie*, Werke 18, 27.

[23] In Kojève's interpretation of Hegel, history ends with a single figure (Napoleon, Hegel himself, or alternatively the modern US, Soviet Union, or Japan). In philosophy this means that absolute knowledge unites its absolute subject and its finite agent in one figure of total knowledge. Kojève says that "absolute knowledge" is not wisdom but the Wise Man (*le Sage*), a human being of flesh and blood, who realizes wisdom or science in his activity; see Kojève, *Introduction à la lecture de Hegel* (Paris: Gallimard, 1994), 323. He continues by saying that the Wise Man is an entirely satisfied human being who knows everything and is completely conscious of himself (*ibid*, 272). He is also morally perfect and can be a model for others. The appearance of the Wise Man is an event in the history of the world: the Wise Man is Hegel, who has perfectly recognized God in

the contrary, the absolute is defined, so to speak, in a "final" manner: from the point of view of its "end" or "goal." This does not mean (simply) that philosophy reaches the absolute when it is able to think the whole of what is and what has been. It means more essentially that reaching the absolute requires the understanding of the final character of the history of consciousness: that although the beginning produces the end, only the end can justify the beginning. This is why absolute knowledge must be defined as the end of the process. Because of the teleological nature of the growth of spirit, the goal of the absolute is "always already there"; but it really appears only when the goal *comes forth* as the *knowledge* of the need to understand the sense of the spirit from its "end." Against this idea, Heidegger raises his own "eschatology of being" that consists in thinking the sense of being and of time as something that is *still to come*.²⁴ Correlatively, Heideggerian thinking is finite (and not absolute) because it is a question addressed to something that is merely coming, and to this coming itself. The general idea is that when Hegel's "end-oriented thinking" "closes" history, Heidegger's "coming thinking" only "opens" it to the possibility of coming events. Hegel's philosophy is incapable of welcoming any new event; it cannot be surprised: in it, everything is fulfilled.²⁵

Heidegger is by no means the only one to interpret Hegel in the framework of Christian theology. This is indeed one way to interpret Hegel, but in my opinion, it is an unnecessarily backward-looking interpretation, and this is why I would like to approach the question from a different angle.

I would like to take seriously Hegel's claim that philosophy is the highest form of absolute spirit and, in this sense, something other than religion. Furthermore, the "theological" interpretation of absolute knowledge leads to a picture of a supra-temporal, purely logical spirit. But isn't such an interpretation of Hegel in the end too unilateral—in particular, because it detaches Hegel's thought from the "concrete life" that was, after all, a

---

Napoleon. Knowledge exists empirically in Hegel's book, *i.e.* in the *Phenomenology of Spirit*, which annuls time and refuses the possibility of a future (*ibid.*, 384).—Of course there is no textual support for these claims.

²⁴ "Der Spruch der Anaximander," in Heidegger, *Holzwege*, 323; *Off the Beaten Track*, 247.

²⁵ In her book *L'avenir de Hegel: Plasticité, temporalité, dialectique* (Paris: Vrin, 1996), Catherine Malabou has tried to show that a dimension of futurity belongs to Hegel's thought. Derrida, in his article "Le temps des adieux: Heidegger (lu par) Hegel (lu par) Malabou" (*Revue philosophique de la France et de l'étranger*, 1998), points out that this does not lead to an assimilation of Hegel and Heidegger: while the future can *surprise* Hegel, Heidegger's thinking has been entirely constructed on the *horizon of the future*.

genuine question for him? As I said, the idea of an absolute knowledge is ambiguous: it is not only a *rationalization* of reality; it is the rationality of *reality*. To what extent can absolute knowledge preserve the finite, historical, figural, and representative reality from which it arises?

Such questions also motivate Heidegger's interpretation of Hegel. When he is not simply trying to ward off the "accomplishment of metaphysics," when he is on the contrary trying to account for the family resemblance between himself and Hegel, his interpretation is more nuanced than the one presented above. The identification of the absolute with God-*logos* is only one aspect of his interpretation. On another level, he recognizes a vertiginous proximity between himself and Hegel, when it comes to seizing *finite existence*. Following this lead, Heidegger writes, "we shall try to encounter Hegel on the *problematic of finitude*. This means, according to what we said earlier, that through a confrontation with Hegel's problematic of infinitude, we shall try to create, on the basis of our own inquiry into finitude, the kinship needed in order to reveal the spirit of Hegel's philosophy."[26] In 1929, Heidegger suggests: "Hegel is opposed to the idea that eternity would be an 'abstraction from time'... eternity in its absoluteness is on the contrary something that time liberates from itself and that is still not torn away from time... the essential problem: doesn't Hegel say that the genuine concept of eternity is born from time and thus it reveals its finitude? Is time the origin of eternity?"[27] Heidegger does not follow up on this lead, however. But following him, we can state that it is possible to read Hegel as a thinker of finitude. This does not mean a reduction of Hegel to Heidegger, but the discovery of a different idea of finitude than Heidegger's.

In order to understand this idea we have to return to the question of the relation of absolute knowledge to time. In the passage quoted by Heidegger, when "spirit annuls time," Hegel is speaking about the "time of nature," which at first is simply hidden in objective reality. The concept surely destroys the idea of time as a detached, external form of intuition. But on the other hand, the concept also *produces* its own time and in particular the "absolute memory" (*Erinnerung*) that coincides with neither natural time nor a timeless idea.

---

[26] *Hegels Phänomenologie des Geistes* (winter semester 1930–1931), GA 32, 55; trans. Parvis Emad and Kenneth Maly, *Hegel's Phenomenology of Spirit* (Bloomington: Indiana University Press, 1988), 38.
[27] *Der deutsche Idealismus*, GA 28, 211.

How does this happen? I quote more key passages from the three last pages of the Phenomenology:

> In this knowledge, spirit has brought to a close the movement of giving shape to itself... Spirit has won the pure element of its existence, the concept. [...] Conversely, to every abstract moment of science, there corresponds a shape of appearing spirit per se. Just as existing spirit is not richer than science, so, too, is spirit in its content not poorer. [...]
>
> Science contains within itself the necessity to empty itself of the form of the pure concept [...].
>
> Knowing is acquainted not merely with itself but also with the negative of itself, that is, its limit. To know its limit means to know that it is to sacrifice itself. This sacrifice is the self-emptying within which spirit exhibits its coming-to-be-spirit in the form of a *free contingent event*, and it intuits outside of itself its pure *self* as *time* and likewise intuits its *being* as space. This final coming-to-be, nature, is its living, immediate coming-to-be; *nature*, that is, spirit emptied of itself, is in its existence nothing but this eternal self-emptying of its *durable existence* and the movement that produces the *subject*.
>   However, the other aspect of spirit's coming-to-be, *history*, is that *mindful* (*wissende*) self-*mediating* coming-to-be—the spirit emptied into time. However, this emptying is likewise the self-emptying of itself; the negative is the negative of itself. This coming-to-be exhibits a languid movement and succession of spirits, a gallery of pictures, of which each, endowed with the entire wealth of spirit, moves itself so slowly because the self has to take hold of and assimilate the whole of this wealth of its substance. Since its consummation consists in spirit's completely *knowing* what *it is*, is spirit *knowing* its substance, this knowledge is its *taking-the-inward-turn* within which spirits forsakes its existence and gives its shape over to recollection (Erinnerung). In taking-the-inward-turn, spirit is absorbed into the night of its self-consciousness, but its vanished existence is preserved in that night, and this sublated existence—the existence which was prior but is now newborn in knowledge—is the new existence, a new world, and a new shape of spirit. Within that new shape of spirit, it likewise has to begin all over again without prejudice in its immediacy, and from its immediacy to rear itself once again to maturity, as if all that had preceded it were lost to it and as if it were to have learned nothing from the experience of the preceding spirits. However, that *inwardizing re-collection* (*Er-innerung*) has preserved that experience; it is what is inner, and it is in fact the higher

form of substance. [...] The goal of this movement is the revelation of depth itself, and this is *the absolute concept*. (PhG, 588, 591; Pinkard, §807-808)

According to Hegel, "time is the existing concept itself" (*die Zeit ist der daseiende Begriff selbst*) (PhG, 45-46, 584; Pinkard §39, and §801). The passage underlined by Heidegger, in which "spirit necessarily appears in time, and it appears in time as long as it does not grasp its pure concept, which is to say, as long as it does not annul time" only describes the natural time found in sense perception: indeed, pure disparition is the essence of this time. But spirit does not remain such a pure I detached from nature. On the contrary, it creates time again as its own dimension, and henceforth time is regarded as spirit's own dimension in reality. This is how spirit "sacrifices itself," "externalizes itself" and only exists as a "free contingent event," that is to say, as time and space, in other words, as nature insofar as nature *is* for Hegel the "being-otherwise of spirit." Furthermore, spirit "sacrifices itself" by becoming history, in which things do not disappear, like in nature, but they are on the contrary conserved in the "night of self-consciousness." The own-most existence of spirit is history, which does not destroy time but on the contrary unfolds it as the proper dimension of the absolute subject.[28]

---

[28] According to Heidegger, Hegel understands history only as the provisional being-otherwise of the idea, and this is why he rejects Hegel's philosophy of history entirely (*Identität und Differenz*, 33-34). Nevertheless, Hegel does say *that* the idea must be historical and briefly shows *why* this is so—but he never develops properly the "metaphysics of time" that would finally explain the historicity of the idea; see Hegel, *Vorlesungen über die Geschichte der Philosophie: Einleitung; Orientalische Philosophie*, ed. Walter Jaeschke (Hamburg: Meiner, 1993), 29 et seq. Several commentators have reacted against Heidegger's categorical rejection of Hegel's philosophy of history and followed Hegel's thesis of the historicity of the idea. Generally the demonstration of the historicity of the idea goes hand in hand with the rejection of the idea of the "end of history." The best book on the subject is Oskar Daniel Brauer, *Dialektik der Zeit: Untersuchungen zu Hegels Metaphysik der Weltgeschichte* (Stuttgart-Bad Cannstadt: Frommann-Holzboog, 1982), see esp. 155-196. See also Stefan Matjeschack, *Die Logik des Absoluten: Spekulation und Zeitlichkeit in der Philosophie Hegels* (Berlin: Akademie Verlag, 1992), 308-335. A convincing analysis of the question is also given by Christophe Bouton, in *Temps et esprit dans la philosophie de Hegel. De Francfort à Iéna* (Paris: Vrin, 2000), 272-298, and idem., "Hegel penseur de la 'fin de l'histoire'?" in "Hegel penseur de la 'fin de l'histoire'?," in *Après la fin de l'histoire: Temps, monde, historicité*, eds. J. Benoist & F. Merlini (Paris: Vrin, 1998), as well as Franck Fischbach, in *L'Être et l'acte: Enquête sur les fondements de l'ontologie moderne de l'agir* (Paris: Vrin, 2002), 85-88. Behind these analyses one can feel the influence of Jean-Luc Nancy's *Hegel: L'inquiétude du négatif* (Paris: Hachette, 1997) and Cathérine Malabou's *L'avenir*

These images must not be understood as if the absolute were a stabile subject, a consciousness facing a stabile object or more precisely the subject's representation of its object. Spirit is not one of the *poles* of this pulse of "self-sacrificing" and "rediscovery": it is the *process itself*. Let us look at it more closely.

For Hegel, the essence of spirit is that its *being is an act*.[29] In order to be true to its concept, the act must not remain potential but must be realized precisely in contingent reality. This is why, also according to the *Science of Logic* and the *Encyclopedia*, the absolute idea is "liberated" when it becomes nature, that is to say, contingent spatio-temporal happening.[30] Only then can it progressively become history, which is the proper origin of the idea. The Phenomenology describes the same process from the point of view of absolute knowing: the absolute cannot know itself if it does not let go and abandon itself to the negativities of nature and history. The absolute is this "free contingent event" and "the night of self-consciousness." It only knows itself when it "reveals this depth." At the same time, it finds something new and surprising: a new form produced by a sort of unconscious imagination of nature and of the past. The exteriority of spirit is productive and inventive: it delivers something unheard-of, of which the absolute had no idea. Maybe it was already "contained" in it—but when the absolute is defined as *knowledge*, *unconscious* contents cannot exactly be considered to be a part of the absolute. Finally, on the level of absolute knowledge, the absolute "reveals the depths" precisely when it finds this "imagination" that is its own-most substance. Then it realizes that its "recollection" is not a simple *storage* of past representations but an unconscious *activity*, through which such representations are synthesized into something *new*. When Heidegger criticizes the "metaphysics of representation," he thinks that the representation is conserved *as such* in its being-otherwise. But for

---

de Hegel, 220–221. Michel Haar, in his "Structures hégéliennes dans la pensée heideggérienne de l'Histoire" (*Revue de métaphysique et de morale*, Jan-March 1980), shows strikingly how close Heidegger's own thinking of historicity is to Hegel's philosophy of history.
[29] Hegel, *Vorlesungen über die Geschichte der Philosophie: Einleitung; Orientalische Philosophie*, 8; see also Fischbach, *L'Être et l'acte*, 57 et seq.
[30] *Wissenschaft der Logik*, Werke 6, 573; *Science of Logic*, 843.

Hegel, on the contrary, imagination is a productive dimension and not one that conserves.[31]

I would now like to end with an interpretation that is not shared by all, and that I cannot, *stricto sensu*, claim to be the only possible one, because now we are on a level that Hegel himself discusses in only a very limited way. I think that at the end of the Phenomenology, at the moment of its "Golgotha," the absolute disappears in the nightly darkness of nature and forgetfulness *over and over again*. There is no end of history; on the contrary, the very finality of thought keeps history moving. I find it absurd to say that at the culminating point of the Phenomenology the movement of the absolute would be stopped by a particular historical figure, were it Christ or Napoleon himself. The idea of the completion of the movement of the absolute as the Parousia of the absolute is not as absurd, but I find it, too, powerless: it is based on the idea that only the thinking of the future, and not of the past, can keep thought open to new events and prevent the dogmatic closure. The thinking of the "coming" might be more effective than the thinking of the past, but the latter is not powerless either. The past can be over, its thinking cannot be—and if it were, the whole of the project of history of philosophy and philosophy of history would be devoid of interest.

The absolute that is revealed in the last pages of the Phenomenology is not a particular figure; nor is it an extreme vision of the "pure light" of knowing described by Heidegger. The absolute is a free act and idea. Because it is an act, it cannot remain simply potential. Because it is an idea, it cannot be an object of a calm internal intuition. The idea is properly present only in the *act* of knowing itself: seen from the point of view of such an act, the eternal idea is the *goal* of the action and the historical idea is its *result*, but none exists without the other. This is why the idea has to have its "temporal existence" with all its tearing, restlessness, and negativity. The absolute is a double movement: on the one hand it has to be realized as particular figures, on the other hand it has to crush each and every one of them, precisely because they are particular and not true to the infinity of the idea. This is why the absolute is the movement of an infinite *figuration and defiguration*. It is not a series of modifications of an unlikely archetype; it is the very movement of figuration. It is not a simple principle of metamor-

---

[31] Cf. *Enzyklopädie der philosophischen Wissenschaften III*, Werke 10, § 455; trans. M. J. Petry, *Hegel's Philosophy of Subjective Spirit* (Dordrecht: Reidel, 1979), §455.

phosis but the movement in which the absolute's figures are born and die. The absolute exists most perfectly in this act of its realization. It is neither the acting subject, nor the object that results from such an action, but it is the action itself. The process engenders the subject and the object, not the other way round.

Thinking the absolute is thinking this movement. Such a thinking "reveals the depth" by bringing out the *activity* of birth and death of particular figures. The activity itself cannot be an object of a calm representation. Only the concept can describe it—because the concept is its own movement. When thinking reaches the goal of spirit, it understands the paradoxical structure that keeps it going. The paradox of thought is that the idea seems simultaneously to *precede* the act in which it is realized, and to *result* from it. The eternal idea is the goal of the activity, the historical idea is its result, and yet the eternal idea does not pre-exist its realization, because it only exists historically. As Otto Brauer says: the idea is an artist: "it has to make itself what it knows itself to be, but it does not know what it is before it has made itself."[32]

This is why I think that the absolute knowing never "ends," but starts over and over again. It is not a simple image of this movement, but a going along with the movement itself.

Hegel scholars are generally aware of the possibility of opposing this kind of *processual* interpretation of the absolute to the *systematic* one (where the end of history is admitted, as well as the closure of the process of thought in absolute knowing). Actually, Hegel offers elements consistent with both interpretations without really resolving the antagonism between them.

Choosing the processual interpretation, I stress that "infinity" is mainly the infinity of the *thought* of *finite* reality, and that "reason" is not an independent entity beyond the finite world but the *desire* of reason *in the world itself*, the desire that produces the reason of a reality that does not have it in the beginning. Now, such a thought of the *logos of the finite world* comes very close to Heidegger's *thinking of being*, much closer than Heidegger would like to admit. But does it go so far as to coincide with it?

In the end, it does not. Hegel urges us to think *what* happens; he also realizes the need for thinking *that* it happens—that *happening (Geschehen)*

---

[32] Brauer, *Dialektik der Zeit*, 156.

is the proper mode of truth.³³ For him, the historical event is the origin of truth, and as far as there is no ideal world behind the events, truth is manifested in the very event. Hegel goes as far as this: he opens the antagonism between ideality and historiality, he urges us to think about it as the main antagonism of thought, but, in the end, he never writes the "metaphysics of time" that ought to have explained this complication properly. Heidegger, on the contrary, *thematizes* precisely the question of the happening of truth. For instance, in "Zeit und Sein," he obliges us to think, beyond events themselves, the "giving" of time and being—*es gibt Sein* and *es gibt Zeit*—that "gives" the events, and this *givenness* itself is the ultimate theme of thought. In this sense, Heidegger would clearly thematize something that Hegel only felt obscurely, for instance when the latter spoke, not so very clearly, about the "chalice of the realm of spirits that lets infinitude foam forth." In this sense, Heidegger's profound question of the finiteness of truth encourages us to re-read Hegel in order to find his answer to it. This is the real *translation of thought* he obliges us to engage in: not a simple change of *words*, but a *transformation of the question* that calls forth the words, too.

---

³³ This is explained very well by Jean-Luc Nancy in "La surprise de l'événement," in Nancy, *Être singulier pluriel* (Paris: Galilée, 1996).

Hegel's *Phenomenology of Spirit*
Some Problems and Perspectives

CARL-GÖRAN HEIDEGREN

In the mid-1990s, I published a running commentary on Hegel's *Phenomenology of Spirit*.[1] To my knowledge it was the first full-length commentary in a Scandinavian language. Furthermore, there existed at the time no complete translation of the Phenomenology into any Scandinavian language. Since then a Norwegian, a Danish, and recently a Swedish translation have been published. Being a sociologist, I have in later years only occasionally returned to Hegel and the Phenomenology. Thus, what I will do in the following text is to recall some of the problems I was struggling with when I wrote my commentary and to present some aspects of an interpretation.

Where not to start: The preface

The Phenomenology begins with a famous preface. It is certainly an important text for the understanding of Hegel's philosophy. However, I don't think that the key to the Phenomenology is to be found there. The preface was intended as a preface to the whole of the system Hegel planned to publish, and not particularly to the Phenomenology. Therefore, in my view the preface should be read after the reading of the Phenomenology, just as Hegel wrote it after having finished his manuscript in October 1806. In the following, I will make use of some formulations taken from the preface (which Hegel sent to the publisher in January 1807).

---

[1] Carl-Göran Heidegren, *Hegels Fenomenologi: En analys och kommentar* [Hegel's Phenomenology: An analysis and commentary] (Stockholm/Stehag: Symposion, 1995).

Right now I just want to draw attention to an important clue to the spiritual atmosphere that animates the Phenomenology and to Hegel's mood while writing the book. I'm thinking of the oft-quoted lines in the preface: "Besides, it is not difficult to see that ours is a birth-time and a period of transition to a new era. Spirit has broken with the world it has hitherto inhabited and imagined, and is of a mind to submerge it in the past, and in the labour of its own transformation" (§11; 18).[2] A few months later, in August 1807, Hegel wrote in a letter to a friend about "the great constitutional lawyer in Paris,"[3] i.e. Napoleon, the personalized world soul whom Hegel had seen riding through Jena at the time he was finishing the manuscript to the Phenomenology. At the time, Hegel thus obviously had great expectations that a new world was in the making and, so it seems, he saw a connection between his book project and this process of change.

Where to start: The introduction

In my view, close attention should be devoted to the introduction to the Phenomenology, which comprises about ten pages. There Hegel presents an operation by which consciousness investigates itself—both what it takes to be the truth or being-in-itself and its actual knowledge. "Consciousness simultaneously distinguishes itself from something, and at the same time relates itself to it, or, as it is said, this something exists for consciousness. ... [W]hatever is related to knowledge or knowing is also distinguished from it, and posited as existing outside of this relationship; this being-in-itself is called truth" (§82; 76).[4] This difference between *knowing* and *truth* is called the *opposition of consciousness*. However, consciousness does not have any direct access to the True as it exists in itself, and so it seems that it

---

[2] The first reference is to Miller's translation of the Phenomenology, G. W. F. Hegel, *Phenomenology of Spirit*, trans. A.V. Miller (New York: Oxford University Press, 1977), the second is to volume 3 of the Suhrkamp edition, G. W. F. Hegel, *Phänomenologie des Geistes. Werke 3* (Frankfurt am Main: Suhrkamp, 1970). Compare the words with which Hegel closed his lectures at Jena in September 1806: "We stand at the gates of an important epoch, a time of ferment, when spirit moves forward in a leap, transcends its previous shape and takes on a new one. [...] Philosophy especially has to welcome its appearance and acknowledge it, while others, who oppose it impotently, cling to the past." Quoted in Shlomo Avineri, *Hegel's Theory of the Modern State* (Cambridge: Cambridge University Press, 1972), 64. All translations from the German texts are my own.
[3] *Briefe von und an Hegel*, vol. I., ed. Johannes Hoffmeister (Hamburg: Meiner, 1952), 185.
[4] In my quotations from the Phenomenology I have left out the italics.

does not have any standard by which to measure its knowledge. But according to Hegel, consciousness provides its own standard by which it investigates its knowledge. "Thus in what consciousness affirms from within itself as being-in-itself or the True we have the standard which consciousness itself sets up by which to measure what it knows" (§84; 77). Based on the distinction between knowing and truth, Hegel presents a procedure by which consciousness investigates itself, and which gives rise to an internal dynamic and development by which consciousness progresses from one shape to another. When the opposition of consciousness is done away with, is finally overcome, we have reached the realm of absolute knowing, i.e. the standpoint of Hegel's system. Thus, the primary goal of the Phenomenology is to overcome the opposition of consciousness, the opposition between knowing and truth. As long as this opposition exists, consciousness has further experiences to make. This is the Phenomenology as an *epistemological project*.

I would like to suggest as a heuristic principle for the interpretation of the Phenomenology to start out from this internal dynamic by which consciousness investigates itself, and see how far the different chapters of the book lend themselves to an interpretation based on this dynamic.

Two perspectives: "For consciousness" and "for us"

In the introduction, Hegel also makes an important distinction between two perspectives represented in the Phenomenology. One is the perspective of the *consciousness* that takes on different shapes and makes various experiences; this perspective is called "for consciousness." The other perspective is from the standpoint of absolute knowing, i.e. from the standpoint of the *author* of the Phenomenology; this perspective is called "for us" or "we." The latter perspective is also to a certain extent the perspective of the *reader* of the Phenomenology, being on his or her way towards the standpoint of absolute knowing.

The organization of each chapter in the book, or rather of each shape of consciousness, is in my view the following. First, Hegel presents a certain shape of consciousness from the perspective of "we" or "for us," for example sense-certainty, perception, etc. Then the dialectical movement of consciousness takes place, the process by which consciousness investigates itself, now from the perspective of "for consciousness" itself. Finally, a transition to the next shape of consciousness is effected by means of a *determinate negation* or the *reversal of consciousness*, once again from the perspective of "we" or "for us." It is not always easy to trace this organization in three steps in the different chapters, nor is it always an easy task to decide where the dialectical movement of consciousness begins and where it ends, but still I think it is possible to make out these moments in each chapter. In fact, that the three steps can be distinguished from one another is a precondition for Hegel's phenomenological method—the dialectic of consciousness, as presented in the introduction—having any plausibility at all.

Two titles

Next, I want to address two problems located so to speak at the gate to the Phenomenology.

The first is the problem of the *two titles*. The book was first to appear under the title "Science of the Experience of Consciousness," but it finally appeared under the title "Science of the Phenomenology of Spirit." Does this change of title indicate that the conception of the book changed during the time of writing it? I don't think so. In fact, Hegel introduces a notion of spirit rather early in the text, at the beginning of chapter IV, in terms of "I that is We and We that is I" (§177; 145), and furthermore announces: "What still lies ahead for consciousness is the experience of what Spirit is" (ibid.). Thus, the science of the experience of consciousness comprises the experience of what spirit is.

How then to interpret the change of title? In the preface, Hegel presents us with the idea of a *ladder* that takes the individual to the standpoint of science, i.e. absolute knowing. "The individual has the right to demand that Science should at least provide him with the ladder to this standpoint, should show him this standpoint within himself" (§26; 29). Now, obviously, you can climb a ladder upwards as well as downwards, you can ascend it as well as descend it, and this goes for Hegel's ladder too. My thesis is that from one perspective—climbing the ladder upwards—"Science of the Experience of Consciousness" is the more adequate title, and from the other perspective—descending the ladder—"Science of the Phenomenology of Spirit" is the more adequate. In the first case we have to do with the formative education of consciousness, in the second case with the reflection of spirit into itself, with substance becoming subject. Hegel stresses this double perspective in the following sentence from the preface: "In this respect formative education, regarded from the side of the individual, consists in his acquiring what thus lies at hand, devouring his inorganic nature, and taking possession of it for himself. But, regarded from the side of universal spirit as substance, this is nothing but its own acquisition of self-consciousness, the bringing-about of its own becoming and reflection into itself" (§28; 33).

Two divisions of content

The second problem relates to the *two divisions of content*. The running text is divided into eight chapters with Roman numerals. However, in the table of contents at the beginning of the book, Hegel inserted a second division with capital letters in combination with the Roman numerals.

Roman numerals	Capital letters
	A. Consciousness
I. Sense-Certainty	
II. Perception	
III. Force and Understanding	
IV. The Truth of Self-Certainty	B. Self-Consciousness
A	A
B	B
V. The Certainty and Truth of Reason	C.AA. Reason
A	A
B	B
C	C
VI. Spirit	BB. Spirit
A	A
B	B
C	C
VII. Religion	CC. Religion
A	A
B	B
C	C
VII. Absolute Knowing	DD. Absolute Knowing

Do the two divisions of content indicate a change in the conception of the book? The eight chapters with Roman numerals are very disproportionate. In the original publication from 1807, chapter one on sense-certainty comprises 16 pages, chapter two on perception 21 pages, whereas chapters five and six, on reason and spirit respectively, comprise 214 and 249 pages. This led Otto Pöggeler, a well-known Hegel scholar, to assume that Hegel must have lost control over the process of writing somewhere in the chapter on reason (V).[5] This is a rather fantastic idea: imagine a famous philosopher losing control over what he was doing, and ending up writing a book that he had not intended to write. This is indeed a very postmodern way to conceive the coming into being of the Phenomenology: a text more or less without an author.

Hegel from the beginning probably had in mind a correspondence between the structure of the Phenomenology and the development of categories in his Logic. Towards the end of the Phenomenology we read: "To each abstract moment of Science [Logic] corresponds a shape of manifest Spirit as such [Phenomenology]" (§805; 589). The problem is that Hegel's Logic was in state of flux at the time he wrote the Phenomenology. It did not yet have the shape of the later *Science of Logic* from 1812–16, and it no longer had the shape of the Jena manuscript on Logic and Metaphysics from 1804–05. The best guess of what his Logic looked like at the time is probably the very rudimentary sketch that Hegel presents towards the end of the so-called *Jenaer Realphilosophie* from 1805–06: "absolute being, becoming other (relation), life and knowing—knowing about knowing, spirit, spirit knowing itself."[6] This division can be broadly related to the Roman numerals.

The division with capital letters is also puzzling. A triad, A-B-C, passes over into a quadruple, AA-BB-CC-DD, all four being subdivisions of the chapter C in the triad. Furthermore, the chapter C has no heading of its own. I think that the most adequate title for the chapter C would have been reason in the broad sense of speculative reason, and not reason in the phenomenological sense of "the certainty of consciousness that it is all reality" (§233; 179). You can't go beyond speculative reason, and therefore the following

---

[5] Otto Pöggeler, "Die Komposition der Phänomenologie des Geistes," in *Materialien zu Hegels "Phänomenologie des Geistes,"* eds. Hans-Friedrich Fulda & Dieter Henrich (Frankfurt am Main: Suhrkamp, 1973), 350.
[6] G. W. F. Hegel, *Jenaer Systementwürfe III. Gesammelte Werke* (Hamburg: Meiner, 1976), 286.

chapters AA-DD are all subdivisions of the chapter C. I will come back to this issue, the structuring of the Phenomenology, in a later section.

Lordship and bondage

Some words must be said about the chapter on lordship and bondage (IV.A), probably the most famous and well-known part of the Phenomenology. How does this chapter fit into the aim of the book as outlined in the introduction: the overcoming of the opposition of consciousness? One interpreter, John N. Findlay, coming to this chapter, talks about "a sudden turn from an epistemological to a practical, social level of argument."[7] If we want to avoid introducing a problematic split into the Phenomenology, between an epistemological argument and some kind of social-historical argument, we have to argue that Hegel's epistemological project has an essential social and historical dimension. This is in my view one of the most difficult problems that an interpretation of the Phenomenology has to face. I will touch on it here and there in what follows, especially in the last section, giving some hints about how I want to address this question.

Furthermore, it is important to distinguish between more or less free interpretations of the dialectic between the lord and the bondsman, interpretations that are in some way inspired by Hegel, and interpretations that claim to capture Hegel's intention with the chapter. The problem with Alexandre Kojève's famous interpretation is that it is a very free interpretation which at the same time claims to capture Hegel's intention with the chapter and the whole book.[8]

All in all, I think it is possible to distinguish between substantial and formal-structural interpretations of the chapter on lordship and bondage, between social-historical and psychological interpretations, and between intersubjectivity-oriented and subjectivity-oriented interpretations. Kojève's interpretation, for example, is a substantial, social-historical, and intersubjectivity-oriented interpretation. Furthermore, I think there are basically three options here. Either you opt for an interpretation saying that we are dealing with two self-consciousnesses, actually two human beings, engaged

---

[7] John N. Findlay, *Hegel: A Re-examination* (New York: Oxford University Press, 1976), 96.
[8] Cf. Alexandre Kojève, *Introduction to the Reading of Hegel*, ed. Allan Bloom, trans. James H. Nichols (Ithaca and London: Cornell University Press, 1980 [1969]).

in a real struggle with one another, having the outcome that the one becomes the master over the other. Or you opt for an interpretation saying that we are dealing with some kind of struggle that takes place within a solitary self-consciousness. Or you argue that the social-historical and psychological is just a semblance (leading the reader astray), and that Hegel as a matter of fact is discussing relations between logical categories.

Although I am not in agreement with Kojève, I strongly favor a substantial, intersubjectivity-oriented interpretation, with a certain social-historical accentuation. However, such an interpretation must go hand-in-hand with an interpretation that does not lose sight of the principal aim of chapter IV, to investigate "what consciousness knows in knowing itself" (§165; 136), or of the primary goal of the Phenomenology, to overcome the opposition of consciousness. The strongest argument for an inter-subjectivity-oriented interpretation I take to be the one based on the structure of the whole chapter on self-consciousness. If we were having to do with the cleavage and internal struggle of one self-consciousness, we would already have reached the shape of consciousness that Hegel calls the unhappy consciousness (IV.B), a shape that in fact comes after the chapter on lordship and bondage (IV.A). About the unhappy consciousness, relating this shape of consciousness to what has gone before, Hegel writes: "the duplication which formerly was divided between two individuals, the lord and the bondsman, is now lodged in one" (§206; 163).

In the chapter on lordship and bondage, we are dealing with two willful, egocentric self-consciousnesses. Each wants to be recognized as independent by the other, but without in its turn recognizing the other as independent. The conflict escalates into a struggle for life and death that finally crystallizes in the relation between the lord and the bondsman. Quite interestingly, the outcome of the ensuing dialectic between the lord and the bondsman is not a relation of mutual recognition. In fact, the chapter comes to a rather abrupt end. One would have liked to know a little more about how the bondsman relates to the lord after having caught at least a glimpse of his own independence, and how the master reacts to the experience of actually being dependent.[9] The essential result of the dialectic is instead the *breaking down of the willfulness* of self-consciousness, as a precondition for being able to obey one's own reason. If fear of the lord, as Hegel says, is the

---

[9] Johannes Heinrichs, *Die Logik der "Phänomenologie des Geistes"* (Bonn: Bouvier, 1974), 189f.

beginning of wisdom, then respect for and obedience to the law is a further step away from willfulness towards the respect for reason itself.

Language as the existence of Spirit

I think it is possible to discern a rudimentary philosophy of language in the Phenomenology, one that focuses on the *performative* and *pragmatic* aspects of language. The notion of spirit was introduced in chapter IV as an I that is We and a We that is I. Later on in the text Hegel states that language is "the existence of spirit"—*das Dasein des Geistes*—or that language is "self-consciousness existing for others" (§652; 478). Furthermore: "The I that utters itself is heard or perceived; it is an infection in which it has immediately passed into unity with those for whom it is a real existence, and is a universal self-consciousness" (§508; 376). Universal self-consciousness here is the name for the We in the formula: I that is We and We that is I. Thus, the I that is We comes into existence in language (although not only in language).

Now let us turn to chapter VI.B, "Self-Alienated Spirit," or to be more precise, the subchapter called "Culture and its Realm of Actuality" (VI.B.I.a). This chapter presents or at least alludes to the historical developments in France from late feudalism via absolute monarchy to the world of the French Revolution. It portrays how the proud warrior nobility becomes a fawning and flattering court aristocracy, and how the center of gravity in society shifts from state power to wealth. Hegel here presents a number of *asymmetrical* relations of recognition to which correspond different forms of *language use*. Consciousness is here literally doing things with words. The general lesson to be learned seems to be that language can be used both to stabilize and to undermine a social order, that language can be a conservative just as well as a subversive force in society.

a) First we have the feudal lord and his vassals: on the surface, a heroism of mute service or the giving of advice for the general good. This is according to Hegel the *language of unselfish advice*. However, under the surface we find a being for-itself, a willfulness that hasn't renounced itself.

b) Next we have the absolute monarch and his courtiers: here we find the *language of flattery*. The flattering courtiers surround the monarch, eager to tell him that he is the incomparable one. But, according to Hegel, the real basis of state power is about to pass over into wealth. The monarch becomes nothing but an empty name, dependent upon wealthy societal fractions and interest groups.

c) Next comes the rich man and his clients: here we have the *language of ignoble or base flattery*. Wealth has now become the center of gravity in society and "self-consciousness has its own language in dealing with wealth" (§520; 384). The language of base flattery praises and takes possession of what it knows to be without any intrinsic being (money as worthless in itself, but a means to everything).

d) Finally, in the shape of Rameau's nephew (taken from Diderot's dialogue with the same name), who is a kind of Bohemian and social parasite, we find the *language of disunity and disruption*.[10] The language of disruption represents a rebellion against the power of wealth. For the nephew nothing is holy anymore—neither state power nor wealth; the nephew speaks the language of inversion and subversion or the *language of wit*. This is a use of language that is found in a society that is on the verge of a revolutionary upheaval. The language that turns everything upside down precedes and foreshadows the world being turned upside down.

Hegel in this chapter of the Phenomenology draws attention to the *social uses* of language. It is of crucial importance not only *what* is said, but also *how* it is said, *why* it is said, and to *whom* it is said.[11] To different social relations correspond different uses of language.

In the chapter "Religion in the Form of Art" (VII.B) we also find a kind of phenomenology of different uses of language[12]. What Hegel discusses in this chapter is the Greek experience of art as the highest expression of the divine. In this chapter, language plays the role of bringing the human and the divine closer to each other; we are witnessing the progressive humanization of the divine. The following uses of language can be distinguished, beginning already in the previous chapter on natural religion (VII.A):

- the *enigmatic* language of the hieroglyphs
- the *alien* language of the oracle
- the *captivating* language of the hymn

---

[10] The manuscript to Diderot's *Rameau's Nephew* was found in St. Petersburg several years after the death of its author, and it was translated into German by Goethe in 1805.
[11] Cf. Daniel J. Cook, *Language in the Philosophy of Hegel* (The Hague: Mouton, 1973), 86.
[12] Ibid., 102ff. See also Günther Wohlfart, *Der spekulative Satz: Bemerkungen zum Begriff der Spekulation bei Hegel* (Berlin: de Gruyter, 1981), 168.

- the *intoxicating* language of the Bacchant
- the *retelling* language of the epic
- the *dialogical* language of the tragedy and the comedy

Some of these uses of language are deficient because they are not understandable to everyone, being either a privileged wisdom like the alien language of the oracle, or an unarticulated expressiveness like the intoxicating language of the Bacchant. Furthermore, the retelling language of the epic is deficient because it tells about things that have happened in the past. The divine is here and now, in the sense of forever, and it speaks a language that everyone understands. The dialogical language of the tragedy and the comedy approximates this. At the same time, comedy represents the disenchantment of the Greek religion of art. Its truth is to be found in the proposition: "the Self is absolute Being" (§748; 545). Behind the mask of the comedian, self-consciousness finds only itself.

All through the Phenomenology Hegel seems to be struggling to find a language that is adequate to *conceptual thought*. Language is the existence of spirit, of spirit in the sense of an I that is We and a We that is I. Towards the end of the chapter on spirit (VI.C.c) we find the remarkable sentence: "The word of reconciliation is the objectively existent Spirit [...], a reciprocal recognition which is absolute Spirit" (§670; 493). We have traversed a long road from the utterances of sense-certainty (I): "Here is a tree" and "Now is night," to the word of reconciliation that is absolute spirit. In the following chapter on religion (VII), consciousness then experiences what absolute spirit is: the self is absolute being, and its reversal, the absolute being is self.

Hegel's remarks on language in the main text of the Phenomenology continue in the preface in the discussion of what is called the *speculative sentence* or *proposition* (cf. §58–§66; 56–62).

Spheres of experience

Returning to the question of the structure of the book, I would like to suggest that the Phenomenology is structured by way of a number of *spheres of experience* that consciousness traverses on its way towards absolute knowing (VIII), towards the standpoint of Hegel's system. More precisely, consciousness traverses the following spheres:

- the experience of something other than itself (I-III / A)
- the experience of itself in opposition to all otherness (IV / B)
- the experience of itself in the world (V / C.AA)
- the experience of itself in history (VI / BB)
- the experience of itself as absolute in the form of picture-thinking (VII / CC)

These different spheres of experience present answers to the question of what consciousness knows

- when it knows something other than itself (I-III / A)
- when it knows itself in opposition to all otherness (IV / B)
- when it knows itself in the world (V / C.AA)
- when it knows itself in history (VI / BB)
- when it knows itself as absolute in the form of picture-thinking (VII / CC)

This is a structuring of the Phenomenology primarily based on the dialectical movement of consciousness itself. Its point of departure is neither of the two divisions of content—neither the one with Roman numerals, nor the one with capital letters. I am not saying that it solves all the problems related to the difficult question of the structure of the Phenomenology, but it is my best attempt.

The infinite judgment

What Hegel calls the *infinite judgment* seems to play an important role in the Phenomenology. The infinite judgment is, so to speak, a failed judgment, a judgment that fails in one of two forms: either in the form of an empty tautology ("the particular is particular") or in the form of an absurd judgment ("spirit is not red, yellow, sour, etc."). The examples are Hegel's own.[13] The first form Hegel calls a *positive-infinite* judgment, the second he calls a *negative-infinite* judgment. In the *Science of Logic* we read: "in the negative-infinite judgment the difference [between the subject and the predicate] is so to speak too big for it to remain a judgment, the subject and

---

[13] G. W. F. Hegel, *Wissenschaft der Logik II*, Werke 6 (Suhrkamp: Frankfurt am Main, 1969), 324–325.

the predicate have no positive relation at all to one another; in the positive-infinite judgment on the other hand we have only the identity [between the subject and the predicate], and because of the complete lack of a difference it is no longer a judgment"[14].

In the Phenomenology, the infinite judgment appears in the following two forms: as an empty tautology: I = I, and as the reification of self-consciousness: the self is a thing. In both of these forms the opposition of consciousness is not overcome but has collapsed into either a positive-infinite judgment (I = I) or a negative-infinite judgment (self = thing). In the first case, the difference between the subject and the predicate is non-existent; in the second case, the difference is too large.

It is my contention that the infinite judgment primarily makes its appearance at certain *turning points* in the Phenomenology, or to be more precise, marks the transition from one sphere of experience to another. The infinite judgment represents the coming to an end or the closing of a certain sphere of experience and at the same time the opening up of a new sphere of experience.

Let me give a few examples. Towards the end of chapter III, "Force and the Understanding," we find a positive-infinite judgment: I = I, and a transition to another sphere of experience is made. The infinite judgment is here reached through the notion of infinity: "Since this Notion is an object for consciousness, the latter is consciousness of a difference that is no less immediately cancelled; consciousness is for its own self, it is a distinguishing of that which contains no difference, or self-consciousness" (§164; 134). Towards the end of chapter IV we find a negative-infinite judgment, the reification of self-consciousness: the self is a thing, or as Hegel formulates it in a later chapter: "The Unhappy Self-Consciousness renounced its independence, and struggled to make its being-for-itself into a Thing" (§344; 260, cf. §229; 175f.). And towards the end of chapter V, in the discussion of the matter-in-hand or *die Sache selbst*, we find again a positive-infinite judgment (cf. §420; 311).

However, sometimes the infinite judgment appears also within a certain sphere of experience, for example in the chapter "Observing Reason" (V.A). The last shape of observing reason is phrenology, i.e. the attempt to answer the question what the I or self is by studying the shape of the skull, a pseudo-science whose wisdom is summarized in the sentence: "the being of

---

[14] Ibid., 325.

Spirit is a bone" or "the self is a Thing" (§344–5; 260). This is a crude reification of the self, a negative-infinite judgment, and consciousness passes over into rational self-consciousness trying to actualize itself through its own activity (V.B).

As to the reification of self-consciousness, there is another side of the coin. This is the speculative truth contained in the statement: the self is thinghood, ultimately the self is absolute being, just as well as its inversion: the absolute being is self.

Recognition

Finally, I come to the theme of *recognition* in the Phenomenology. My argument here is to begin with the idea that recognition is a continuous theme in the book, and not something that plays a role only in the chapter on self-consciousness (IV). In fact, the word *Anerkennung* and its different forms are most frequent in the last chapter on spirit (VI.C.c).[15] Thus, Vittorio Hösle has argued that beside the goal of overcoming the opposition of consciousness, there is a second goal for the development in the Phenomenology, namely "the overcoming of unjust, unreasonable, asymmetrical relations of intersubjectivity,"[16] i.e. one-sided forms of recognition. How do the two goals of the Phenomenology relate to each another? One way to answer this question is: The first goal can be reached only by way of reaching the second. In order to overcome the opposition of consciousness asymmetrical relations of intersubjectivity must be overcome.

Hegel introduces the notion of *mutual recognition* at the beginning of chapter IV.A, in terms of a double movement of two self-consciousnesses: "Each sees the other do the same as it does; each does itself what it demands of the other, and therefore also does what it does only in so far as the other does the same. Action by one side only would be useless because what is to happen can only be brought about by both" (§182; 146–7).

The struggle that takes place in "Lordship and Bondage" is, as mentioned before, a struggle between two *willful* self-consciousnesses. However, no mutual recognition can be achieved on the basis of willfulness. Willfulness

---

[15] Joseph Gauvin, in collaboration with Charles Bailly et al., *Wortindex zur Phänomenologie des Geistes* (Bonn: Bouvier, 1977).
[16] Vittorio Hösle, *Hegels System: Der Idealismus der Subjektivität und das Problem der Intersubjektivität*, 2 vol. (Hamburg: Meiner, 1987), 383–384.

must therefore be broken down. This is the lesson from chapter IV.A. Thus, we have to find a more solid foundation or base for a mutual recognition. In chapter IV.B this base is sought in *thought*, in chapter V in *reason*, and in chapter VI in *institutionalized reason*. As thinking beings, we are all alike; thought is so to speak a common ground for all of us, an element of intersubjectivity. Thought as reason is no longer standing over against reality, but is "the certainty of consciousness that it is all reality" (§233; 179), that reason is to be found in reality. Finally, spirit is institutionalized reason: customs and laws that are valid for all of us. It all turns on realizing a certain kind of *like-mindedness*.[17] Like-mindedness, among other things, means having the same standards of rationality, of what is to count as true and false, right and wrong, just and unjust, etc. Achieving such a like-mindedness means, from the side of the individual, being socialized into a certain world, and, from the side of mankind, a long and winding historical process of formation. This like-mindedness has its seat in thought, in reason, in spirit as institutionalized reason, and in spirit unfolding in history as the *history of institutionalized reason*. What consciousness experiences in chapter VI is essentially that institutionalized reason has a history, a history that takes the reader from the Greek city-state, via the world of culture, to the postrevolutionary Europe of Hegel's time. At the end of chapter VI, we reach an intersubjectivity that is free of asymmetrical relations. I quote the following sentence once again: "The word of reconciliation is the objectively existent Spirit [...], a reciprocal recognition which is absolute Spirit" (§670; 493). Now consciousness has experienced or at least caught a glimpse of what spirit is: an intersubjectivity free from asymmetrical relations.[18]

What is still missing is universal self-consciousness, or the *community*, as a mediating third element: realizing the formula I = We = I (Thou). This mediating third is first the *religious* community (VII.C), and then the *philosophical* community (VIII).[19] Once again it is relevant to refer to

---

[17] I pick up this notion from Robert B. Pippin, *Hegel's Idealism: The Satisfactions of Self-Consciousness* (Cambridge: Cambridge University Press, 1989), 146f, 155, 160.

[18] Remember Hegel's announcement at the beginning of chapter IV: "What still lies ahead for consciousness is the experience of what Spirit is" (§177; 145).

[19] A deficient form of community appeared already in the chapter on conscience (VI.C.c), a community of moral geniuses whose "divine worship" is "the utterance of the community concerning its own Spirit" (§656; 481–2). Hegel here probably has in mind the romantic coterie at Jena in the late 19th century, which to him represented an inward flight from reality.

language: "Language only emerges as the middle term, mediating between independent and acknowledged self-consciousnesses" (§653; 479). I think that Hegel, as he saw it, standing at the dawn of a new epoch, held the very optimistic conviction that the philosophical community is not necessarily a community of the few, but that every creature endowed with the capacity of thought, endowed with reason, can take part in it. The following quote from the preface points in this direction: "We must hold to the conviction that it is the nature of truth to prevail when its time has come, and that it appears only when this time has come, and therefore never appears prematurely, nor finds a public not ripe to receive it" (§71; 66). The very optimistic message of the Phenomenology seems to be that everyone can climb up on Hegel's ladder to the realm of philosophy and take part in the philosophical community: a potentially unlimited community of communication speaking the language of conceptual thought.

To summarize, my main points on the topic of recognition are:

1. Recognition is a continuous theme in the Phenomenology, not something that plays a role only in chapter IV.A.

2. The theme of recognition is closely related to the definition of spirit that Hegel introduces in chapter IV: I that is We and We that is I.

3. There is an interconnection between the theme of recognition and the rudimentary philosophy of language to be found in the Phenomenology.

4. The themes of recognition, spirit and language are essential to the Phenomenology also as an epistemological project, as a social and historical epistemology.[20]

Conclusion

Two hundred years have gone by since the publication of the Phenomenology, and we are still struggling to unravel its mysteries. Rather than

---

[20] Here it must be said that the last chapter of the Phenomenology, on absolute knowing (VIII), does not lend itself very well to an intersubjectivist reading. The overcoming of the opposition of consciousness now seems to be disconnected from the topic of mutual recognition. Hegel, according to Habermas, in the last instance favors a kind of knowledge which is supposed "to be categorically superior to all knowledge emerging from the co-operative quest for truth of participants in the rational discourses of a self-justifying culture." See Jürgen Habermas, "From Kant to Hegel and Back Again: The Move Towards Detranscendentalization," in *European Journal of Philosophy*, 1999, 7:2, 148.

having presented clear-cut answers and definite solutions, I have drawn attention to some problems that pertain to the Phenomenology and hinted at some possible lines of interpretation. The Phenomenology is certainly one of the most charismatic texts in the history of philosophy. Therefore, I am quite convinced that in two hundred years, if there still is human life on earth, people will be sitting in small circles all over the globe, trying to come to grips with the problems of the Phenomenology. What about sense-certainty? What about lordship and bondage? What about the unhappy consciousness? And, last but not least, what about absolute knowing?

Hegel's Anomalous Functionalism

STAFFAN CARLSHAMRE

The section in the *Phenomenology of Spirit* on "observing reason" is one of the least studied parts of the work, which is a pity because it contains some things very pertinent to contemporary philosophical concerns. The only passage I will treat in any detail here is the discussion concerning the observation of biological organisms (§§254–297),[1] but I will start with a few remarks concerning the place of observing reason within the Phenomenology as a whole, and of the observation of organic life within observing reason.

"Observing Reason" is the first main section of the reason chapter. In Hegel's formal scheme, the chapter on reason has a double numbering that may seem confusing at first, but on closer inspection reveals itself to be entirely logical. The preceding chapters, on consciousness and self-consciousness, are called A and B, respectively. As Hegel's basic progression is always through triads, one expects the following chapter to be C, and then for the numbering to start again on a new level. In keeping with this, the two chapters following reason, on spirit and religion, are numbered BB and CC, and one would expect them to be preceded by a chapter AA. Between these two series we find the chapter on reason, and, lo and behold, it is called C AA. The only natural reading of this is that reason has a double role in the dialectical progression: it is both the last stage of the first triad and the first stage of the second.[2]

---

[1] Hegel's *Phenomenology of Spirit* is cited in the translation by A. V Miller (New York: Oxford University Press, 1977), with paragraph numbers.
[2] As Robert Pippin pointed out at the Translating Hegel symposium, there is a problem reconciling this analysis with the fact that chapter CC is immediately followed by the final chapter DD, on absolute knowing. My best answer is that this is a kind of mistake, probably reflecting a genuine uncertainty on Hegel's part about what to do with the final chapter. If absolute knowing really is the final stage of the dialectic, it should be the third

This is also reasonable with regard to the content. In the overall flow of the Phenomenology, the dialectical waltz is syncopated by another rhythm in two-step, moving back and forth between objectivity and subjectivity. Sense-certainty takes the world as naively given and itself as pure registration, perception concentrates on the contribution of the subject, while the understanding rediscovers itself in objective reality. On the next level up, consciousness as a whole is concerned with objectivity, while self-consciousness is concerned with the subject—in reason, self and world are reunited as self-consciousness rediscovers itself in the world, in the form of an object. But precisely in virtue of this, reason is also ready to play the role of the first, objective stage in the next large triad where spirit represents the subjective pole and religion combines the two in a spiritualized rendition of the world.

The same principles apply to the disposition of lower levels, within the collection of collections of Chinese boxes that is the *Phenomenology of Spirit*. Sense-certainty, for example, begins with naive objectivism, goes on to naive subjectivism and ends up with a synthetic unity that is the foundation of the first, objective, stage of perception. According to the same pattern, reason itself has three parts, and observing reason is the first one, concerned with reason as manifested in the object, as observed by reason. Put in another way, observing reason is concerned with *science*, as the most sophisticated attempt to capture reality in entirely objective terms.[3] And, of course, observing reason again has three main sections that relate in the same way, concerned with the observation of physical nature, with the observation of the psyche, and with the psycho-physical relation between the body and the mind, respectively.

The passage about living organisms, in turn, is situated at the end of the discussion of nature, just before the transition to the observation of self-consciousness. Natural as this may seem from a modern point of view, it is not a self-evident choice as far as Hegel is concerned. Living things are intermediate between inorganic nature and consciousness. In *De anima* Aristotle treats plants and animals as having souls, in virtue of the functional organization that is their defining characteristic for Hegel as well,

---

stage of a triad, but religion already occupies the only available slot. As it is, I think the final chapter is best regarded as belonging with the preface, as a comment from the outside rather than as a proper part of development of the spirit—it is really an epilogue.

[3] Here I use the word *science* in an ordinary way, of course, and not as a translation of Hegel's "Wissenschaft," which he uses for the highest form of philosophy.

and the main previous discussion of living things in the Phenomenology is located at the beginning of "Self-Consciousness" rather than at the end of "Consciousness." Had he been less strongly attached to his formal scheme, Hegel would, perhaps, have treated life as a separate stage between inorganic nature and self-consciousness. As it is, he hesitates about where it belongs, but he is clearly more interested in the differences between living things and inorganic nature than in their similarities.

What gives Hegel's discussion of science its contemporary interest is largely his thorough anti-reductionism, and the fact that he opposes reductionism for conceptual rather than for metaphysical reasons. In keeping with this, the main point of his treatment of biological categories is his argument that they are not reducible to the categories of physics and chemistry. More precisely, he argues that there can be no proper scientific laws connecting the two domains—as hinted in the title of this article, his argument to that effect bears a certain resemblance to Donald Davidson's argument for the anomalousness of the mental.

Nature

Observing reason as a whole is concerned with the nature of scientific *concepts* and their relation to scientific *laws*. The beginning of the scientific attitude is the naive conviction that the world itself is reasonable and that you can find reason in the world by just paying attention—i.e., by observation. In a way, we seem to be back at the level of sense-certainty, where consciousness appears to itself as doing no more in the acquisition of knowledge than registering the way things are. But in truth, we are at a higher level where reason is in charge and controls what it shall experience.

The active role of reason in the epistemic process is deepened as we go along. At the first, taxonomic, stage it goes no further than to classify particular phenomena in general terms. The desire for knowledge is expressed through the effort to describe everything there is, to extend what we know, through voyages of discovery and ever more powerful instruments of observation. Soon, however, the spontaneous will to chart the unknown and describe what one finds in nature starts to run into problems. It is easy enough, says Hegel, to see that there is something special about the elephant, the oak or the substance of gold, but when we push further and try to distinguish genera and species in what soon threatens to become a chaos of animals, plants, and natural substances, we loose our foothold and find it increasingly difficult to draw the line between what are really separate species and what is mere individual variation. The solution is to create systematic taxonomies, built on unified criteria, but this already implies that reason abandons its passivity and increases its own command:

> Through this distinction between what is essential and what is unessential, the Notion rises above the dispersion of the sensuous, and cognition thus makes it clear that it is just as essentially concerned with its own self as with things. (§246)

Are the kinds that we discern, and the criteria we employ, grounded in the nature of things or are they just tools manufactured by us? As usual, Hegel distinguishes different grades and levels in this respect, before he connects the classifications most worthy of being taken as both real and reasonable to the concept of law.

Easiest of natural things to demarcate by essential characteristics are, according to Hegel, animals, and the reason for this is that animals divide themselves into kinds. The individual animal upholds and defends its own identity against external attack—by a somewhat dubious argument, Hegel draws the conclusion that they are best classified by the tools they use for this purpose, i.e., by the shape of teeth and claws. Plants are lower on the ladder of conceptuality and do not sustain their individuality in the same active way—they stand, says Hegel, "on the boundary-line of individuality." But in the interest of reproduction they uphold at least one essential distinction, namely the distinction according to sex, and so we classify them by their reproductive organs.

While the details of this account are decidedly passé, the underlying point is important. There are no real individuals in inorganic nature, new things can be fashioned at will by composition or partition, and in many cases the actual demarcation between different things is obviously artificial and imposed by the observer. And the higher degree of individuality of animals and plants is connected to their more intimate relation to conceptuality—the animal does not need to wait for an observer to be classified, it incorporates its concept and itself recognizes its kin. In inorganic nature, on the contrary, not even the boundaries between different substances are absolute: in chemical reactions given substances are transformed into new ones with unpredictable features.

Reason looks for what is constant in experience but cannot find it on the level of observable properties, because the nature of things is to change. What first appears as an essential property of an abiding thing reveals itself as a fleeting stage of a process. What is constant must be sought on another level, in the laws that govern change, but the search for natural laws will force a decisive change in the formation of scientific concepts.

At the outset, observing reason takes it for granted that laws shall be accessible to direct observation, that they shall be given as correlations between observable properties. But it soon runs into two sorts of trouble with this approach. First, purely empirical correlations are never truly universal, they always admit of exceptions and special cases, that we in turn want to understand and submit to strict laws. Second, even if an empirical correlation should happen to be universally valid, it lacks the *necessity* of a true law. The necessity of a true law stems from its conceptual form rather than from empirical observation, which by itself can reach no further than to contingent probabilities.

So what is it, according to Hegel, which confers necessity on a true law? It has to do with the relation that reason instinctively seeks to establish between what is given in experience and the conceptual structures it applies to it.

> That a stone falls, is true for consciousness because in its heaviness the stone has in and for itself that essential relation to the earth which is expressed in falling. Consciousness thus has in experience the being of the law, but it has, too, the law in the form of a *Notion* [*Begriff*]; and it is only because of the two aspects together that the law is true for consciousness. The law is valid as a law because it is manifested in the world of appearance, and is also in its own self a Notion. (§250)

The stone falls because it is heavy, but heaviness is nothing but a disposition to fall. It sounds as if Hegel thinks of natural laws as analytic, as conceptual truths of a kind, and so he does, to some extent. The terms of a scientific theory are defined in relation to each other, and the laws of the theory express the relevant relations. Take the concept of *mass*, to stay close to the example in the quote. Mass is measured by weighing, which in itself is a relational procedure—as demonstrated by the use of scales to establish sameness of mass—and its role in Newton's mechanics is defined by the laws of inertia and gravitation. Would something that did not obey these laws really be mass?[4]

(The concept of mass is also a good example of the important phenomenon that Hegel calls "reflection." The mass of a thing is essentially a *relation* that it has to other things, but it appears to us as a *property* of the thing itself: the relation is "reflected" back into it. Unpacking such reflected relations is one of the main tasks of the Phenomenology.)

The urge to transform empirical correlations into conceptually grounded laws is, according to Hegel, built into the praxis of science, for example in the use of controlled experiments, with the aim of purifying proposed laws from accidental circumstances and reach the really essential factors.

> The inner significance of this investigation is to find the *pure conditions* of the law, and this means nothing else [...] than to raise the law into the form of Notion, and to free its moments completely from being tied to a specific being. (§251)

This is a first point where Hegel's view bears a striking relation to Davidson's. The idea of a reciprocal relation between laws and the concepts used to formulate them plays a key role in Davidson's argument for the non-reducibility of the mental, which relies on a specific account of conceptual holism, according to which the physical and the mental constitute separate conceptual totalities, held together by separate unifying principles. In the case of the mental domain, the relevant unity is constituted by the principles of rationality, as reflected in the principle of charity, while the physical domain is held together by "constitutive laws" for which one should not "force the decision" whether they are analytic or synthetic—Davidson even uses the term "synthetic a priori" for such laws.[5]

---

[4] Thomas Kuhn, who views the relation between concepts and theories in science in a similar way, has famously argued that there is no contradiction between the theories of Newton and Einstein, because they do not use the same concept of mass: for Newton gravitational and inertial mass are the very same thing, while they are different quantities in relativity theory.

[5] D. Davidson, "Mental Events," in *Essays on Actions and Events* (Oxford: Oxford University Press, 1980), 221.

Living things

The next step is to go from inorganic to organic nature. As we saw, non-living things, according to Hegel, have no real individuality—for a stone, there are no immanent criteria of identity that define the border between transformation and annihilation. A living thing, on the contrary, incorporates the law of its own development, it exists in the form of a law-governed process and preserves itself through change.

One has to remember, of course, that Hegel was writing before Darwin, and at the beginning of modern science, before the softening of the borders between physics, chemistry, and biology. His worldview was dominated by the ontological hierarchy that he, by and large, inherited from Aristotle. There are distinct levels in nature, which differ not only in conceptual complexity but also in value: the living is more valuable than inorganic nature, conscious life has more value than organisms without consciousness, and so on. The relations between different levels are always at the center of Hegel's attention but there is no reduction: each level has emergent properties that could not be predicted on the basis of lower levels—this goes for chemistry as well as for biology.

The essential characteristic of biological organisms is their finality, i.e., that they are susceptible to functional or teleological explanation. The focus of Hegel's discussion is the nature of functional laws and the relation of functional organization to inorganic nature, to the body and to the physical environment of the organism.

He starts out with a discussion of correlations between features of organisms and general characteristics of their *milieu*—examples are the thick fur expected of animals in cold climates, and the typical shapes of fish and birds that seem adapted to life in water and air, respectively. Lacking the Darwinian framework, Hegel has no theoretical way to treat such associations, and he brushes them aside as mere empirical correlations, susceptible to exceptions and lacking the inner necessity of true laws.

A teleological explanation explains why something is or happens in a certain way by invoking a goal, something that it achieves or to whose realization it contributes. In the usual case, the goal is beyond the phenomenon to be explained, something external to the process whose goal it is—I take the bus to the airport in order to be in Paris later in the day. But the basic biological functionality is different, according to Hegel. A biological organism is its own *telos* and creates itself only in the sense that it preserves itself, recreating what it already is. Hegel associates this kind of self-relation to self-consciousness, and from a philosophical perspective we can see the living thing as an incarnated concept. But this conception is beyond observing reason, which is bound to treat the relation between the function and the organism as a connection between two things, a correlation to be observed.

> In this way, the organism appears to the observing consciousness as a relation of two *fixed* moments in the form of immediate being—of an antithesis whose two sides, on the one hand, appear to be given to it in observation, and on the other hand, as regards their content, express the antithesis of the organic *Notion of End* [*Zweckbegriff*] and *actuality* [*Wirklichkeit*]; but as the Notion as such is effaced therein, the antithesis is expressed in an obscure and superficial way, in which thought has sunk to the level of picture-thinking [*Vorstellen*]. Thus we see the Notion taken to mean roughly the *inner*, and actuality the *outer* and their relation produces the law that *the outer is the expression of the inner*. (§262)

It is worth noting the word "roughly" in this passage. The opposition between the inner and the outer is invoked many times in the Phenomenology, but always accompanied by critical reflections. We first meet it in the section on force and the understanding, as a way of thinking about the relation between the super-sensible world and the world of appearance, and it recurs as a way of viewing the relation between consciousness and the body. In each case, Hegel argues that the idea of a relation between two independent entities is ultimately untenable.

The biological functions that Hegel uses as examples are "sensibility," "irritability," and "reproduction." The choice of these three goes back to Aristotle's discussion of the basic functions of the soul in *De anima*. Aristotle identifies the mental with the biologically functional, and ascribes "souls" to plants and animals, not in the sense of having consciousness, but, precisely, in the sense of having certain types of functional organization. The "reproductive soul" is common to plants and animals, and amounts to the capacity to reproduce, i.e., to grow and procreate. What sets animals apart from plants is that they also have the capacities of perception and movement—it is the latter faculty that Hegel refers to as "irritability."[6]

---

[6] As Hegel himself points out, the ensuing discussion is primarily relevant to animals, rather than to living things in general.

Hegel's first question is about the relation between the function and the biological structure that we take to be its organ or carrier—for example the relation between sensibility and the sensory nervous system or between irritability and the motor system. How can we observe such a relation? The metaphor of an outer and an inner already seems to imply that the game is lost, for what does it mean to be "inner" here except to be inaccessible to observation? To be empirically correlated with the outer, the inner must already be observable, it must, in Hegel's terms, itself have an external shape (*Gestalt*):

> We have now to see what *shape* the being of inner and outer each has. The inner itself must have an outer being and a shape, just as much as the outer as such; for it is an object, or is itself posited in the form of being, and as present for observation. (§264)

So what is the outer aspect of a function, its observable *Gestalt*? It is, of course, the functional behavior, what Hegel calls a "doing" (*Tun*). A law that connects function and structure ultimately regards the relation between the activity of the organism and its "ruhendes Sein," but the conception of such a law gives rise to new problems, akin to those that Davidson points out with regard to the possibility of strict psycho-physical laws.

The functional capacities belong to the organism as a whole, ultimately serving its self-reproduction, and they also form an integrated totality. Particular capacities, like sensibility or irritability, are dependent moments of this totality: there can be no sensibility without irritability, says Hegel, or the reverse, and there is even a necessary correspondence between the two, implying that an organism cannot have "more" of one capacity without having more of the other. Why would that be so?

Sensibility is the capacity to register differences in the environment, while irritability is the capacity to react to them. To have a high degree of sensibility is to be able to discriminate subtle differences between stimuli. But what does it mean to say that an organism itself recognizes a difference, that two stimuli are different not only for us but for the organism itself? It is obviously not sufficient that its sensory apparatus reacts differently to them, i.e., occupies states that we, as external observers, can discriminate—in that sense a stone, for example, would have a subtle capacity to register temperature differences in its environment, but there is presumably no temptation for us to ascribe the capacity to discriminate hot and cold to the stone itself.

The natural suggestion is that the organism discriminates between different stimuli by reacting differently to them, or at least by being able to react differently—there is a conceptual connection between its sensory repertoire and its behavioral repertoire. The same thing can be argued from the opposite direction: if we ascribe a complex repertoire of behaviors to an organism, we implicitly ascribe to it representational capacities of corresponding subtlety—the difference between goal-directed behavior and just being moved around, like a stone, implies the capacity to recognize when to start and when to end.

But is this not just to postpone the problem—what makes two reactions different, apart from the possibility of an external observer to tell them apart? Presumably it has to do with some difference that they make with regard to the self-preservation of the organism, with its capacity for reproduction. When the organism correlates differences in stimulations with differences in behavior in a way that furthers its survival and reproduction, we have grounds to say that these are differences for the organism, and not just for us. With this, we have arrived at Hegel's conclusion: that the different functional capacities are abstract moments of a conceptually intertwined totality.

The important contrast is between being an abstract *moment* of a totality, in this sense, and being a concrete *part* of something, in the way that the sensory nervous system is a part of the body. While the sensory function is conceptually intertwined with the other life-functions, the different parts of the body are conceptually independent of each other. One can illustrate the point with the help of Aristotle's famous example of the eye: there are no anatomical properties that in themselves make something an eye; something is an eye only as a functioning part of a living body. But to view something as a living body, in this sense, is to make a conceptual jump from the anatomical description to the functional, to see what the organism does in the light of its end, self-preservation.

And this also completes the analogy with Davidson's argument for the anomalousness of the mental. It is the fact that functional capacities constitute a conceptually linked totality of a specific kind that makes them irreducible to phenomena that do not belong to the relevant circle.

Hegel and Exposure

VICTORIA FARELD

One of the major achievements of the *Phenomenology of Spirit* is not only, as Marx said, that Hegel grasped man's historical, self-transformative nature—that man is the product of his own work.[1] What's remarkable in Hegel's work is also the idea that man's independence presupposes his dependence, which is suggested by his notion of recognition (*Anerkennung*). The desire for recognition describes a process where one appears as a self only when being recognized by others. Hence, to appear as an independent self one has to stand in relation to what is other than oneself, one has to be dependent. This is a major insight conveyed by the *Phenomenology of Spirit*, with consequences, I contend, that even today remain to be worked through.

One way of trying to consider what it might mean to be involved in relations of dependence in order to attain independence, is to understand the nature of this dependence as, I will suggest here, a human condition of *exposure*. I will read the Hegelian dialectic as a series of such exposings.

The complex relations of interdependence in the *Phenomenology of Spirit* invite various interpretations. Indeed, the notorious struggle between lord and bondsman seems to be inexhaustible when it comes to generating new readings. Beginning right after Hegel's death, every generation has had its own versions of his dialectic, adapted to tackle the urgent issues of its own time.[2] One of many actualizations of the Hegelian struggle for recognition is to be found in Jean-Paul Sartre's preface to Frantz Fanon's *Les condamnés*

---

[1] Karl Marx, "Critique of the Hegelian Dialectic and Philosophy as a Whole," in *Economic and Philosophical Manuscripts of 1844*, trans. Martin Milligan (Moscow: Progress Publishers, 1959 [1844]), 165.

[2] For an account of Hegelianism, see for instance John Edward Toews, *Hegelianism: The Path Toward Dialectical Humanism, 1805–1841* (Cambridge, Mass.: Cambridge University Press 1980); Wolfgang Essbach, *Die Junghegelianer: Soziologie einer Intellektuellengruppe* (Munich: Wilhelm Fink, 1988).

de la terre (*The Wretched of the Earth*), from 1961. In this preface, Sartre uses Hegel's idea of interdependence, which characterizes the relation between lord and bondsman, and transforms it into a political appeal to Europeans to listen to the testimonies of colonized people, because, as he says: "It's enough that they show us what we have made of them, for us to realize what we have made of ourselves."³ This understanding of the constitutive relations of interdependence establishes dialectic as a rebounding movement, suggesting that the key to my self-knowledge is in the hands of the other. But it also, and more interestingly, says something else: As I am essentially dependent on the other, the denial of the other is at the same time a denial of myself.

However, as we know, Sartre himself was primarily interested in trying to overcome this dependence, by seeing the struggle for recognition as a struggle to maintain an exclusive subject position.⁴ He didn't acknowledge that the flipside of this fear of *the other*—of being devoured by the other or reduced to an object—is indeed the fear of *oneself* as exposed.

Understanding interdependence in the *Phenomenology of Spirit* as a condition of exposure will allow me to reflect upon the implications of being ex-posed, of being posed outside oneself in the constitution of oneself through others. This implies that there is vulnerability in the very formation of the self, that one is constitutively dependent on others and thus not fully apparent or accessible to oneself, as part of one's very possibility of emerging as an "I."

Moreover, understanding this dependence as exposure will allow me to shift focus from recognition to *recognizability*, that is, to the question of who is *recognizable* as someone to be recognized. This involves a shift of focus from the relation between self and other to the social space and the practices governing this space, in which people *appear* as recognizable to each other. If we focus on recognizability as an essential part of the social process of recognition, the following questions appear: How do humans beings become recognizable? Under which conditions, under which social norms, is an individual recognizable as someone to be recognized as a unique individual? And what are the mechanisms that make some people unrecognizable? I will end with an argument for the contemporary relevance

---

³ Jean-Paul Sartre, "Preface," in Frantz Fanon, *The Wretched of the Earth*, trans. Constance Farrington (New York: Grove Press 1963 [1961]), 12.
⁴ Jean-Paul Sartre, *Being and Nothingness: An Essay on Phenomenological Ontology*, trans. Hazel E. Barnes (New York: Philosophical Library 1956 [1943]), 242–243.

of a certain way of thinking dialectically, by exploring the condition of what I call being made dialectically redundant—a situation where some people appear as non-recognizable, by being dialectically abandoned.

What interests me with the question of exposure in the *Phenomenology of Spirit* is therefore, one might say, how we can translate a certain way of thinking—which in my view is deeply Hegelian—into a contemporary language, and make it into an interpretative tool in contemporary philosophical debate. What I am proposing is not a reading of Hegel that is attentive to the historical contexts of his philosophy, but rather one that actively seeks other contexts for his ideas.

This means that I have understood translating Hegel in the widest sense possible. How can we make use of Hegel? What can a way of thinking dialectically offer us today? In answering these questions, I will partly depart from Hegel. Translating Hegel will here imply transforming Hegel; an act by which something is necessarily lost and yet something else is hopefully gained. In that sense, what I will try to do is itself fairly Hegelian. I will stick with Hegel by (in a way) leaving him behind, I will be Hegelian by (in a certain sense) being post-Hegelian, in line with what the German philosopher Günter Figal has said, that you think better without Hegel by thinking with him.[5]

Aristophanes and alienation

I would like to begin this exploration of the exposed self in the Phenomenology, not with Hegel himself but with Plato, with one of his dialogues, the *Symposium,* which provides an interesting starting point for discussions about exposure and dependence in the *Phenomenology of Spirit*.[6] In this dialogue, Aristophanes tells a well-known, mythological story about the essence of love and desire. He traces these phenomena, love and

---

[5] Günter Figal, *Für eine Philosophie von Freiheit und Streit: Politik, Ästhetik, Metaphysik* (Stuttgart: Metzler, 1994), 133.
[6] I am indebted here to Jay M. Bernstein, especially to his interpretation of Hegel's *The Spirit of Christianity and its Fate*, in *On Christianity: Early Theological Writings*, trans. T. M. Knox (New York: Harper Torchbooks, 1948), as an early text that provides an underlying thought structure for the Phenomenology as well. See Bernstein, "Conscience and Transgression: The Exemplarity of Tragic Action," in Gary K. Browning (ed.) *Hegel's Phenomenology of Spirit: A Reappraisal* (Dordrecht: Kluwer, 1997), and Bernstein, "Conscience and Transgression: The Persistence of Misrecognition," *Bulletin of the Hegel Society of Great Britain*, vol. 29, 1994.

desire, back to the very first people inhabiting the world and what befell them. The very first men were round, Aristophanes says, their bodies were circle-formed, and their strength and independence threatened the gods. The gods, however, didn't want to kill them, since they needed the sacrifices and worships from the people in order to be true gods. So, instead of killing them, Zeus decided to make them weak and dependent, by cutting each one of them in half. And since then, Aristophanes tells us, we are, each one of us, still searching for the other part of us, this second half, which was originally taken away from us. This is, he continues, what love and desire are all about: a longing to be whole again, to recuperate an original unity.[7]

Aristophanes' story is generally read as a description of romantic love, driven by a desire to fuse with the other and become one, and thus overcome a condition of alienation by finding oneself again. This interpretation can be compared to a very influential understanding of the process of alienation running throughout the *Phenomenology of Spirit*. This interpretation says that we are to understand the desire that drives history in the Phenomenology as spirit's longing for completion, as a process of recuperating a lost unity. History is spirit (as originally one) alienating, externalizing, shattering itself, and gradually recollecting itself again, in order to gain concrete forms through history, and thus realizing itself by finally reuniting with itself in an absolute unity. Hegel's famous lines about spirit as an "'I' that is 'We' and 'We that is 'I'"—about becoming an individual by being part of a community—is understood in a similar way, as a process of de-alienation, of finding oneself in, and becoming one with, one's community.[8]

In line with this view is an understanding of Hegel's idealism as a unity of thought and being. In one of the key passages in the Phenomenology, Hegel writes that "die Substanz wesentlich Subjekt ist," about grasping "the True, not only as *Substance*, but equally as *Subject*."[9] This has been interpreted as a fusion of reality and consciousness in an all-inclusive totality, where the subject no longer stands in opposition to the substance but fuses with it. Thought and world, or thought and being, become one.

---

[7] Plato, *Symposium*, ed. and trans. C. J. Rowe (Warminster: Aris & Phillips 1998), 189a–193e.
[8] G. W. F. Hegel, *Phenomenology of Spirit*, trans. A. V. Miller (Oxford: Oxford University Press, 1977), 110; Hegel, *Phänomenologie des Geistes, Werke* vol. 3, eds. Eva Moldenhauer & Karl Markus Michel (Frankfurt am Main: Suhrkamp 1993), 145.
[9] Hegel, *Phänomenologie des Geistes*, 28; *Phenomenology of Spirit*, 10.

The pattern is familiar: We start from identity, an identity that constitutes its difference, but only to return to identity, to a higher form of identity with difference as part of it.[10] Or, we start from unity, we were cut in half, but only to return to unity.

A common critique of this understanding is that alienation and difference are nothing but moments to be overcome, as spirit (as well as the subject) develops through a dialectical transcendence of otherness, and becomes at home in this otherness by internalizing it, appropriating and assimilating it, and recognizing itself in it. Hence, difference, according to this understanding of the Hegelian dialectic, only exists to the extent that it originates from and returns to identity. This is the well-known criticism outlined by critics like Adorno, Deleuze, and Lévinas who are very uncomfortable with a dialectic that can only cope with plurality by submitting it to identity.[11]

Let us now return to Aristophanes' speech. What is truly interesting with this story, I claim, is that the search for the "perfect" other—which is a search for oneself, for I am actually looking for (the other half of) myself—is that it is a never-ending story. I can never find myself, because what I find is always another, someone who is not me, who is different from me, separated from me. It is ultimately a story about the impossibility of finding oneself in the other, about the unbridgeable split that exists between me and the other, and which exists within me, since a part of me is always already lost.

It is important to emphasize that Aristophanes tells this story from the point of view of a *lost unity*. We have never been circle-formed. We have never been in this mythical unity, for we have always been split from the very beginning. We know of this unity only from the perspective of the split. So, what we have is a notion of wholeness and unity as *always already lost* to us.

This means, of course, that the desire for fusion with the other—which is also a way to become one with oneself—can never be satisfied, wholeness

---

[10] Cf. Charles Taylor's "expressive" interpretation in his *Hegel* (Cambridge: Cambridge University Press, 1975), see for instance 59, 107. In relation to recognition, see Robert Williams, *Hegel's Ethics of Recognition* (Berkeley: University of California Press, 1997), 170, 180–185, 226.

[11] Cf. Theodor W. Adorno, *Lectures on Negative Dialectics: Fragments of a Lecture Course 1965/1966*, ed. Rolf Tiedemann, trans. Rodney Livingstone (Cambridge: Polity, 2008); Gilles Deleuze, *Difference and Repetition*, trans. Paul Patton (London: Continuum, 2004 [1968]); Emmanuel Lévinas, *Totality and Infinity: An Essay on Exteriority*, trans. Alphonso Lingis (Dordrecht: Kluwer, 1969 [1961]).

can never be realized. This interpretation of Aristophanes' speech can be compared to an understanding of the Hegelian dialectic, which sets alienation as one of its permanent and most prominent features. What drives history in the Phenomenology, in this view, are the constant failures and repeated attempts to satisfy the desire for completion, and thus the impossibility of overcoming alienation.[12] Since desire is driven by difference, a fusion between self and other would be the end of all experiences. Difference would disappear into sameness and desire would disappear into *status quo*. History would indeed end.

If there is no final return to identity in the Phenomenology, the negation of negation—*Aufhebung*—is not a restored unity, but rather the return of the negated.[13] Identity is there for us, but only as a unity that is *always already* lost, which is the very possibility of our appearing as selves.

Exposure and expropriation in the *Phenomenology of Spirit*

In the following, I will remain within this second line of interpretation of the Hegelian dialectic, as I would like to explore the idea of unity as lost, by suggesting that we understand it in relation to exposure. Since we are dependent on what is other than ourselves to appear as selves, the unity which is "I" is always already lost, as a precondition for the self that I am. Being ex-posed—posed outside of myself—means that I have lost this unity from the very moment I appear as an "I." This perspective makes possible, in my view, a shift of focus from the Hegelian struggle for recognition as an *appropriation* of oneself or of the other, to an *expropriation* of oneself.

In the German noun *Eigentum*, "property," we find the adjective *eigen*—"proper," as in its Latin origin, *proprietas*, from *proper*, "own." The word reveals a connection between ownership and being one's own, which characterizes the notion of property that dominates the philosophical tradition from Locke onwards, where property is linked to the proper person, *proprius*. This notion of property, referring to both objects and to persons, is intimately connected to the idea of freedom as autonomy. Just as

---

[12] Cf. Jean-Luc Nancy, *Hegel: The Restlessness of the Negative*, trans. Jason Smith and Steven Miller (Minneapolis: University of Minnesota Press, 2002 [1997]), 4–7.
[13] Cf. Slavoj Žižek's reading of Hegel in *The Ticklish Subject: The Absent Centre of Political Ontology* (New York: Verso 2000), 76–79.

the utmost property is one's own person, the ultimate freedom is being in possession of oneself.[14]

Hegel questions this idea of the individual as originally in possession of itself, by letting its *Eigentümlichkeit*, its singularity, only appear through its actions, through what it creates and attains. The individual is, Hegel claims, what it has become through its own activity.[15] To have *Eigentum*, "property," is for Hegel to appear as will and to manifest oneself as one's own. That is why Hegel makes a distinction between "possession" [*Besitz*] and "property" [*Eigentum*], the former being incorporated and consumed whereas the latter is maintained and given a social form, which others can recognize.[16] One sees oneself as an independent person in and through one's property, Hegel says, as one makes oneself into reality by making the outer world into one's own, through appropriation of it and externalization of oneself in it. To have property is thus to manifest oneself as will and to be one's own.[17]

The self-externalizing act [*Selbstentäusserung*] of making the world into one's own and appearing as someone in the world is also, however, a process of alienation [*Entfremdung*], of being at odds with oneself and the world.[18] What Hegel tells us is that making the world into our own—which is the same as making our selves into our own in the world—is a double-

---

[14] John Locke, *Two Treatises of Government: A Critical Edition with an Introduction and Apparatus Criticus by Peter Laslett* (Cambridge: Cambridge University Press, 1960), §27, 305: "every Man has a *Property* in his own *Person*"; §44, 316: "Man (by being Master of himself, and *Proprietor of his own Person*, and the Actions or *Labour* of it) had still in himself *the great Foundation of Property*."

[15] Hegel, *Phänomenologie des Geistes*, 294-297; *Phenomenology of Spirit*, 237-240.

[16] G. W. F. Hegel, *Grundlinien der Philosophie des Rechts oder Naturrecht und Staatswissenschaft im Grundrisse*, *Werke*, vol. 7, §45, 107; §51 and Zusatz, 115; *Hegel's Philosophy of Right*, trans. T. M. Knox (Oxford: Oxford University Press, 1967), §45, 42, §51, 45 and additions to §51, 237.

[17] To be an abstract person (with rights) is for Hegel therefore connected to the right to have property. See Hegel, *Grundlinien der Philosophie des Rechts*, §§39-40, and 57, 98-102, 122-123; *Hegel's Philosophy of Right*, §§39-40, and 57, 38-40, 47-48. See also Hegel, *Enzyklopädie der philosophischen Wissenschaften im Grundrisse (1830)*, eds. Friedhelm Nicolin & Otto Pöggeler (Hamburg: Meiner, 1991), §§488-492, 392-393; *Hegel's Philosophy of Mind: Being Part Three of the Encyclopaedia of the Philosophical Sciences (1830)*, trans. William Wallace and A. V. Miller (Oxford: Clarendon Press, 1971), §§488-492, 244-245.

[18] Hegel, *Phänomenologie des Geistes*, 366: "[D]as Dasein ist vielmehr die Verkehrung jeder Bestimmtheit in ihre entgegengesetzte, und nur diese Entfremdung ist das Wesen und Erhaltung des Ganzen"; *Phenomenology of Spirit*, 299-300: "[E]xistence is really the perversion of every determinateness into its opposite, and it is only this alienation that is the essential nature and support of the whole."

edged activity. It is not only an act of appropriation, of gaining something, but just as much an act of ex-propriation, of losing something that belongs to the proper, to *proprius*, to one's own.[19]

The two moments of alienation emphasized by Hegel, *Entäusserung* and *Entfremdung* (in Miller's translation: "externalization" and "alienation") can help us to further complicate the connections between self and ownership. Like *Entäusserung* or dispossession, expropriation means to be forced to release one's property, what belongs to oneself, to another. However, the dialectical movement of self-expropriation involves, I claim—just like Aristophanes' story—a *double* movement. What you lose, or what is taken away from you, you have never owned. The unity is always already lost, *ex-proprius* occurs at once with *proprius*.[20] You appear as a self only by simultaneously being dispossessed of yourself.

In line with this view, the desire for recognition could be understood as a force toward self-expropriation. This means that the dialectical relation between me and the other, which makes me exposed, is not to be understood as a movement where something inner is externalized and shattered in my encounter with the other, but rather as manifesting that this unity which is "me" is always already lost to me, as a precondition for my self-relation.

To put self-expropriation at the center of self-constitution is an effort to challenge the historical connections between *Eigentum* and *Eigentümlichkeit*, between "property" and "individuality," and to question the influential idea that access to oneself (to what is proper, so to speak) occurs via the possession of oneself. Being one with oneself (*bei sich sein*) presupposes, therefore, a certain loss of self.

This perspective focuses not only on how one appears as a self through one's relations to others (which in my view has been too much at the center of attention in contemporary discussions of recognition), but also, and

---

[19] Hegel, *Phänomenologie des Geistes*, 363–365; *Phenomenology of Spirit*, 297–299. See also 360: "das *unmittelbar*, d.h. *ohne Entfremdung* an und für sich geltende Selbst ist ohne Substanz […]; *seine* Substanz ist also seine Entäusserung selbst, und die Entäusserung ist die Substanz"; 295: "this activity and process whereby the substance becomes *actual* is the alienation of the personality, for the self that has an absolute significance in its *immediate* existence, i.e. without having alienated itself from itself, is without substance […]; *Its* substance, therefore, is its externalization, and the externalization is the substance."

[20] Cf. Jean-Luc Nancy, preface to *The Inoperative Community*, ed. Peter Connor, trans. Peter Connor et al. (Minneapolis, Minn.: University of Minnesota Press, 1991), xxxvii: "'to be exposed' means to be 'posed' in exteriority […] having access to what is *proper* to existence, and therefore, of course, to the proper of *one's own* existence, only through an 'expropriation.'"

primarily, on how these relations dispossess the self, expose the self. Moreover, this perspective makes it possible to shift focus from the dyadic relation between self and other, to the social space that enables and regulates this relation.

Non-recognizability and dialectical redundancy

Let us now turn to Hegel's idea of ethical life, *Sittlichkeit*, understood as a theory of how the individual emerges as an individual in the state. As such, Hegel's discussion of ethical life is an account of the social norms governing subject-constitution. This implies a shift of focus to the more interesting question, in my view, which is not about recognition but rather about *recognizability*. It concerns what conditions the self's encounter with the other, how we appear as recognizable to each other, how this space of appearance is structured.[21] In this part, I would like to explore how Hegel's idea of *Sittlichkeit* could be used analytically in relation to questions of recognizability.

With the notion of *Sittlichkeit,* Hegel insists that one can only become an individual by inhabiting and embodying a particular form of social life. The freedom one gains as an individual is a result of one's taking part in a social life, in an ethical community, and of having subjected oneself to the norms and customs governing this life. This is, of course, an inversion of the leading contract theories of Hegel's day, which he criticizes. For Hegel, freedom is always the result of a certain form of subjection, and the individual is the result of a certain form of social life. This means that for the individual to emerge—that is, to be recognized as an individual—it has to be part of this social space of mediation, where one's particularity as an individual is *recognizable* in the name of the common. The particular individual is, according to Hegel, the result of a mediation, which transforms the individual from something in a state of abstract and unrecognizable particularity without any social content, into something that is

---

[21] Cf. Judith Butler, *Frames of War: When is Life Grievable?* (New York: Verso, 2009), 4–15. Butler here distinguishes recognizability from recognition: "If recognition is an act or practice undertaken by at least two subjects, and which, as the Hegelian frame would suggest, constitutes a reciprocal action, then recognizability describes those general conditions on the basis of which recognition can and does take place," ibid., 6. See also Judith Butler, *Giving an Account of Oneself* (New York: Fordham University Press, 2005), 27–29.

particular in a way that is recognizable. This can only occur, he claims, for citizens in a state, in which one's particularity appears by being given a concrete form that is recognizable to others.²² Or as Etienne Balibar has put it, a bit more radically: individuality, for Hegel, is a social institution.²³

If we push Hegel's idea of subject-constitution within the state a bit further—if we radicalize it in line with what Balibar suggests—it makes possible a discussion of the normative and normalizing aspects of the subject's appearance as a recognizable subject in the state. How we are, as subjects, always already included in a certain space, and subjected to the norms and practices governing this space. How we are called into being in this space by being conferred a name, by being made addressable and thereby recognizable to each other.

I argue that to become recognizable *at all*, one has to be involved in dialectical relations of mediation. Again, if we understand this situation in terms of exposure, it becomes clear that we are exposed in relations of mediation, as our self-relations are mediated from places outside of us. There is also, however, a mode of exposure which appears as a result of being posed outside of this space of mediation *itself*, of being made, what I call, dialectically redundant.

In Latin, there is a well-known distinction between two words that are both used to describe the other, namely "alter" and "alius." This distinction could be useful to explain what it might mean to be made dialectically redundant. The word "alter" refers to a particular somebody, a specific other to whom one has established a certain relationship (it could be one of violence or struggle, it could be one's enemy, as long as there is a relationship, by which the other is defined). "Alius," on the contrary, is an unspecific, undefined stranger; too different or too distant, to establish a relationship to. "Alius" is not even recognizable as someone specific.²⁴

Hegel himself mentions this distinction between "alter" and "alius" in the *Science of Logic*, to stress the difference between otherness related to reciprocity and unspecific otherness.²⁵ And even if "alius" for Hegel can be

---

[22] Hegel, *Grundlinien der Philosophie des Rechts,* §§141–157 and 260, 286–304, 406–407; *Hegel's Philosophy of Right*, §§141–157 and 260, 103–110, 160–161.
[23] Etienne Balibar, "Ambiguous Universality," *Differences*, vol. 7, No. 1, 1995, 58–63.
[24] Florence Dupont, "Rome ou l'altérité incluse," *L'étranger dans la mondialité, Revue rue Descartes*, No. 37, 2002, 42–46. See also Giorgio Agamben's use of this distinction in his "Friendship," *Contretemps*, No. 5, 2004, 6.
[25] G. W. F. Hegel, *Wissenschaft der Logik: Erster Teil* (Hamburg: Felix Meiner, 1990), 112; *Hegel's Science of Logic*, trans. A. V. Miller (Amherst, N.Y.: Humanity Books, 1998) 117.

embraced by dialectic, it is obvious that a dialectical way of understanding the dynamics of relations presupposes the structural reciprocity, which characterizes an "alter" relationship: the other has to be someone specific. In this sense, a dialectical relation is indeed inclusive—in line with the critique of dialectics for not letting anything exist outside of it—as it cannot account for a situation of radical exclusion, where one is made invisible, treated with indifference, or appears as non-recognizable.

With this in mind, using a certain way of dialectical thinking to reflect upon what governs recognizability could be criticized as a futile endeavor, as the important question of non-recognizability—what makes some people unrecognizable to us—seems to have no place within a dialectical frame of thought. Precisely at this point, however, where the Hegelian dialectic seems to have encountered its limits we find its pertinence for our discussion, by focusing on what the dialectic itself produces as exclusions and redundancies.

No matter how inclusive dialectic seems to be, as many critics have pointed out, there has always been an outside to it, which is intimately connected to its inside: a dialectical rubbish heap, remainders, surplus, supplements or whatever we might call that which exceeds—and secures—the dialectical setting.[26] Hegel himself made the Africans dialectically redundant in his world history.[27] Frantz Fanon made us aware of how the colonial situation put the structural reciprocity of the Hegelian dialectic out of play.[28] A similar way of putting it would be: The colonizer regarded the colonized as "alius," there was no dialectical, no alter, relationship. In contrast to Hegel's slave, the colonized was dialectically abandoned.

To be treated as "alius" is indeed to be exposed, to be posed outside the space of addressability, because what actually ends up outside the dialectical relation appears as non-recognizable. What you say is not intelligible, or maybe not even heard, your face cannot be recognized as a human face, or as the face of a unique individual. This exposure appears to us, I claim, in the form of non-recognizability.

---

[26] Cf. Jacques Derrida's treatment of Antigone in the Phenomenology as an element which "assures the system's *space of possibility*" by exceeding it; see Derrida, *Glas*, trans. John P. Leavy, & Richard Rand (Lincoln: University of Nebraska Press, 1986 [1974]), 162a.
[27] For a discussion of Hegel's treatment of Africa, see Achille Mbembe, "Out of the World," trans. Steven Rendell, in Mbembe, *On the Postcolony* (Berkeley: University of California Press, 2001) 176ff. See also Ronald Kuykendall, "Hegel and Africa," *Journal of Black Studies*, vol. 23, No. 4, 1993, 571–581.
[28] Frantz Fanon, *Black Skin, White Masks* trans. Charles Lam Markmann (New York: Grove Press, 1967 [1952]).

Let us return to Hegel to try to specify what dialectical redundancy, or dialectical abandon, might mean here. In contrast to what Hegel calls "abstract universality," which tries to claim its universality by negating particularity and by positing itself as the opposite of the particular, Hegel outlines what he calls "concrete (that is, 'true') universality" (*konkrete Allgemeinheit*).[29] The concrete universal cannot be abstract commonality, but is, one might say, always the result of a construction, of a mediation that has its constitutive condition in particularity, and can only appear in relationship to it. True universality, according to Hegel, is thus not an abstract point of departure—*we are all human beings*—but has its very origin in particularity.

Now, what does this mean in relation to recognizability? Since the universal is never there from the start, we have to give it some concrete form, and claim universality, through particularity. What happens when you are made dialectically redundant is that your particularity cannot be intelligible as part of a commonality. The universal claim—*I am a human being, I have a right to have human rights*, to use Hannah Arendt's expression[30]—turns out to be an abstraction that doesn't have any concrete social and political significance. It lacks concrete form, as it has not been dialectically mediated. You end up referring to a universality, which claims its universality by reducing particularity to mere abstraction, and which makes individuals appear as abstract, separate, identical—and non-recognizable—units, as they don't have any social, mediated, content.

And, not surprisingly, it turns out that those who are in a situation in which they have nothing else to refer to than an abstract humanity, who cannot claim any particularity (for instance if they don't have any documents to prove their particular identities), they tend to be not recognized as human individuals when it comes to human rights.[31]

---

[29] Hegel, *Grundlinien der Philosophie des Rechts*, §303, 474; *Hegel's Philosophy of Right*, §303, 198. Hegel, *Enzyklopädie der Philosophischen Wissenschaften*, §552, 431; *Hegel's Philosophy of Mind*, §552, 282. See also *Phänomenologie des Geistes*, 436–438; *Phenomenology of Spirit*, 359–361.

[30] Hannah Arendt, *The Origins of Totalitarianism* (New York: Schocken Books, 2004 [1951]), 375.

[31] See Maria Johansen, "Some Versions of a Paradox: A Non-Sovereign Approach to the Rights of Man," *Documenta Magazine*, No. 1-3, 2007, http://magazines.documenta.de/frontend/article.php?IdLanguage=1&NrArticle=794; Giorgio Agamben, *Homo Sacer: Sovereign Power and Bare Life*, trans. Daniel Heller-Roazen (Stanford: Stanford University Press, 1998); Jacques Rancière, "Who is the Subject of the Rights of Man?," *The South Atlantic Quarterly*, vol. 103, No. 2-3, 2004.

It turns out that one has to be someone specific, a unique individual—and the important thing here is that one has to be *recognized* as such (again: by proving one's particularity)—in order to be *recognizable* as human in general. So, interestingly enough, being human in general, is in a way being *too particular*; being particular in an unmediated and thus non-recognizable sense.

But moreover: if you cannot refer to anything *common* that makes you *specific*, or anything *universal* that makes you *particular* (a citizenship, a profession, an ethnic identity, etc.); if you are just you, you are deprived of a dialectical relation, you are dialectically abandoned, because your particularity will not be intelligible, your universality will lack any concretion—and you will appear as non-recognizable. To be made dialectically redundant in this way is indeed to be in a no man's land: you cannot claim particularity and you cannot claim universality.

It is well known that many people today in liberal, Western democracies live in such a no man's land. The so-called irregular migrants, *les sans-papiers*, tend to be deprived of the "right to have human rights." They are as Giorgio Agamben says included in society by being excluded from it, as they are defined by a system (as "illegal" or "criminal") of which they cannot be part and within which they cannot act (being deprived even of the legal status of the criminal).[32] When Arendt discusses the paradox at the core of human rights in *The Origins of Totalitarianism*, she captures very succinctly, in my view, this movement of being made dialectical redundant and, as a result, non-recognizable:

> The paradox involved in the loss of human rights is that such loss coincides with the instant when a person becomes a human being in general—without a profession, without a citizenship, without an opinion, without a deed by which to identify and specify himself—and different in general, representing nothing but his own absolutely unique individuality which, deprived of expression within and action upon a common world, loses all significance.[33]

She also says interestingly that the misery for the refugees "is not that they are not equal before the law, but that no law exists for them; not that they are oppressed but that *nobody wants even to oppress them.*"[34] Being deprived

---

[32] Agamben, *Homo Sacer*, 17–29.
[33] Arendt, *The Origins of Totalitarianism*, 383.
[34] Ibid., 375, my italics. Saying that nobody has an interest in oppressing them is, of course, not the same as saying that they are not victims of oppression and brute

of all legal status they have no place in the world where they can act; They are *abandoned*, as they have been deprived of the structural reciprocity which characterizes a dialectical space of mediation and thus cannot act within the very relations by which they are defined, existing in "the abstract nakedness of being human and nothing but human."[35] They live among us as if they were not here, unrecognizable to us, as the political system's own produced remainders—as what both exceeds and secures the abstract idea of universal rights.

Being exposed

Using Hegel and a way of thinking dialectically when discussing questions of recognizability makes visible that these issues are intimately connected with dependency and exposure. Being made dialectically redundant is *one mode*, I claim, in which exposure appears to us. Understanding exposure as constitutive of subjectivity does not imply, however, making it into a common, unchanging feature for all human beings, as part of the essence of being human. What I am interested in is to try to analyze how exposure appears to us in various forms, how it manifests itself in different social practices, rather than giving it some general and independent status.

Although our involvement in relations of dependence makes us exposed in our self-constitution it is not the relations as such which manifest exposure, but rather different splits and ruptures in these relations. This point has been emphasized by Judith Butler in her most recent works. She argues that loss and mourning could be seen as specific modes by which vulnerability and exposure appear to us.[36]

I would like to suggest that another form by which exposure manifests itself to us is a situation of dialectical redundancy. In this situation, exposure turns out to be an *indeterminacy* in what is human, rather than

---

exploitation, which is indeed the case for many irregular migrants today. The point is that they are made invisible and inaudible, in a sense superfluous within the political system, by being excluded from, but yet defined by, the political realm.

[35] Ibid., 377. See also ibid., 381 where she writes: "It seems that a man who is nothing but a man has lost the very qualities which make it possible for other people to treat him as a fellow-man."

[36] Judith Butler, *Precarious Life: The Powers of Mourning and Violence,* London: Verso 2004); Butler, *Giving an Account of Oneself;* Butler, *Frames of War.* See also Catherine Mills, "Normative Violence, Vulnerability, and Responsibility," *Differences,* vol. 18, No. 2, 2007, 133–156.

something common to all humans as a given. It shows us that what is recognizable as human depends upon the norms governing the space of mediation, in which we emerge as subjects. Exposure, in this sense, thus reveals that what it is to be human is never given, it has to be recognized. Nothing about us is recognizable to us in general, without mediations through socially regulated practices. So, what ultimately counts as human is conditioned by the socio-political processes determining recognizability.[37] Instead of saying something general about all humans being exposed, as an abstract point of departure for a political philosophy, a more interesting and important question would thus be to ask how exposure appears to us in its particularities, and to investigate its different forms and manifestations within a certain socio-political setting.

And Hegel can help us here. He can help us to think about ourselves as necessarily caught up in relations of absolute dependence. We can use Hegel, I suggest, in discussing the consequences of this condition of dependence. Not as an abstract and general idea—'I am necessarily in the hands of others when I try to define myself', or, 'we are as human beings dependent on each other'. Rather: what *does it mean*, not as an abstract knowledge, but spiritually—*geistlich*—in a Hegelian sense, as part of our reflective self-understanding? What does it mean in our experiencing the world if we really make it into knowledge of ourselves and of our being in the world? How do we live this knowledge?

If we think of ourselves as exposed, in different ways, we should not continue to outline ideas of political and ethical agency based on notions of the subject as autonomous or self-transparent. Hegel insisted that the world as we experience it changes as a result of our own activity. But more importantly, he emphasized that we, as experiencing subjects, are constantly transformed by the experiences we undergo—experiences that make us other to ourselves. Instead of trying to overcome this condition of exteriority or exposure, we should try to reconsider what agency, autonomy, and responsibility might mean to us, starting in our lived experience of being exposed.

---

[37] Cf. Mills, 146–149; Butler, *Precarious Life*, 146–147.

The Place of Art in Hegel's Phenomenology

SVEN-OLOV WALLENSTEIN

Art, mythology, and religion in Hegel's early writings

Hegel's critique of the Romantic aspiration to place art above philosophy is well known, as is the element of self-criticism that this entails.[1] In the Jena period, from his first real public appearance in 1801 with *The Difference Between Fichte's and Schelling's System of Philosophy* onwards, Hegel undertakes a critical re-evaluation of his earlier views, which had been developed in the writings from Bern and Frankfurt. In these earlier texts, the capacity to found an ethical order, a *Sittlichkeit*, was ascribed first and foremost to religion, but also to an art understood in the general and broad sense in which the state itself can be taken to be a work of art, as in the case of the Greek *polis*. But at the present moment, Hegel says in 1801, there is a "need for philosophy," i.e., an overcoming of the divisions of modernity that would take place through the work of reason and of the concept, and not through an aesthetic intuition.

Hegel's analysis of the ethical order began with a study of early Christianity, though the aim of the analysis was to intervene in the present, by investigating the possibility of a religion that would combine the virtues of Kant and the French Revolution, and would be able to regenerate a unified world. But as Hegel's analysis progressed, Christianity and in particular the church appeared as a world separated from everyday life, and the city of God as an ideal city, i.e., a mere representation and a negative counter-image that was unable to produce a true reconciliation. This is why, after acknowledging the necessary failure of Christianity to achieve the goal of freedom and reason, Hegel turned to the Greeks, and to a kind of

---

[1] The standard work is still Otto Pöggeler, *Hegels Kritik der Romantik* (Munich: Fink, 1988).

aestheticized view of the *polis*, which now appeared as the place where reason and freedom were truly realized.² The beautiful religion of the Greeks could in this sense be taken as an ideal in the full sense, and Hegel explicitly defined the Greek *polis* as a work of art.³ The city-state was instituted by the work of art, but it was also itself a work, a harmonious unity where the political and the aesthetic ceaselessly passed over into each other.

A decisive influence for Hegel's turn to the Greeks seems to have come from Hölderlin. Together they developed these ideas in terms of what they called "popular education" (*Volkserziehung*), to the point that they even planned a division of labor between them, so that Hölderlin would deal with art and Hegel with religion.⁴ Hegel now systematically opposed the Greek beautiful religion to the "positivity" of the Christian religion, where this education had been transformed into a transcendent law and a merely external cult, and Hölderlin's *Hyperion* and the successive versions of the tragedy *Empedocles* could be taken as attempts to work this out in the literary form of a "modern tragedy." The background for this was undoubtedly Schiller's *Letters on Aesthetic Education*, but in asking the question of how the idea of reason could be made *effective* in a contemporary world that is characterized by division and sundering, they wanted to go beyond the merely "beautiful appearance" that Schiller proposed as the domain of art.

The most densely formulated version of this vision is the so-called "System Program of German Idealism," a text dating from 1796, though excavated from the obscurity of a Berlin library and published only as late as 1917, by Franz Rosenzweig. The text has itself been handed down to us in a fragmented state, and its author remains unknown. Hegel, Schelling, and Hölderlin have all been suggested as likely candidates, and contemporary

---

² For a discussion of the context of Hegel's early theological fragments and the development of *Sittlichkeit*, and of how a reinterpreted Christianity became one of a series of different utopian modes projected back in history, see Christoph Jamme, "*Ein ungelehrtes Buch.*" *Die philosophische Gemeinschaft zwischen Hölderlin und Hegel in Frankfurt 1797–1800*, Hegel-Studien, Beiheft 23. On the ideas of Greece, see Jacques Taminiaux, *La nostalgie de la Grèce à l'aube de l'idéalisme allemand* (The Hague: Nijhoff, 1967).

³ See, for instance, the passages in *Jenaer Systementwürfe*, Gesammelte Werke vol. 8 (Hamburg: Felix Meiner, 1976), 263.

⁴ See *Briefe von und an Hegel*, eds. Johannes Hoffmeister & Friedhelm Nicolin (Hamburg: Felix Meiner, 1981), vol. I, 24f. Hegel's response to Hölderlin's proposal is lost.

consensus opts for Hegel.⁵ This fragment brings together philosophy, religion, morality, and politics under the rubric of a new "mythology," in which abstract ideas were to be cast in sensible form, and the merely externally associated limbs of the social body joined together as in a living organism. The ideas of practical reason (i.e., the heritage of Kant's second Critique), the anonymous author suggests, need to be brought into contact with a speculative or "grand physics," so that they cease to be merely unattainable ideals, just as the state, previously considered as an external "machine,"⁶ needs to be transcended in the direction of a higher idea where all men can be united and perceive their own individuality as stemming from a higher principle of reason, which is to be found in the idea of beauty:

> Finally, the idea that unites all [previous ones], the idea of beauty, the word understood in the higher Platonic sense. I am convinced now, that the highest act of reason, which—in that it comprises all ideas—is an aesthetic act, and that truth and goodness are united as sisters only in beauty. The philosopher must possess as much aesthetic capacity as the poet. The people without an aesthetic sensibility are philosophical literalists [Buchstabenphilosophen]. Philosophy of the spirit is an aesthetic philosophy.⁷

---

⁵ Cf. Christoph Jamme and Helmuth Schneider (eds.), *Mythologie der Vernunft* (Frankfurt am Main: Suhrkamp, 1984), which contains a selection of important philological and philosophical interpretations of the text, by Rosenzweig, Otto Pöggeler, Dieter Henrich, Anne Marie Gethmann-Siefert, and Xavier Tilliette.

⁶ The image of the state-machine in fact has Kantian roots; cf. for instance the paragraph "Beauty as a Symbol of Morality" in the *Critique of Judgment* (§59), where Kant discusses two different ways of symbolizing the state: if it is controlled by "internal popular law" it is represented by an "animated body," if it is controlled by a "singular absolute will," by a "mere machine." Both of these cases are however "symbolic representations," and this symbolism, in merely transferring a "rule for reflection" from one object to another, would be precisely what a text like the *Älteste Systemprogramm* attempts to transgress by posing the aesthetic idea as the highest.

⁷ "Zuletzt die Idee, die alle vereinigt, die Idee der Schönheit, das Wort im höheren platonischem Sinne genommen. Ich bin nur überzeugt, daß der höchste Akt der Vernunft, der, indem sie alle Ideen umfasst, ein ästhe[ti]stischer Akt ist, und das Wahrheit und Güte, nur in der Schönheit verschwistert sind—Der Philosoph muß ebenso viel ästhetischer Kraft besitzen / als der Dichter, die Menschen ohne ästhetischen Sinn sind unsre Buchstabenphilosophen. Die Philosophie des Geistes ist eine ästhetische Philo[sophie]." *Das älteste Systemprogramm,* quoted from the transcription in *Mythologie der Vernunft,* 12f. The slash indicates the break between recto and verso page of the manuscript.

The double movement of the aestheticizing of the political and the politicizing of aesthetics that was to become one of the most fateful legacies of Romanticism here finds one of its essential roots. It is only as united under the spell of the aesthetic idea, the *idea tou kalou* derived from Plato's *Phaedrus* and *Symposium*, that morality, philosophy, and public life can come together, which also signifies that the role of the philosopher will have to be transformed: he must not only be endowed with an aesthetic sensibility equal to the poet, but should in fact in himself include and transcend both the figure of the philosopher and the poet, just as the imagination in its upward flight passes beyond the strictures of both the understanding and sensibility, and leads us towards a new conception of reason. Aesthetic ideas are thus not only meant as fiction—which, as we saw, was the aporia encountered by Schiller in his *Letters on Aesthetic Education*—but as effective interventions in reality.

The question becomes to what extent this can take place in the modern world. For Schiller, the remoteness of the ideal is precisely what teaches us not to confound it with reality, and prevents it from becoming a deception, whereas for Hölderlin and Hegel this distance, which subsequently would be worked out as an idea of "aesthetic autonomy," condemns the work to an exile in the space of the imaginary. This problem will echo throughout the history of modern art and its attempts to become politically effective and to transcend its dimension of autonomy or the "aura," as in the famous exchange between Benjamin and Adorno in the second half of the 1930s, or later in Marcuse's idea of "repressive desublimation," and it extends into the last decade's debates between modernism and postmodernism.

But Hegel soon withdrew from the heights of the aesthetic idea. Unlike Schelling, who opted for the possibility of reunifying the world through a work of art, which he famously saw in the modern epic created in Dante's *Divine Comedy*,[8] Hegel came to fundamentally distrust the Romantic vision, and from the *Differenzschrift* onwards, it is philosophy and conceptual thought which for him holds the key to the reconciliation of the modern world. The short essay from 1800, the year before the *Differenzschrift*, on Schiller's drama *Wallenstein* points to the fact that there can be no such thing as a modern epic: modernity is inherently prosaic, it does not allow for a return to religious or aesthetic ideals, and the heroism of Schiller's

---

[8] See his "Über Dante in philosophischer Beziehung" (1803), first published in the two-year collaborative project undertaken with Hegel in Jena, *Kritisches Journal der Philosophie*.

protagonist leads him to be destroyed by the disenchantment of the modern world, and ground down by the "prose of relations" (*Prosa der Verhältnisse*), of which Hegel would later speak in his analysis of the modern novel in the Berlin lectures on aesthetics.[9] This does not of course mean that art would simply have become useless, only that its role can no longer be to give a unified representation of the world; it can hold up a mirror to us that shows a broken reflection, but the true unity of self and image can only come through a second-order reflection *on this reflection*, i.e., by *speculation*, which is the true task of philosophy.

This would mean that Hermann Glockner's thesis that there is something like an "aesthetic foundation"[10] for Hegel's system, as this develops from the early Jena writings and onwards, cannot be sustained. Glockner's thesis can be used in a weaker form to imply that the system itself has an aesthetic quality, or that it is based upon aesthetics as its first (chronological or logical) part. But it can also be read as a more open suggestion, which is what I would like to do here, i.e., as a question that bears upon Hegel's actual *use* of artworks, how they are intertwined with the logical structure of his thought, to what extent they are essential to its very articulation, and in this sense would be located neither beneath nor above philosophy, but as it were *within* it. And it is this question that I would like to pursue in relation to the *Phenomenology*, the work that concludes Hegel's Jena period, and where he is supposed to have finally overcome the romantic temptation.

The multiple uses of art in the Phenomenology

In the Phenomenology, Hegel draws on several of his earlier analyses, and inscribes them in an overarching structure, which is the path of spirit coming to itself, or is the "experience of consciousness" as it gradually comes to overcome its distance towards the world, and to understand that substance must be understood as subject, and the subject as substance. The world, as substance, must be grasped as a meaningful totality, for which the

---

[9] The conflict of the modern novel in fact lies "zwischen der Poesie des Herzens und der entgegenstehenden Prosa der Verhältnisse"; see *Vorlesungen über die Ästhetik, Werke*, eds. Eva Moldenhauer & Karl Markus Michel (Frankfurt am Main: Suhrkamp, 1986) vol. 14, 219f, and vol. 15, 392f.

[10] "Die Ästhetik in Hegels System der Philosophie" (1931), rpr. in *Beiträge zum Verständnis und zur Kritik Hegels, Hegel-Studien*, 1965, Beiheft 2, 425–442.

mediated unity of self-consciousness is the model, but subjective consciousness must in turn understand that it itself is part of a larger substantial order of an intersubjective nature. Whether these two orders can be truly united is the key issue for Hegel; the kind of unification that the Romantics sought in art and aesthetic intuition can however no longer be the final answer, but at best only a preliminary form, destined to be superseded by higher and more complex forms of mediation, with the unity achieved in the philosophical concept as the ultimate goal.

The question would be: what happens to the earlier understanding of art in the phenomenological model? Is it simply rejected and relegated to a prehistory supposed to have been overcome in the System of Science? In point of fact, references to art and literature permeate the whole of Hegel's text. They are however always anonymous, as if constituting a kind of tacit knowledge woven into the fabric of the experience of consciousness, and are indeed always more or less inexact; Hegel paraphrases and translates from memory, he cuts and edits at will, but always with the intent of integrating the references into the movement of his own discourse.

Beginning with the second section of the chapter on reason, the literary references multiply: the paraphrased quote from Goethe's first version of *Faust* that opens the analysis of "Pleasure and Necessity," where Hegel points to the contradiction in Faust's desire to achieve instant gratification in fusing with the other, while still retaining the autonomy of self-consciousness; the following step, which analyzes "the law of the heart," weaves together references to Rousseau's *Julie, or the New Héloïse*, Schiller's play *The Robbers*, Jacobi's *Woldemar*, and perhaps also Hölderlin's *Hyperion*. Later we encounter the unfortunate Don Quixote, Goethe's *Wilhelm Meister*, and also many other scattered references.

In the following chapter, on spirit, it would be possible to unearth a logical development organized around three successive readings of literary examples. The first section, "True spirit, ethical life," famously draws on Greek tragedy, and particularly Sophocles's *Antigone*, which Hegel quotes in a typically free manner, in order to establish the irreducible conflict of the power of the family and the netherworld, incarnated in the figure of Antigone, and the power of the state and the *polis*, incarnated in the figure of Creon. The second section, "Spirit alienated from itself: Cultural maturation" (*Bildung*), cites Diderot's dialogue *Rameau's Nephew* in order to show the vertiginous re-evaluation of all values brought about by the completion of cultural maturation on the eve of the revolution. And the third and final section, "Spirit certain of itself: morality," in its analysis of the "beautiful soul," looks to novels, what seems to be Goethe's *Wilhelm Meisters Lehrjahre* and once more Jacobi's *Woldemar*, and quotes directly from Novalis's *Heinrich von Ofterdingen*. And then, of course, at the very end of the chapter on absolute knowledge, we find the slightly altered quote from Schiller's *Die Freundschaft*, which points to the necessity for spirit to go out of itself into the *contingency* of history in order to come back to itself as *grasped* history. These two forms, Hegel writes, introducing the final quote by a dramatic dash, together constitute "the Golgotha of absolute spirit, the actuality, the truth, the certainty of its throne, without which it would be lifeless and alone; only—*Out of the chalice of this realm of spirits / Foams forth to him his infinity*" (§810).[11]

I will not continue with more examples, since my proposal here is not to add to the collection of poetic and/or literary images and borrowings scattered throughout the text of the Phenomenology, but rather to say something about the logic of the collection. This logic is, I will argue, in fact *double*—art appears to play two roles.

On the one hand, it is an *object of analysis*, and its role is circumscribed within a historical narrative that treats it in terms of its capacity to provide us with an adequate presentation of the movement of the concept. In the Phenomenology, art thus gradually emerges from out of its intertwinement with religion until it reaches the state of "absolute art"—and this is where it seems to *end*, in Greek comedy and a momentary state of happiness, both unprecedented and without sequel, where man feels completely at home in the world, but at the price of almost entirely evacuating his own substance. In this, the *Phenomenology* can be taken to affirm that philosophy must overcome art, and to prefigure the later statements in the Berlin lectures on art as a "thing of the past," something that must be superseded by philosophy as an adequate way of grasping the concept in the medium of thought itself.

On the other hand, artworks often seem to function as something that we, following Jean Starobinski in his discussion of Freud,[12] could call

---

[11] All citations from the Phenomenology are taken from the translation by Terry Pinkard, with paragraph numbers. The translation is available at: http://web.mac.com/titpaul/Site/Phenomenology_of_Spirit_page.html.
[12] See Jean Starobinski, "Hamlet et Freud," preface in Ernest Jones, *Hamlet et Oedipe* (Paris: Gallimard, 1967). For a discussion that takes its cues from Starobinski, but then proceeds to show how the work, when positioned as a model or tool, also acquires the capacity to talk back, and to challenge the hegemony of theoretical representation as

"operators." By using this term Starobinski suggests that Hamlet and Oedipus are not just objects for Freud's discourse, but more like sieves or epistemological grids that constitute integral parts of the project of psychoanalysis—they are a privileged representation of the subject's desire in its relation to castration. Similarly, in Hegel, artworks often appear to operate as models for thought at strategically located junctures in the text. The idea of the "operator" indicates that they are located halfway between *concepts*, which as such would be indispensable, and *illustrations*, which would be merely sensuous and particular representations of properly conceptual structures. They belong to the sphere of the imagination, of the *Mitte*, which since Kant had always been given the role of unifying the architectural whole, although neither as a foundation nor as *telos*, but as a properly interstitial element.

This use of art as a philosophical *tool*, while not simply contradicting the later thesis on art as a thing of the past with respect to its "highest aim," in fact draws Hegel close to some of Schelling's ideas about art as an "organon," and it opens up the possibility of a different type of exchange between art and philosophy that constitutes one of the most vital aspects of the Hegelian heritage in contemporary philosophy of art. This however requires that we examine more closely the distinction between art as an object of philosophy, which can be treated systematically, and an art that somehow insinuates itself into philosophy and informs its discourse in a more oblique way.

The systematic treatment

Let me begin by giving a brief overview of the *systematic* treatment, which we find in the section entitled "The Religion of Art" (*Die Kunstreligion*), which is located in the middle of the chapter on religion. As the title indicates, the treatment of art is systematically interwoven with and even subordinate to the treatment of religion, which takes us from its first and simplest forms, where art has not yet appeared, through Greece, where it does appear. and forms the strange compound "Kunstreligion" (which Hegel sometimes even calls "artificial religion," "künstliche Religion," a

---

such, see Jean-François Lyotard, "Freud selon Cézanne," in *Des dispositifs pulsionnels* (Paris: UGE, 1973).

religion as it were based in artifacts), and up to Christianity, where art recedes into the sphere of memory and *Er-Innerung*.

Hegel first takes us through an analysis of "natural religion," which starts in the "luminous essence" (*das Lichtwesen*), a pure beginning or a gift of being which is also, as Derrida has pointed out,[13] a sacrifice, an expenditure of luminosity, or the "creative secret" (§685) of birth. This secret must however appear and enter into representation, and the thought that errs through nature and generates a "sublime" lack of measure in its random forms, must acquire a defined shape. No artworks are yet mentioned here, but in the later Berlin lectures on aesthetics Hegel will connect this sublimity to, for instance, Hebrew poetry, or to various early forms of architecture. Now, this necessary shaping occurs in the subsequent and slightly enigmatic section, "Plant and Animal," in the form of pantheism and a peaceful religion of flowers, which soon passes over into the violence of the religion of animals. Out of this destructive violence, which "grinds down," as Hegel says, the beings that exist for themselves, the final moment in natural religion emerges, which is also the first recognizable artistic agent: the "Artisan" (*der Werkmeister*). His work is still instinctual, and it produces the rectilinear and planar shapes of the understanding, in pyramids and obelisks. The work that appears is however not yet spiritual, but must receive this spiritual quality from the outside, as in the case of the pyramids, which enclose a deceased placed within them, or as themselves a dead body that must be given voice by the rising sun, as in Herodotus's description of the colossi of Memnon. In his work with external reality the artisan however gradually comes to intertwine the geometric and the organic, and "free architecture" (§694) begins here. In the later lectures, Hegel would develop this much further, and explicate the link between architecture as the first art of space, matter, and gravity, which inscribes death and the underworld in a movement towards the Greek luminosity.[14]

---

[13] See the discussion in *Glas* (Paris: Galilée, 1974), 331ff.

[14] Hegel's rich treatment of the first phases of architecture has received surprisingly little comment, although it in fact provides many keys as to why the schema of "architect-tonics" imposes itself as a model for the philosophical system. In addition, this treatment also displays a rich variety of synthesizing and interpretative moves that need to be made for a history of art to have a *beginning*, in the passage from "pre-art" (*Vorkunst*) to art. I discuss this in more detail in "Hegel and the Grounding of Architecture," in Michael Asgaard and Henrik Oxvig (eds.): *The Paradoxes of Appearing: Essays on Art, Architecture, and Philosophy* (Baden: Lars Müller Publishers, 2009).

In Greece and the religion of art, then, spirit truly becomes an artist, but it does so on the basis of a fusion of art and religion. In the later Berlin lectures, Hegel would more clearly separate art and religion, and also present an infinitely more detailed analysis of the individual arts that correlates them with historical phases. In this later version, the Greek moment contains the sensible appearing of the idea, and freestanding sculpture constitutes the paradigmatic form, whereas the subsequent Christian moment ascribes this role to painting, although art *as such*, as the presentation of truth, has been relegated to a secondary position in relation to religion. In the Phenomenology, these different developmental lines are still intertwined, and Greece is understood as the moment of an "absolute art," which will be just as condemned to disappearance as is the Greek *Sittlichkeit*.

In the Phenomenology, Hegel discerns three steps in the Greek development, the *abstract*, the *living*, and the *spiritual* work of art, all of which can be understood as the gradual emergence of self-consciousness and the becoming-human of the divine powers. When this process is completed, art will fade away, together with the Greek gods, and the systematic treatment comes to an end.

The first moment takes us from sculpture to the hymn, and finally to the cult, and "abstraction" here means that the constitutive moments of art have still not formed an integral unity. In this process, gods and humans begin to draw closer to each other, and the animal and natural shapes are relegated to the obscure memory of the "unethical realm of the titans" (§707). The proper appearance of the god however requires a higher element than the merely external space of sculpture, and this will be *language*, in the form of the hymn and the oracle, which are finally brought together in the cult and the sacrifice, where the fruits that are consumed are at once a spiritualization of matter and a descent of the gods. The cult joins together the subjective interiority of worship and the external space of sculpture, and makes art into a common and collective event.

In the second moment, the *living* work of art, we see a development leading from the Mysteries to the Olympic games, and the emergence of a human universality. This is the feast that man gives in the honor of himself, where the human figure takes the place of archaic sculpture, and the beautiful body of the athlete or the fighter receives the worship earlier bestowed on the statue. Once more, however, the equilibrium between inner and outer is lacking, and this time, too, language proves to be the medium in which it is to be achieved, which will take us into the third and final moment.

This is the *spiritual* work of art, where Hegel traces a development from epic to tragedy and comedy, which gradually removes the gods from the stage until man finally encounters nothing but himself, and this, as we will see, is the brief and transitory moment of what Hegel calls "absolute art." In the epic, the spirit of different groups comes together in a kind of pre-state community (for which the *Iliad* and the war against Troy seem to be the paradigm), and here the interaction between man and gods already shows the redundant nature of the divine powers in a way that prefigures the comic dissolution: the actions of the gods merely duplicate those of the humans, and as such they are nothing but a "farcical superfluity" (§730) that initiates their process of dying. In tragedy language then appears in a more pure form, where the protagonists take the stage in order to express their inner essence, and where the hero with his determinate character presents a further step of humanization. And finally, in comedy we witness the "the depopulation of heaven" (§741): the gods are divested of their substance and everything returns to consciousness and the self. This moment "is, on the part of consciousness, both that of well-being and of letting-oneself-be-well which is no longer to be found outside of this comedy." (§747) This, then, is absolute art, the moment of artistic confidence, which is also the end of art as well as the first death of God in the narrative of the Phenomenology. The moment of absolute art is a moment of irony, a happiness that treats everything lightly, and plays upon the use of masks and dissimulations in order to affirm its own lack of substance.[15]

The next section, "Revealed Religion," looks back at this transformation from the opposite end, or more precisely from a vantage point *beyond the end* of classical art: as we noted, the elevation of the self in comedy is just as much a loss of spirit, and Hegel now describes the pain inherent in the "harsh phrase *that God has died*" (§752) as a transition. On the one hand, the oracles are gone and the statues have become corpses, faith has abandoned the hymns and the old artworks are "beautiful fruit broken off from the tree" (§753)—all of which can be understood as a nostalgic trope

---

[15] Which is of course a very tricky moment that may be read both with against dialectics; cf. Werner Hamacher, "The End of Art with the Mask," in Stuart Barnett (ed.): *Hegel After Derrida* (London: Routledge, 1998).

derived from Winckelmann,[16] but also as that which makes possible our modern aesthetic appreciation of these works by wresting them away from their original soil. This is developed further in the lectures on aesthetics, and we can seen this idea germinating in the image of the young girl, who in a gesture of mourning, but also of generosity and grace, offers the works to us and our *Er-innerung*, to the interiorizing that takes place in our memory and our art-historical institutions.[17] On the other hand, the death of the old gods is also the precondition for the birth of the new God, which is a response to the pain of unhappy consciousness and the emptiness of a situation where "the self is the absolute essence," in the form of the descent of the absolute to man—which in turn prefigures the second death of God, this time a more profound death out of which philosophy itself will arise.

Art as operator

What then of the other role of art? As we have already noted, references to, and hidden quotes from, works of art are scattered throughout the text of the *Phenomenology*. A first remark would be the following: if in the systematic explication presented above they appear as more and more fulfilled and perfected indications of a development of consciousness, as stepping-stones on the way toward the historical caesura which divides the death of the ancient gods from the birth of the Christian God, they are also, as singular works, powerful agents that assume a much more active and organizing role than simply being illustrations of a development, which I above attempted to capture by the term "operator."

Let me clarify what I mean with two examples. Both are located at similar critical junctures in the chapter on spirit—the first functions as the paradigm for the dissolution of Greek ethical life, the second as the endpoint of the process of cultural formation (*Bildung*), which opens onto a kind of pre-revolutionary nihilism—and in this they constitute a kind of interior rhyme in the text, a cumulative effect that allows the second reading to inform the first, and which also organizes the narrative that they seem

---

[16] In fact, Winckelmann can just as much as Hegel be read as a theorist of the rise of aesthetics as a modern predicament: the loss of the Greek origin creates the space of art-historical, aesthetic, and museological discourse.

[17] Jean-Luc Nancy reads this passage as the advent of a discourse on art as autonomous and self-conscious form, which requires the detachment from religion; see *Les Muses* (Paris: Galilée, 1994), 75–97.

merely to illustrate. These two cases are, of course, Sophocles's *Antigone* and Diderot's *Rameau's Nephew*.

If the Greek polis can be taken as a work of art, as an aesthetic-political unity, which Hegel indeed had claimed in his earlier writings, then the action performed by a work like Sophocles's *Antigone* is the tearing apart of this beautiful unity, the revealing of its irrevocable *disunity*. The properly tragic dimension of tragedy is that both parties—in this case Creon and Antigone—are in fact right, and both of them simply fulfill a duty, the law, divine or human, that has been allotted to them, without being able to see the justification for the actions on the part of the other: "Since it sees right only on its own side and sees only wrong on the other, the consciousness that belongs to divine law beholds on the other side merely human and contingent *acts of violence*; and that consciousness which belongs to human law beholds on the other side the obstinacy and *disobedience* of inward being-for-itself" (§465). This is not just simply a conflict between the subjectivity of the heart and the objectivity of duty, but between two equally unavoidable duties (family-state, woman-man, divine-human), and both Creon and Antigone emphasize the objective and non-personal dimension of the law whose command they are carrying out. This incapacity to see the perspective of the other is what brings down the beautiful totality of the *polis* and of Greek ethical life, and when the spheres of family and state have come to be opposed, the process of disintegration is irreversible: old and young are pitted against each other, the state must attempt to undermine the authority and inwardness of the family, while the family, and more precisely femininity, the "polity's eternal irony" (§474), overtakes the government's universal purpose and transforms it into a private family enterprise.

My interest here is not so much the significance of tragedy as a literary artifact, or the tragic as an ontological and/or existential structure in Hegel's philosophy, but the way in which the example orients the logic of the narrative. What Hegel intends to show is that the individual in the beautiful ethical life is embedded in a social order that must be broken up for the infinity of subjectivity to appear, and in the section entitled "The ethical world, the human and divine law, man and woman," which precedes the references to *Antigone*, he provides us with an account of the equilibrium between human and divine law, man and woman, state and family. This account, I would like to propose, is obviously already structured by the analysis of Sophocles, in its highlighting two features that will become the key issue in the play: the family that provides the death of the individual with a higher meaning through the ritual of burial and joins the earthly and the chthonic order, and the inner structure of the family, where Hegel stresses the relation between brother and sister as a pure recognition, untainted by any desire. This latter relation, Hegel concludes, implies that "the moment of the *individual self*, as recognizing and being recognized, may here assert its right because it is bound up with the equilibrium of blood relations and with relations utterly devoid of desire. The loss of a brother is thus irreplaceable to the sister, and her duty towards him is the highest" (§456). This indeed makes little sense as an analysis of Greek ethical life in general, and the function of this passage seems rather to be its prefiguring of the reading of *Antigone*; or, in the perspective that I would like to suggest here, Sophocles's play functions as an operator or a grid through which Greek ethical life can appear in a particular way, and the literary text intervenes not only as an illustration of a thesis established independently of it. Greek ethical life was for Hegel always underway towards the tragic dissolution staged in Sophocles's play, or inversely: Sophocles's play is the hidden attractor that makes it possible to depict this life as always underway towards tragedy.

My second example is the similar strategic use of Diderot's *Rameau's Nephew*, which, I would argue, provides the argument in the subsequent analysis of cultural maturation with its direction, and in this functions in a similar fashion as *Antigone*. We must first note that Hegel does not understand *Bildung* in the sense of a culture acquired through a reading of a certain set of canonical texts, but as a progressive estrangement and externalization of the self in which the individual must shed his natural determination, all of which leads to a kind of nihilism, even though this is a term that Hegel himself does not use (nor, it must be added, could it have been available to him, since it emerges out of a certain nineteenth-century reading of the Hegelian completion of metaphysics). This analysis forms a part of the most entangled and layered sections of the *Phenomenology*, and here I can only trace a particular line that ends in Diderot, although I believe that it has bearings on the whole.

Hegel suggests a developing opposition between state power, substance, or the collective order, and the individual's quest for personal wealth. These two are however only opposed on the surface, and, drawing on his reading of British political economy, Hegel shows how the individual in his pursuit of his own pleasure and gain in fact might contribute to the well-being of the whole. On the basis of this dialectical opposition Hegel then proceeds to analyze the emergence of an increasingly complex social order, within which the individual understands state power both as his own essence and as that which deprives him of individuality, in a process that takes us from the feudal order, through the arrival of the absolutist state and up to the revolution. From my perspective, it is crucial that Hegel systematically accounts for this development as a series of what could be called language games—from the "language of the counsel" (§504), to the "heroism of flattery" (§510), and the "empty name" (§511). These processes, where on the one hand state power comes to be concentrated in a point that eventually escapes definition since it is situated at the limit of language, and on the other hand wealth develops into an independent system, no doubt characterized by an opposite but equally empty verbosity, generate a torn, split, and lacerated world, which is expressed in the "language of laceration" (*die Sprache der Zerissenheit*), which Hegel understands as the "perfected language of this entire world of cultural maturation as well as its true existing spirit" (§519). This language is precisely what unfolds in *Rameau's Nephew*, which can be understood as the completion of cultural maturation in a vertiginous reversal of all values, and at the end of the *ancien régime* it already appears to herald both the Marxist analysis of universal commodification and Nietzsche's diagnosis of nihilism: everything is for sale, all values can easily be converted into their opposite, and the only reasonable stance is to understand and affirm the complete bankruptcy of reason.

Now, could we not say that the inevitable conflict of Creon and Antigone, and even more so the inversions and reversals of Diderot's dialogue on the eve of the contemporary age, are indeed akin to the movement of dialectics itself? Not only do they portray the necessity of *Zerrissenheit* and the movement of *Verkehrung*, but they in fact provide Hegel with two of the most powerful ways to think dialectics: the idea of a necessary and determinate contradiction, and the possibility of an infinite negativity. In this they propagate their effects far beyond the confines of the analysis of "the religion of art," and they indicate the presence of the artwork as what I have called a *tool*, an *operator*, or perhaps what we, following Adorno, could call a "model." This second position of the work, no longer an object simply *outside of, in front of, before* philosophical discourse, in fact testifies to the way in which Hegel's language does not simply dominate its objects, which is how he is often perceived, and particularly so with respect to artworks, but allows them to unfold their own analytic powers inside a philosophical discourse that is itself in search of its own definition.

Understanding as Translation
How to read Hegel's *Phenomenology of Spirit*
PIRMIN STEKELER-WEITHOFER

On some problems of reading philosophical texts

Reading is translating. This claim seems to contradict Wittgenstein's insight that understanding is *not* interpreting. But whereas Wittgenstein is right with respect to immediate language use, for example when we understand spoken language by reacting or answering correctly in a communicative and cooperative way, the situation with writing is different, as was already known by Plato. The problem is this. Texts written in a phonematic way (using alphabets) codify only a certain abstract or formal way of speaking. This means that the actual situation of the speaker is always somehow missing for the reader as a resource for anaphorical references and relevance. On the other hand, the writer does not know the circumstances of the reader, in particular he cannot guard against obvious misunderstandings of his intentions and, what is more dramatic, he cannot foresee diachronic changes in linguistic meaning or use.

As a result, readers and writers always share a cooperative task which is in some respects more complicated and more demanding than the corresponding task of speakers and hearers—if we think of real dialogues and not of merely preaching speeches, which Plato rightly identifies (in his *Phaedrus*) with paper texts. Similar to a preacher, the writer has to do his best to make his text readable for a large and personally unknown audience, given the general system of language and knowledge he lives in. The reader has to support the text by reading it with charity. And this always means, at least in part, to interpret the text, i.e. to translate it into the language she, the reader, would have to use if she wanted to express the same thoughts (contents, meanings) in her situation, her time, given her language and her general knowledge. Correcting malapropisms, as we do it in spoken discourse as well, is only a minor point here. Taking possible changes of semantic systems of default inference including all sorts of connotations into account, is already a more serious matter.

Things get even more complicated when the topics of the texts are not just object-related, as will or should be the case in all sorts of object-centered science. In fact, science is first and foremost a cooperative linguistic enterprise. A necessary condition is logico-linguistic regimentation. Only on its ground can we presuppose more or less well-defined notions of "synonymy" as a relation of "equivalence in relevant meaning" between different scientific texts. In a much less rigid way, the same holds for a given language use and implicit practice of understanding in different vernaculars, i.e. in "natural" or rather "spoken" languages. The problem is that, by necessity, the language of philosophical reflections on science, concepts, and languages rather resembles the use of vernaculars than of terminologically already regimented languages, and that the ideal of a clear and exact philosophical terminology as well as the idea of transforming philosophy into a science with a limited topic or domain of objects to be investigated miss the very point of the enterprise of philosophical reflection, as Plato and Aristotle very well knew. In contrast to this, from Kant to the present day, the possibility and usefulness of formal terminology in philosophy seems to be overestimated and its limits undervalued. In the twentieth century, only Heidegger and Wittgenstein seem to have noticed with due emphasis the deep difference between, on the one hand, what we try to show in philosophical texts—that they can never do more than help us to reflect on forms of our practices—and, on the other hand, what we say about already well-determined objects or topics in the sciences.

As a result of this insight—which unfortunately has not yet reached the stage of public knowledge—in the understanding of philosophical texts, the reader first has to figure out at least the main topic and focus, the particular relevance and particular modes of speech, especially when she reads historical philosophical texts.

Even in the object-related case of the sciences, reading historical texts is almost the same as reading texts written in another language. This is much more so for philosophy. Or rather, we should be aware that this may be so, even though we might not feel it at first. At first, we usually assume that we still speak the same German language as, for example, Kant and Goethe, Fichte, Schelling or Hegel. But this is not so. Many words have changed their use, and, what is worse, some conventions and acceptability conditions concerning grammatical constructions have changed. The same problem hold for Descartes and French. Much more complicated problems for understanding, however, are created by philosophical texts that use a language in the same way Spinoza used his Latin. In the corresponding class of authors belong Oswald Spengler, Ferdinand Tönnies, Otto Weininger, Martin Heidegger, and, believe it or not, Ludwig Wittgenstein. Before we even can start to evaluate the possible truths of, or in, these texts, we first have to clarify how to read them. And even though all authors mentioned in the last list certainly write in German, they all make fairly creative use of the German linguistic system—which allows, like ancient Greek though unlike a less "abstract" language as English—for arbitrary nominalizations and explicit topicalizations of all possible parts of speech. As a result, many readers who are not used to more abstract or, as they claim, bureaucratic means of expression, accuse such writers of using idiolects or ascribe ontic hypostizations to them. But nothing could be farther from the truth.

In order to show this, we might, for example, look at Carnap's claim that Heidegger's talk about "das Nichts" was metaphysical. For Carnap's judgment is, in the end, not much more than a sign that he does not interpret the text correctly. For any reader who knows a little bit more about the German used in philosophy at that time sees more or less immediately, first, that Heidegger's logical concern was much more similar to that of Russell and Carnap than these authors knew: Together with Brentano and Meinong, Heidegger knew that we have to distinguish between being a mere object of talk (like numbers, unicorns, or dead or non-existing kings of France) and being something that really exists. Hence, the basic question of critical philosophical ontology is not, as Quine claims, what can be a value of a variable in a formal domain of speech, but what it means to refer language and practice to the real word. In citing the *locus classicus* of modern philosophy, Leibniz's question, Why or on what ground is there some real thing and not rather nothing? Heidegger shows and says among other things, first, that we should not read the "why" as asking for a sufficient efficient cause, but for the form of distinguishing between real things and possibilities from merely verbal entities and possibilities; second that the word "nothing" always is relative to an already presupposed domain of objects we talk about. If we say, for example, that the expression "the largest prime number" refers to nothing, we do not mean that it refers to something called "nothing." Rather, the word nothing denies the possibility of any proper reference. Things get even more complicated when we say that in empty space there is nothing or when we say that there is nothing feared in *Angst*, because *Angst* as a *Stimmung* is not intentionally directed in contradiction to, for example, fear of sickness or death.

Nobody says that Carnap and his followers should *like* Heidegger's expression "Das Nichts nichtet" or be content with it. But since it is clear that Heidegger was himself more than aware of the fact that the sentence contains the neologism "nichten," Carnap should better put more effort into a sufficiently accurate attempt to understand what Heidegger obviously wants to express. For Heidegger tries to say in his words more or less the same as what Russell, Carnap and all other "anti-metaphysical" analytic philosophers are proud of saying themselves—and even more than this, as we can see in a sentence like the following: "there is nothing *angst* refers to whereas *fear* always fears some specific possibility." Of course, talking about angst and fear here is talking about concepts together with the real phenomena they distinguish, not to any hypostatization of entities or powers. As a result of these short remarks on how to read Heidegger we can already see: Carnap is barking up the wrong tree. My claim is that most criticism of Hegel in traditional analytic philosophy is of the same nature.

In fact, it is about time to re-evaluate the "on dit" or hearsay of twentieth-century analytic philosophy about what has to be criticized as transcendent metaphysical claims (about nothing, without reference and content) and what is only a lack of linguistic understanding when it comes to different ways of abstracting and topicalizing by using the linguistic form of nominalization. Intuitive resentment against allegedly all too grand and speculative or "metaphysical" sentences that want to say something about "the West" or "the East," "the community" and "society," "man" and "woman," about Being-in-the-world or an allegedly non-thinking science is no real help here. The same holds for a priori resentments about talking about objective or absolute spirit and things like understanding, reason, desiring, in order to come closer to the topic of Hegel's *Phenomenology of Spirit*, at least with our examples. From a really logical point of view, which, as such, goes far beyond merely formal logic, the understanding of such abstract or generic expressions is, ironically, fairly similar to the understanding of mathematical ways of speaking, from talking about the equilateral triangle in elementary geometry to, say, specific differential equations. In both cases it does not make sense to ask to express "the same content" in everyday language, whatever the late Wittgenstein sometimes seems to say against this view. He is right, however, to criticize any overestimation and awe which some readers manifest with respect to generic or structural talk or abstract mathematical theories. In the same vein, if we are linguistically competent, we neither should abuse nor misunderstand, nor avoid generic statements about "the German(s)" or "the Roman(s)," to say nothing of "the Jew(s)." The same holds for talking about "understanding," "desiring," "reason" or "objective spirit." We rather should face the problems we have when we use such ways of talking, or else we also do not understand claims about "the world," "the logical form of sentence" or "the superstition" (of our belief in causality), as we read them in Ludwig Wittgenstein's *Tractatus*.

The first reason for the difficulties of understanding generic sentences about general structures has to do with the fact that we today generally tend to read a sentence, say, about "the German(s)" or "woman" or, to take some other examples, "the mountain lion" or "the triangle" in a *universal*, not in a *generic* way. Precisely this change in our attitude towards nominalizations and a lack of understanding of their generic use is the culprit behind most misunderstandings especially of German philosophy from Kant to Heidegger.

In a universal reading, these expressions refer to the set *of all singular* Germans or women or triangles. In fact, today, this reading comes to mind first. It always was a possible reading. But in earlier times, every sufficiently learned person knew that it was not the only one. For in generic sentences about the German(s) or the mountain lion we express only *default* truths when we say, for example, that the mountain lion eats rabbits or that Nazi Germany had a biologistic (mis)conception of nationhood and talked in an incredibly sweeping way about a struggle for survival of the German "Volk." But not all mountain lions eat rabbits. And not even a majority of singular Germans supported Nazi ideology. Nevertheless, the rather primitive "folk-science" of biologism was a leading motive for many of the terrible deeds committed by and in Nazi Germany.

Just as no structured social and political history of institutions, ideas and people can be told without generic sentence, but only singular stories about lives, opinions, happenings and deeds of singular persons, no philosophical analysis of conceptual structures can be expressed without generic sentences. Hegel addresses this very topic by thinking about the logical status of "the speculative sentence(s)." As such, any speculative sentence is generic. And its "truth" is of a specific form. In order to show why for such sentences neither the principle of the excluded contradiction nor the excluded middle or third holds, we can compare the speculative sentences with a tradition of moral advice from Seneca to La Rochefoucauld, La Bruyère or Gratian, and all corresponding proverbs. There are, for example, deep "dialectical truths" in the Greek sentence *gnothi seauton* in the sense of "be self-conscious" or in the Latin sentence *festina lente*, "proceed slowly." But sometimes our judgments and actions have to be *fast*, not *slow*, *decisive* and *courageous*, not too *cautious*, *timid*, or *self-reflective*. The first to notice the need for dialectical considerations on the generic status of sentences about concepts and virtues like those of temperance or justice, was, obviously, Socrates, as we can see in Plato's dialogues. Hegel belongs to the still very few readers of Plato who realize precisely this. As a result, he sees that we have to learn to use generic sentences in a logically correct way. This holds for philosophy as well as for the sciences or everyday discourse. And this means that we cannot use generic sentences in a schematic or formalistic way, as if they could be read as universal quantifications about all singular cases. We cannot even use all the geometrical truths about, say, straight lines and plane surfaces, when we use them in judgments about real (solid) things or ("empty") space. We can use them only on the ground of general experience—*Erfahrung*—which is not to be confused, as is often done in English texts, with a set of prior sensations and perceptions of some kind. Experience as *Erfahrung* is rather a practical competence.

This is already a central remark on Hegel's speculative analysis of mind in his Phenomenology. The topic of the book is, altogether, not only in the beginning, *the experience of consciousness* (with itself, namely in a properly understood self-consciousness), in German: *Die Erfahrung des Bewusstseins (mit sich selbst, nämlich im Selbstbewusstsein)*. What Hegel wants to articulate and make explicit are levels of generic insights that develop by making these experiences explicit. We make these experiences in *using* the concepts that are the results of previous generic understandings; and we develop these understandings in critical reflections by noticing the problems and one-sidedness of any merely schematic or thoughtless use of previous understandings. As a result, all the following (speculative, generically reflective and in the end logico-conceptual) sentences about mind are totally true: Mind in the sense of the competence of human sapience (necessarily) is (inner) sensation (*Empfindung*), (outer) perception (*Wahrnehmung*), consciousness (*Bewusstsein*) and understanding (*Verstand*). Mind (necessarily) is (reflective) self-consciousness (*Selbstbewusstsein*), (subjective) reason

(*Vernunft*) and objective spirit (*Geist*). Nevertheless any of these sentences can be at the same time wrong, namely in the sense that they all are one-sided and express *only necessary* conditions for full human sapience. Therefore, and because of their generic form, each one of them can be easily misunderstood. Only if we take them together do we arrive at a true picture: Human sapience is much more than (animal) sensation. It is more than (animal) perception, guiding (animal) desire. It is also much more than the (important but by far not sufficient) faculty of following rules (in Kant's and Hegel's sense of understanding or *Verstand*)—and so on.

But there is another problem as well. In order to avoid possible misunderstandings of generic sentences we might think that we better avoid these sentences altogether. In fact, much of Wittgenstein's philosophy can be seen as supporting this view: The misunderstanding of speculative or philosophical reflections would indeed come to an end if we stopped doing philosophy. If this were what Wittgenstein said, he would be the unhappy protagonist of modern *Zeitgeist* and its naïve understanding of language, which asks for verbalized expressions, avoids abstract nominalizations, prefers showing something by examples to saying it in the mode of all too grand and easily misunderstood generic sentences, and does not see that examples usually can be properly understood only together with the generic sentences they illustrate, just as allegories and metaphors are *less* illuminating than analogies: In analogies we transfer the model-structure of some *Urbild* to the realm we want to talk about by *saying* what the comparison between the *Urbild* and the realm can *show* us. In other words, we use the same words and sentences in describing the structure of the *Urbild* and of the intended realm, such that the result of any analogy is a kind of (more or less strong or weak) isomorphism, as, for example, the isomorphism between Plato's *polis* and *psyche*, Hegel's *state* and *soul*, and Plato's and Hegel's *society* and *mind*.

If I am right, we not only have to translate Hegel's German into French, English or, for that matter, Swedish, but we have to translate it into the idioms of modern German. Of course, we cannot do this in a narrow and formal sense of the adverb "literally." What we do instead is to add comments to the original text.

This is all the more important since we cannot separate concepts form generic knowledge. In fact, this is one of the most important, and deepest, of Hegel's own insights: the very meaning of words and sentences depends on the general knowledge of a time expressed by generic sentences.

Therefore, we should bracket the times: by this we create epochs in the literal sense of a series of bracketing of times. Only with reference to an epoch may we assume that meanings are more or less fixed. In other words, the idea of eternal or synchronic meaning is always an idea that abstracts from the relevant epoch and from the fact that there always are diachronic changes of meaning that depend on the development of our knowledge, our institutions, and our forms of life. As a result, without interpretation, and without systematic comparisons between different epochs with different forms and norms of inferential meanings we cannot identify any relevant sameness or identity of content and meaning. This is the very insight of Hegelian dialectics: There are no eternal meanings. But there are possibilities of identifying identities of relevant content despite many changes in detail, if we only keep to the appropriate and relevant equivalence relations. Thus, Greek democracy is, in a sense, the same as modern democracy, and comes with similar problems, even though in other respects modern democracy is fairly different, much more republican in a Roman sense and much more monarchic in the sense of an absolute power of some executive representative, at least for some time.

If we are not aware of logical facts like these, we cannot understand historical texts properly. One part of the corresponding method of interpretation is defining appropriate epochs in which relevant forms of practice and contents of language remain essentially the same. And this means to make the particular forms of an epoch explicit, "die Zeit auf den Begriff zu bringen," which includes an explication of the relevant epochal changes that take place between such epochs. This is, I take it, Hegel's own insight into what I would like to call "historical hermeneutics."

But if we must "translate" Hegel into contemporary philosophy (not into a particular idiom as the proposal of the organizers suggest when they talk of "phenomenology, critical theory, analytical philosophy, etc."), how should we do it? I would not like to talk about "a philosophy" as the proper "heir" of Hegelianism, because I do not think it useful to use any "ism," perhaps not even in textbooks for beginners. The question why Hegel has nevertheless used a label like "absolute idealism" for his contributions to philosophy is, of course, interesting. But it must be answered under the presumption, or rather insight, that there is only one philosophy, and that the idea that one can have one's own philosophy just as a hairdresser has his and a car dealer has his is absolutely misleading. In fact, belief-philosophy is not philosophy. There is a categorical and absolute opposition between philosophy and any belief in "isms."

There is no way of reading Plato or Aristotle, Kant or Hegel, "immediately," without considerable knowledge about the peculiar problems they wanted to solve, the peculiar projects they wanted to further and the peculiar knowledge, language, and perhaps contentions ("prejudices") they took for granted, and perhaps had to take for granted. Therefore, translating Hegel into contemporary philosophy, or rather, commenting on his texts in the language of contemporary philosophy, not only makes Hegel "more readable" for those unfamiliar with Hegel's idiosyncrasies, but is a necessary step in understanding the content of what he says. Contents exist only as that which remains invariant when we say the same thing in different words, be they different words in one language or in more languages. Hegel himself always was occupied with seeing the same general idea behind all changes of particular forms. Teaching differences, as Wittgenstein famously prefers to an allegedly Hegelian teaching to see identities is a nice thing only in its proper place. If there were no transpersonal identities in meanings we never could understand anyone else. Without transcending our own epoch and province we cannot understand others'—Plato's, for example.

Therefore, we better distinguish the necessity of *translation* and *interpretation* of texts from any *assimilation* of their considerations and arguments to our present concerns. That is, we should not project *contingent* interests of today arbitrarily onto Hegel's text. Like Pippin, Pinkard or Brandom, we rather should try to show that modern thoughts are already found in Hegel. As a result, we do not need anachronistic projections of our own concerns onto Hegel's text. In fact, I show at many places how Hegel's thought were influenced by his intelligent reading not only of Kant (and the British philosophers) but especially of Greek authors—of course by also showing how to reconstruct the appropriate reading of Greek thought. In other words, my concern is not so much to discern "what is living and what is dead in Hegel," even though I would not read Hegel at all if I did not find his thoughts interesting for us today.

However, there is no understanding of a text, no interpretation and therefore no translation of a non-trivial text without risks. The reason is clear. No human in the world can say sufficiently important and general (generic) things in such a clear and distinct way that there is only one way of understanding him or his texts. The cooperation between speaker and hearer, writer and reader is always free. Hence, there is always the risk the speaker or writer says or would say: No, I did not mean this. By this, he says: No I do not want you to infer these things you infer from what I have said. I did not want your thoughts to go this way. But if a speaker or writer is dead, he cannot help his texts by judgments like these, as Plato famously has seen and said. The responsibility is now in our hands. And now, of course, different readers today will disagree in their comments. But there is no truth of the matter left that goes beyond our free and open debate which interpretation or translation taken as a proposal of reading might be best—and for which reader. At first, every voice of any interpreter has equal weight, if it conforms in its arguments to the state of art of reading the corresponding texts properly, i.e. if the interpreter uses the virtue of *accuracy* (Bernard Williams) in a sufficient way.

The art of reading is a technique with more or less clear criteria for evaluating the results without all too general words like "depth" and similar hand-waving. The aspects to be judged are: Do we understand the issues? Which parts of the text remain closed territory, mere letters and sentences, without clear conditions of truth and orientation? The feeling of depth often is not much more than the judgment that I do not understand the text. There is nothing valuable in this, not even with respect to poems. In other words: There is a difference between the inferential power of a text and the clarity of an interpretation.

Hence, in a good translation and interpretation, nothing "essentially Hegelian" can get *lost*. But, of course, it might always be a good advice to look into the original texts, just as a judge often better consults the law than his intuition.

I do not believe that Hegel's German, or Heidegger's German, for that matter, was anything near an idiolect. The truth is rather this: These authors exploit some possibilities of using German in a way that presupposes a fairly high standard of philosophical *and* linguistic competence. And of course, they introduce some terminology of their own, as *any* original writer must do, without turning the resulting "scientific idiom" into an idiolect. When Hegel, for example, uses nominalized verbs as in "*das Erkennen*/the knowing" or, much more difficult, "*das Meinen*/presuming," it is absolutely crucial that he refers to performative attitudes, not results, as they are expressed in the "normal" substantive form of languages which stylistically do not allow for free nominalizations as German and Greek. Therefore, "knowledge," "cognition" and "opinion" would be misleading translations, at least in part. But I certainly understand that we have to balance gracefulness and accuracy, or else no one would enjoy reading the text. But, on the other hand, Hegel certainly was absolutely reckless in this, just as Kant and Heidegger: They all have turned question of stylistic grace down if this seemed to be required by the form of precision they strove for.

Questions of translations and interpretation of a philosophical author like Kant, Hegel, or Heidegger cannot be separated from questions concerning the main topics and aims, the overall structure and the path of the argument(s). With respect to Hegel's *Phenomenology of Spirit*, this seems to me even more true than with most other texts in the history of philosophy. Here we have to grasp the idea of the book as a whole. Is it a kind of story about the (ontogenetic and or phylogenetic) development of human sapience and the modern, self-conscious intellect, as people following Marx, Lukács, Kojève down to the Frankfurt school openly or implicitly assume? Or is it rather a series of deconstructions, namely of wrong, but widespread, ideas about ourselves, our knowledge of and practical reference to things, our knowledge of and practical attitudes to ourselves, the individual and social, or rather institutional, status of understanding, reason, intelligence, and "spirit"?

This leads us to the question of Hegel's relation to Kant and to the agenda of Hegel's Phenomenology. In both respects, the traditional historiography of philosophy of the nineteenth and twentieth century, mainly influenced by Neo-Kantians and analytic philosophy, does not get things right at all.

The structure of Hegel's phenomenology of the human mind

In his criticism of Brandom's approach and my own attempts to read Hegel's texts as contributions to an analysis of concepts—or of "the concept" as the system of all conceptual knowledge, for that matter—which adds a modern logico-linguistic or semantic interpretation to this concept-analysis, Herbert Schnädelbach somehow sneeringly talks about a "deciphering" (*Entzifferung*) of Hegel. Obviously, he thinks that such a scrupulous reading and interpretation of singular sentences is not necessary. But such a judgment presupposes that it is clear what Hegel is talking about and where he is heading. But it is precisely this that is not the case. As a result, Schnädelbach's own effort of reading Hegel, like many others, does not go beyond the already well-known hearsay about Hegel, which is the product of the 19th and 20th century's fights between different groups of Hegelians and anti-Hegelians, with Adolf Trendelenburg or Bernard Bolzano as early, Bertrand Russell and Karl Popper as later critical non-readers.

There is of course no space here for a detailed deciphering or interpretation of long passages in Hegel's Phenomenology. I rather sketch the general structure of his thought and argument.

In a sense, Hegel begins with a concern about Kant's basic principle of *transcendental apperception* and Descartes' *res cogitans*, namely with the question what it means that any *Vorstellung*, that is, any presentation or representation of something in the world, must be able to be accompanied by some "I think (of it)." The concern is with the question of what thinking is and who the thinker is. And, indeed, this remains as unclear in Kant's texts as it already had been in Descartes'. Part of the second question is how to understand the *I*, the *self*, the *subject* of thinking and consciousness.

The two questions, what thinking is and who the thinker is, that is, how to understand the subject of thinking, are the two leading questions of Hegel's enterprise in his Phenomenology. The first question is crucial since we should stick, as Hegel famously says, to the age-old insight that thinking marks the difference between the mode of being of *homo sapiens sapiens* and that of the merely animal. The second question is crucial because we know all too well about the traditional ontic hypostatizations of the human mind as a subjective-individual soul in traditional "rational psychology," of a general-generic spirit as a god in traditional theology.

Our two leading questions concerning thinking and its subject now turn into one question, if we ask how to understand *consciousness* and *self-consciousness* properly. Precisely this is the leading question of Hegel's Phenomenology. In fact, the book is, from the beginning to the end of the project and the text, a *phenomenology of (self-) consciousness*. In order to understand this claim properly, we must, however, be aware of the fact that Hegel uses words like "understanding," (subjective, i.e. individual, singular) "(self)consciousness" and "reason" (also) as (sub-)labels for *limited aspects* (or *concepts*) of *spirit*. That is, "spirit" is his word for comprehensive (self) consciousness, which, as such, *contains* all forms of singular and generic (implicit and explicit, practical and reflective) *knowledge* about the essential forms of our human life. As practical know-how, spirit also contains the *experience* of putting these forms into practice. And precisely as practical know-how or competence, spirit is not just the object of our self-conscious reflection, but the mental subject behind all our singular and individual actualizations of (forms or types of) judgments and actions. But this, together with the insight that mind or spirit, fully understood, is as much an *I* or *self* as it is a societal, institutional and, as such, generic, *We* is already a remark about the final results of Hegel's enterprise. This also holds for the corresponding sentence in Hegel's chapter four on self-consciousness. Only later, in the chapter with the title "Spirit," does Hegel make clear in which sense spirit is *the* generic *We* and that this *We* is, in a sense, the actualized form of a joint human life. This form is not a utopian idea or a mere thought, as the English use of the word suggests. It rather is Plato's highest idea: It is the idea of the good, true and beautiful, the *idea tou agathou*. As such, it is the actually used system of norms which is presupposed in all judgments, the real *idea of all proprieties, all kinds of normative judgments about correctness, rationality, truth, and reason*.

According to my reading, Hegel sees here, long before Heidegger and twentieth-century pragmatism, the importance of the ontological difference between the We as an object of discussion, speech, and reflection and the We as the subjects of practical life, of mental attitudes, judgments and actions. And he sees long before George Herbert Mead and his followers that everyone is very much dependent, in his mental capacity, on the possibilities for thinking and speaking, acting alone and acting together, that are provided by the *tradition and social context* he lives in, i.e. by the *we-group* he is part of. This holds even for the possibilities of developing *new* forms and norms of judgments and actions. As a result, the concept of freedom and liberty must be understood in its relation to the situation we are in if we want to understand it realistically and leave utopian imaginations of "absolute" freedom behind as well as counterfactual ideas of total pre-determinations of our judgments and actions. In this sense, it is right to say that understanding freedom of thought and action correctly is the main task of Hegel's philosophy. Hume and Kant aimed at the same goal, but Hume missed it because his picture of man collapses into a picture of a clever social animal, whereas Kant's transcendental arguments for free will as a noumenon mystifies the reality of freedom and action, just as Descartes and Leibniz had done before.

One of the crucial problems of reading Hegel's Phenomenology now is how to understand Hegel's method. What is "phenomenology" in his sense? And how do we have to reconstruct the corresponding argumentative procedure? For one thing is clear: Hegel does not just *describe* the phenomena which are explained by mental powers, faculties, or competences. Nor does he look for basic certainties, as Husserl's phenomenology, at least in its Cartesian phase, still did. Moreover, Hegel is not content with Kant's way of arguing in favor of transcendental presuppositions. Even though it is true that in any human act the specific powers of human mind are involved, just to presuppose these powers, as Descartes and Kant did, does not suffice to understand them. What we need is an account of the reality of mind and spirit, which is much more than, and something different from, a mere argument for its necessary presupposition. We need an assessment of how the different forms of our own mind or mental powers appear to us. We need an account of the development of our own attitude to these powers. We need a reconstruction of the steps, in which we make our mind and spirit explicit, in which self-reflecting consciousness or self-consciousness develops. Such a reconstructtion has to proceed step-wise or dialectically because in each step only certain aspects of mind and spirit are explicitly articulated. As a result, any reconstruction of the logical steps in the development of self-consciousness also has to de-construct the failures, mistakes and one-sidedness of each step in the development of self-consciousness.

Moreover, Hegel sees that theology, natural psychology including physiology, and philosophy compete, in a sense, in their claim of finding the key to a correct understanding of mind and spirit. That is, they all are disciplines that take self-consciousness as their topic. Theology uses the expressive form of myths; psychology the form of self-observation, and philosophy conceptual analysis. To make a long story short, the result of Hegel's analysis here is this: Any correct understanding of self-consciousness and any deep enough knowledge about who we are and what human mind is must to a large contain degree some social philosophy and philosophy of history, and, of course, some deeper understanding of conceptual analysis than we find in traditional formal logics from Aristotle to Frege and their followers down to twentieth-century analytic philosophy.

As a result, Hegel's phenomenology is destructive rather than constructive. In other words, Hegel de(con)structs all the first intuitions about what thinking or mind or (self)consciousness is. This holds at all levels. It starts on the immediate level of the empiricist idea that consciousness is awareness, i.e., a direct perceptual relation either to some object of my inner sense (like sense data and the like) or to physical objects of the outer world (as alleged causes of my sensations and perceptions). In other words, Hegel radically deconstructs, first, the myth of the given in the idea of sense-data we see so to speak *avant la lettre* in Hume and Berkeley, and in Russell, Carnap or Ayer, and then, in an immediate second step, the idea of impressions that would be causally produced by physical objects, which we find as early as Locke, and which extends to Quine's epistemic naturalism, including all the followers we cannot and do not have to name here.

In the third chapter, which stands under the title "consciousness," Hegel, the great foe of immediacy (Sellars), questions the idea that there could be an immediate intentional relation of consciousness between me and the objects of the world. Any such referential relation is, by necessity, conceptually mediated. Therefore, it presupposes some general and generic linguistic and practical competence, as we shall see in the end.

But the first step in Hegel's argument that leads us away from identifying consciousness with immediate awareness or attention consists in an insight into the difference between a merely habitual attitude of desire and an already self-reflexive intentionality and its self-conscious intentions. Self-consciousness as a necessary aspect of human consciousness results from the need to control the proprieties of proper intentional relations. *I* have to control these properties, even in the case when *I* control or judge about the truth or normative correctness of your claims, judgments, or actions. As a result, it sounds as if this "*I*" or "self" is some kind of *higher or spiritual entity called self-consciousness* which is the *master* of all judgments and actions, addressed under the word "soul" as the subject or master of thinking and under the word "will" as the subject or master of action. The body seems to be a slave to this spiritual master. This is an age-old picture of the relation between my self-consciousness and my body.

Hegel shows, according to my reading of his most famous passage of the Phenomenology, the chapter on master and slave, that this picture is not only wrong, it is inconsistent and incomprehensible. Unfortunately, the usual reading which jumps too far ahead into a social reading of joint self-consciousness, of acknowledging other persons (and not just norms and proprieties) misses this crucial point and thus loses track of Hegel's deconstructive arguments in the self-consciousness chapter. In this reading, it becomes totally unclear why stoicism should be wrong in identifying the master with pure thinking, without actions, and skepticism because of its thoughtless pragmatism. A reading of the whole book as a metaphorical *Bildungsroman* or even a mere kaleidoscope is the unhappy consequence of these defective interpretations of the chapter on (subjective, individual) self-consciousness.

Of course, it is not easy to make sense of every move in Hegel's text. His transitions to new chapters or aspects are particularly hard to understand. But it seems clear to me that the transition from the chapter on self-consciousness to the chapter on reason rests on the insight that any judgment of correctness or truth presupposes a distinction between me as the singular subject and normative reason to which I appeal when I say that something is true, right, correct, or—reasonable. The problems of the chapter on reason are, first, to overcome any mystifying dualism between sensibility and reason. "Reason" is no transcendent instance we can appeal to. But what is it then? How can I know about reason? How can reason guide me? And what is it that guides me, if the guide is reason?

One aspect of the chapter on reason is leaving mental subjectivity and solipsism behind and accepting the objectivity of reason. In contradistinction to Kant and most Kantians, Hegel realizes long before Nietzsche, Foucault and the postmodernist critique of the self-declared ages of Reason and the Enlightenment that any appeal to reason can hide a version of subjectivism that is even more dangerous than immediate egotism. The problem is that in a certain moral stance, the stance of Kant's "practical reason," I have, allegedly, the last word about the norms and forms of reason. Thus, I become the master of reason.

Hegel sees that the deep mistake in Kant's philosophy rests on an overestimation of consistency. From the fact that my proposals about what could be jointly acknowledged moral norms are consistent with what I do, it neither follows that what I am doing is ethically right, nor that the norms that *could* be consistently accepted already can function as criteria for *actual moral judgment.*

In other words, Hegel's attack against the "Age of Reason" or Age of Enlightenment and against Kant as the philosopher of pure theoretical and pure practical reason rests on a logical insight, which, in the end, is as easy and true as it is important: Consistency and sincerity are by far not enough. Consistency and sincerity are necessary conditions for true and good judgments and actions. But they are by far insufficient for the truth and the ethical goodness of the judgment or action.

This insight corresponds to the important thesis that Hegel had defended in his habilitation in Jena. The thesis says: *Contradictio regula veri, non-contradictio falsi*—"Contradiction is the limiting rule for what is right, non-contradiction for what is wrong." That is, non-contradiction or consistency can only be used as a delimiting criterion or demarcation for what is wrong. It is not sufficient as a criterion of truth.

Only now can we understand the basic points in Hegel's attack against the "position" of "Reason": What is reasonable in the sense that it is a *possible* form or norm for judgment and action is, as such, not yet true or good. Hence, the mere *possibility* of a consensus, say, about a proposal P to give a normative answer to questions about where people should be allowed to smoke or how to treat embryos, just to name two example, does not suffice *at all* for using P as a norm. In other words, it is not *possible* acknowledgments but *real* agreements that are the foundation of ethical judgments. The same holds for the criteria of "theoretical" truth.

The subjectivity of the standpoint of reason is the subjectivity of mere sincerity. Sincerity is never enough. On the contrary, sincere well meaning without objective accuracy (Bernard Williams) tends to self-righteous hypocrisy. Therefore, the standpoint of morality, which Hegel identifies with Kant's practical reason and its alleged basic principle, the categorical imperative, appear from the standpoint of real ethics as the upshot of subjectivism. Hegel's irony becomes sarcastic when he says that the principle of moral reason thus turns out as a principle of ethical evil. The road to hell is not only paved with good intentions. It is guided by post-signs that say: We all should act in such a way W that *I* or we consistently can think that *all* could and should act according to W. Of course, a defender of Kant may say that he did not *mean* his principle of morality or practical reason this way. But the point is what Kant actually says, not what he *means* in the sense of what he *should have said*, given the problems of interpretation Hegel puts his finger on.

The standpoint of reason is not objective enough. The objectivity of ethics (*Sittlichkeit*) only rests upon real institutions of cooperation in practice and joint evaluation of judgments. Hence, not subjective moral reason but "the state" understood as the overall system of really instituted norms and forms of proper judgment and action is the (generic) "subject" of *Sittlichkeit*, including all ethical evaluations. In short, not subjective reason but the system of epistemic and ethical institutions is the spirit of all laws and norms, laws and norms of truth and knowledge as well as of the ethical good and aesthetically beautiful. Of course, if we understand Hegel's talk about the state in an all too concrete way as the merely *political* system, his analysis and judgments turn problematic. But there is no question that

Hegel's talk about the state has to be read under the guidance of the logico-rhetorical form or trope of *synecdoche*, just as Heidegger's *Sorge* (care, *cura*) or Wittgenstein's Sprach*spiele* (language *games*). To defend, and develop, this thought and claim in detail would, however, require much more time and space.

In the chapter on reason, Hegel deconstructs another attempt to overcome the mystifying idea of a subjective mind by an objective turn, the turn from talking about the soul to talking about the brain. This turn continues at first the course of argument Hegel had developed in the famous passages on master and slave: The real master cannot be the (stoicist) paper tiger of pure thinking. It must be the acting body. From this it is a short step to assume that my self and my brain are essentially the same and that consciousness and self-consciousness consist of the images or picture the brain creates about the world at large and the person's body in this world.

Hegel ridicules this account, as it is still today the leading account of physical and physiological empiricism and scientism. He replaces the soft brain by the hard skull and shows that no observation of living or dead brains or skulls can show us the "mental" or even "intelligent" parts and processes in our behavior and action. In other words, brain watching is, as a scientific approach to understanding the human mind, as superstitious and wrong as trying to find the areas of Haydn's real musical genius or Lenin's alleged political genius by investigating his skull.

Mental processes can only be understood in the context of a social philosophy or theoretical (micro- and macro-) sociology, not in the context of physiology or merely behavioral psychology. These are the results of Hegel's analysis, if we translate them into modern language: The mind is a function of our human social life. It is defined by competent participation in social institutions like language and learning, ethics and legal justice, aesthetics and religion, as tiles for whole domains of actions and judgments, e.g. ranging from dealing with primitive symbols to using mathematical theories in the sciences. In short, mental competence is, in the end, social competence. Hence, the way that leads from any mystifying religious or philosophical psychology into physiology and cognitive psychology is misleading.

Nevertheless, Hegel supports the turn from any mystical domain of the mental to real processes. We cannot or should not just presuppose a spiritual mind or transcendent soul. But the turn to bodily parts is a bad idea. The brain as such is as dead as the skull. And despite its relative magnitude with respect to the rest of the body, it is not the human brain that makes us humans intelligent but the specific use of it by also using our tongue and ears, our hands and eyes, in social institutions involving showing things, playing together, speaking a language, and developing verbally articulated knowledge and science.

From here it is no great leap to the basic or rather most general structures of objective spirit, to the informal communities of families and clans and the formal society and the state. The first is the domain of the sacred, divine, implicit law of kinship. The state is the domain of the positive, and positively and negatively sanctioned law of universal free cooperation in the polis and the state, in a civic society with its institution of property, free division of labor and all the norms of *habeas corpus*, of bodily integrity (which define murder, robbery and kidnapping as crimes). Let me here only remark that Popper totally misses Hegel's point when he overlooks Hegel's radical liberalism in his analysis of property rights.

Desire as a performative self-relation

In the following, I turn from saying to showing, from talking about reading Hegel to presenting a paradigmatic interpretation. I choose the beginning of chapter four in his Phenomenology. The chapter starts with a reflection on the results of the previous chapters: "In the previous modes of certainty, that which is true for consciousness" (i.e. what I would judge as true for example on the ground of my own perception) "is something other than itself." This is so, because I always perceive or know of *something else* than *what I am*, as we rightly say and believe on this level of reflection. "But this notion of truth" (I prefer this translation to "the Notion of this truth") "vanishes in the experience of it" (§166).[1] The reason is that in a second round of reflection we must ask what we mean by *the object that allegedly is directly perceived or known about.*

"What the object immediately was *in itself*—i.e. at first mere being in sense-certainty, then the concrete thing of perception, and finally, for the Understanding, a Force producing sensations or other reactions in observers or other objects—proves to be in truth, not this at

---

[1] All translations from Hegel's Phenomenology are by the author.

all." In other words, we realize that what we take as the object perceived is neither a bundle of sense data nor an object or a power in itself. Such a power would transcend the realm of brute, real and "holistic" (i.e. always rough-and-ready) experience. In other words, what we (say that) we perceive is always already conceptually formed in a fairly complicated and holistic way. We cannot neatly separate sense data; nor can we distinguish "pure" conceptual truth from general experience. We may add that, in a sense, this is already an insight of Kant. Hegel's rather uncharitable reading tends to overestimate Kant's admittedly unhappy talk of a thing-in-itself, as, by the way, most readers of Kant do.

Hegel now continues: "instead, this *in-itself* turns out to be a mode in which the object is only for an other." Despite what I have just said about Kant and his thing-in-itself, Hegel's rephrasing must be taken as a deep insight. For he says more clearly than Kant that the very notion of a thing-in-itself, Plato's *kath'auto*, refers only to things of thought. These things of mere thought belong to a realm of things produced by mere thinking. They are therefore, as such, merely "intelligible." They are merely abstract entities. They exist only for an other, namely for us, not for themselves.

In other words, it would be semantic nonsense to assume that things-in-themselves could produce anything in the world causally (if only subjective sensations). As a corollary, no possible god can produce anything because any such god is merely a thing-in-itself, i.e. a mere thing of our thought or our ways of talking. To assume the contrary would be as nonsensical as to say that numbers could produce thoughts causally.

What we do, however, is this: We "attach," so to speak, to our very concept of any object of possible perception the force of producing the sensations by which we can perceive the object. But here, Hegel's insight into the concept of force is not at issue. I am rather focusing on the difference between consciousness and self-consciousness.

"Consciousness is to itself the truth." […] "With self-consciousness, we have therefore entered the native realm of truth." The emphasis rests on "native" or "*einheimisch.*" The immanent domain of truth belongs to self-consciousness insofar as the topic is knowledge about the very concept of knowledge and truth: "It is a kind of knowledge of itself in contradistinction to knowledge of other things." Hegel says, moreover: "Let us look now how the form or gestalt of self-knowledge appears."

For Hegel, consciousness or *Bewusst-Sein* is actual knowledge in the sense of "being of the opinion that," or of the "belief." He distinguishes it as a kind of mental state from self-knowledge, which he characterizes as a "return from being something else to itself" (*Anderssein*: some other thing to which I might refer). In fact, the very word "self-consciousness" expresses this *return* in an act of reflection in the sense of the Latin *reflectere animum*.

In any self-knowledge, I have to identify something I know of, like my body or my behavior, with being myself, leading my life. At first, it does not matter if this identification is immediate or mediated. In self-knowledge, I turn myself into an *object* or *topic* of my knowledge. This knowledge about myself may partly include my own knowledge about something else. In other words, self-consciousness may have consciousness of something else as its object. This is a first step. The second step is this: I take or treat or acknowledge my own opinion about myself as true. This means that I represent myself in a kind of self-model—first step—and acknowledge the model as fitting to what I am—second step.

The term "subject" often stands for *what I am*, the term "object" often stands for *the topic* ("subject-matter") of my judgments. And *acknowledgement* is a *performative attitude* either to judgments (about myself) or to actions (which might be my own or not). Now, the question arises as to whether a judgment about myself really *is true*, i.e., if *it should be acknowledged*, or if I only *take it to be true*. This very difference shows the *normativity of truth* (of any alleged knowledge or self-knowledge).

Sometimes, I can *make* self-models and judgments about myself *true*, namely by acting in a certain way. In this case, *self-knowledge turns into active and practical self-determination*. But at first, the question of self-knowledge tends to be answered by an "unmoving" (*bewegungslos*) tautology, as in Fichte's formula $I = I$. Such a formula does not help us, however. It does not represent a judgment that has content. This is so because it cannot be false. It is in a sense not a meaningful speech act. It is not a move or action in our language game. It cannot be even understood as having a definite and well-determined meaning. Contrary to this, practical self-determination in intentional actions can be understood much more easily. In fact, it is self-determination, not mere verbal self-comments, that should guide us when we ask what self-consciousness or self-knowledge is. I take this to be the deepest insight of Hegel's *Phenomenology of Spirit* and his analysis of self-consciousness, together with his insight into the "ontological difference" (as Heidegger will call it) between the forms of being *an object of thinking* and the forms of *actively living a life*. In other words, being in the sense of performing forms of life includes being the personal subject or actor of my actions and speech acts. This is the very topic of Hegel's talk about what he calls "Gestalten des Bewusstseins." These are the *forms of our performances* in our actualizations of our competence to live a human life. In such performances—in being who I am, so to speak—self-knowledge or self-consciousness *turns into practical reality*.

The explication of the concept of self-knowledge finds in this practice and action the corresponding *Fürsichsein*. This *Fürsichsein* should be taken as the reality or realization of the concept of self-knowledge in practical life. As such, it is different from merely abstract *Ansichsein*, which is only *what we talk about, not what is in-and-for-itself*. As a result, self-knowledge is "in and for itself" conceptually determined self-knowledge and self-consciousness, and, as such, not at all immediate, but mediated by generic knowledge and by concepts that apply to my own life. The only feature of immediacy we can find here *is the utterly trivial immediacy of the performance itself*. In judgments about myself, I (myself) do and must judge. Hence, in any case of full-fledged self-knowledge, I should be conscious of, or know about, what self-knowledge is conceptually, and how the very concept, the content of our talk about self-knowledge and self-consciousness, relates to sensibility and understanding, rationality and reason, mind, soul, and spirit, i.e., not only to the corresponding concepts, but to *what they are concepts of*.

The generic object of consciousness is the world in its whole extension. The generic *subject* of being, on the other hand, is the *unity of the* (implicit, practical) *self*, which is, in a way, already *self-consciousness*. On the other hand, we can, and should, distinguish the self, which I am, from self-consciousness or self-knowledge, which takes the self, at least formally or grammatically, as the object or topic of its reflections and explications.

The question now is: *What does the unity of the self consist in*? How do we understand the unity of the subject's self-consciousness? And how do we grasp the relation between the self (i.e., of me in the sense of whoever speaks right now and right here) and the world at large? Hegel's answer is: *This unity is desire altogether* ("Begierde überhaupt"). But why on earth is it *desire* that provides us with the *unity of the self*?

The answer might be this: Desire corresponds formally to what Heidegger later calls *Sorge*, care. Desire or caring comes with a peculiar modal time-structure: Formally, I desire to be somebody else than I am right now already when I desire to get something. At the same time, desire is not only a relation to things around me, but a kind of self-relation. Desire or caring are the structures in which I relate to a *possibility*, to what I possible could be, and perhaps will be, namely when the desire gets fulfilled. In this sense, desire is a structural moment of the temporal unity of living a life, being a self, of subjectivity. In fact, Hegel sees, and wants us to see, the intrinsic, conceptual *connection between desire and life*: "Consciousness, as self-consciousness, henceforth has a double object: one is the immediate object, that of sense-certainty and perception, which however *for self-consciousness* has the character of a *negative;* and the second, viz. *itself* which is the true *essence."*

I do not like the English translation "essence" of *Wesen*, even though it is customary to read *Wesen* as the German word for Latin *essentia*. This word *Wesen* refers to being myself as I am, not as I picture myself. This is being an *ousia* or *Wesen* in the sense of Heidegger's *Being*, which means for living beings that they live their life in performing "things" in behavior and action that are typical for such a life.

Hegel continues that this *"essence"* or *Wesen* is present in the first instance only as opposed to the first object. "In this sphere, self-consciousness exhibits itself as the movement in which this antithesis is removed, and the identity of itself with itself becomes explicit for it." "But *for us*, or *in itself*, the object which for self-consciousness is the negative element has, on its side, returned into itself, just as on the other side consciousness has done. Through this reflection into itself the object has become Life. What self-consciousness distinguishes from itself as having *being*, also has in it, in so far as it is posited as being, not merely the character of sense-certainty and perception, but it is being that is reflected into itself, and the object of immediate desire is a *living thing*."[2]

This sentence wants to achieve too much, as Hegel's sentences often do. But the essential thought is fairly straightforward: The unity of the subject or person is *not* defined by actual *memory*. Lockeans claim this down to our times. Think, for example, of Derek Parfit. Memory is, like perception, merely a "theoretical" attitude; and it is, like perception, usually rather passive, and momentary. The unity of the subject or person is the individual life of an individual person, not just some bundles of merely immediate and present feelings, sensations, or memories. In fact, the merely actual feelings

---

[2] "Der Gegenstand, welcher für das Selbstbewusstsein das Negative ist, ist [...] *für uns* oder *an sich* ebenso in sich zurückgegangen als (=wie) das Bewusstsein andererseits. Er ist durch diese Reflexion in sich *Leben* geworden. Was das Selbstbewusstsein *als seiend* von sich unterscheidet [...] ist in sich reflektiertes Sein, und der Gegenstand der unmittelbaren Begierde ist ein *Lebendiges*" (108f).

of self-certainty are not even close to being enough, at least if we overlook the intrinsic time-structure of desire in particular, life in general.

In fact, desire already shows something about the basic temporal structure of animal life. In it, actual life relates to future life. The desire of a subject is, in the end, to live the life of a subject and to continue this life as well as possible. In this sense, the object of desire of a living being is, in the end, its life itself: Most readers think that Hegel is talking about some other living being here. But this is not so, if we read the text with some understanding of the arguments provided.

In other words, it is the living being itself that, in its continued life, satisfies its desire. It does so, of course, not without the means of the surrounding world. Satisfaction as such consists in the peculiar way in which life goes on. This way is not arbitrary. Usually, satisfaction of desire consists in a life that corresponds to the form of life of the living being, just as satisfaction of hunger consists in eating (not, for example, in getting blows on the stomach: this counter-example goes back to Wittgenstein). Satisfaction of thirst consists in drinking, etc.

Hegel rightly turns here from the generic individual to the generic species or genus, even though we might at first be surprised by this turn. The turn is made explicit in the text a little later: There, Hegel explains that the unity of human life consists in the unity of living a human form of life, to which a certain form of "practical reflection on life" is an essential part. One aspect or moment of this reflection is merely subjective self-certainty and self-awareness; another aspect is already much more complicated, it is conceptually mediated, and detached, self-knowledge.

In the end, we find a unity in what we verbally distinguish: a unity of life as the real ongoing process, its generic form, which is actualized in a particular way in the very process and some awareness or better consciousness of this process. Hence, we must distinguish, and at the same time identify, the process and its form, the process and reflection, the subject of the process and reflection, and me as the object I talk about with myself as the subject who is leading my life.[3]

---

[3] "Thus the simple substance of Life is the splitting-up of itself into shapes and at the same time the dissolution of these existent differences; and the dissolution of the splitting-up is just as much a splitting-up and a forming of members. With this, the two sides of the whole movement which before were distinguished, viz. the passive separatedness of the shapes in the general medium of independence, and the process of Life, collapse into one another."

This is the way I read the following sentence: "Life points to something other than itself, viz. to consciousness, for which Life exists as this unity, or as genus."[4]

The unity of performing (my) life in the process of (my) life and present (actual, immediate) reflective self-awareness or attentive reference to myself in my surroundings constitutes the subjectivity of us (as higher animals). We are at the same time "origins and results of our behavior" in the "practical world of our life," as Kambartel aptly says somewhere; and we notice this at least implicitly, in the mode of more or less immediate self-awareness.

This unity of myself as a living being with the "object" of my immediate self-awareness and reflective subjectivity is, according to Hegel "the simple species or genus" of the living being in question. This is so, because it belongs to the form of life of the higher animals in question, with their subjectivity.

The species, genus or life form of the species (of humans or lions, for example) does not exist as such in the singular process of life ("die Bewegung des Lebens selbst"), because a singular animal can be mutilated, sick or only sleeping.

It is true, in reality there are only the individual animals. But the life of each of them refers implicitly to the limited possibilities of living a good life as a member of the species in contradistinction to the possibilities of a bad life, of mishaps and monsters. In this sense, we should not forget that my own life refers in a way "onto something other than what I immediately am," namely, as I read this passage, to a good life. But at first, Hegel identifies this "other" with "consciousness, for which it is this unity as species" or the form of a good life as a member of the genus.

I read this difficult passage or thought thus: In any immediate self-knowledge or self-awareness of mere subjectivity, which we share with quite a number of higher animals, there already is a certain self-control relating to whether or not the normality or satisfaction conditions of a sufficiently

---

[4] "Sie (also die Einheit) ist die *einfache Gattung*, welche in der Bewegung des Lebens selbst nicht für sich als dieses Einfache existiert; sondern in diesem *Resultate* verweist das Leben auf ein Anderes, als es ist, nämlich auf das Bewusstsein, für welches es als diese Einheit, oder als Gattung ist." "Dies andere Leben aber, für welches die *Gattung* als solche und welches für sich selbst Gattung ist, das Selbstbewusstsein, ist sich zunächst nur als dieses einfache Wesen, und hat sich als *reines Ich* zum Gegenstande [...]. Das einfache Ich ist diese Gattung oder das einfache Allgemeine, für welches die Unterschiede keine sind, nur, indem es *negatives Wesen* der gestalteten selbständigen Momente ist; und das Selbstbewusstsein hiermit seiner selbst nur gewiss, durch das Aufheben dieses Andern, das sich ihm als selbständiges Leben darstellt; es ist *Begierde*." (111).

good life of being a member of my species are fulfilled: This either/or allows, of course, for a broad range of (intermediary) cases. The only point is that we often realize ("know") that such conditions are not fulfilled, and often we realize that they are fulfilled. As such, this control is, in its present immediacy, always a mere subjective control of satisfactions or non-satisfactions of merely subjective desires in the sense of animal appetites. Such a desire or appetite includes, negatively speaking, the avoidance of pain and other sensations of pain (*Schmerzempfindungen*). The attitudes are given in the natural life form of the species. The immediate attitudes or dispositions of behavior consist in being immediately led by avoidance of pain and the striving to fulfill my desires. In other words, desire and pain show the very core of subjectivity and reflective self-awareness in a quite fundamental way.

So we see that Hegel's desire is a title for the life-supporting appetite of subjectivity. Only higher animals have it. Plants do not, at least if we do not ascribe to them spiritual properties arbitrarily. Plants are not subjects, not because they are not individuated as higher animals, but because the form of their life, their Aristotelian *kinesis*, is totally different. They do not show the same form of movements in pursuing goals and desires and avoiding pain as animals do.

In short, Hegel uses the title-word "desire" as a synecdoche, as a label for the actual unity of life performances of living beings that have, and show, subjectivity. The fundamental self-certainty now can be seen thus: It is realized in immediate states of pain and desire and the "feelings" of satisfaction or the end of pain or uplifting of pain.

But now, Hegel talks about some "other life," "which as such is the species." What does it mean that its *Fürsichsein* is the species? In what sense is this other life self-consciousness? And what does it mean to say that as such it is "at first only as this simple being (*Wesen*)," which has itself as a pure I as its object ("sich als reines Ich zum Gegenstande")?

I admit that it is not too clear what the expression "this other life" refers to. Some readers think that Hegel is already talking about two persons here. But I read the consideration and arguments differently. In the end we shall see that and why thinking and comprehending, intention and action are possible only in a we mode. When Hegel here already talks about *us*, he wants us not to loose sight of this goal. The difficult task of interpretation is, therefore, to read the sentence "*Self-knowledge achieves its satisfaction in another self-consciousness*" in its context appropriately.

In order to do so, I start with a short reflection on the nature of an "immediate desire" in the sense of an animal appetite—in contradistinction to the nature of an intention which is always already mediated by a conceptual determination of what is intended and how the intention governs the action in my attempt to fulfill the intention.

Desire as such is only an immediate, present, state of desiring. If it is already directed to an object, it presupposes some *awareness and attention*. This is still a rather meager concept of consciousness. It is, so to speak, animal consciousness or mere *vigilance*. As such it is present directedness to objects in the actual world around me. The faculties of awareness, attention and vigilance do not differentiate yet between (higher) animals and men. In contrast to this, intentions are embedded in trans-present actions by which we pursue the goal of fulfilling presently perhaps inhibited desires and wishes.

An animal and sometimes humans, too, have a desire for something, if they want to incorporate it somehow directly. Ownership is a kind of institutionally extended incorporation, as Hegel rightly sees. I want something, if I want to make it somehow into something that is my own.

In both cases, the goal is, as Hegel says, to deny or sublimate the difference between being something other and being my own.[5]

It might appear plausible to think already here of some fight between different persons for property, power, and respect. In a sense, the path to this thought is not too long. It would lead us to a life and death struggle insofar as property rights are a question of power and dominance: Personal power, especially the dominance of masters over slaves and serfs, can survive only by some backing by threats of sanctions. Only fear of punishment or even death can move the slaves to obey the order of the master. On the other hand, in a certain way, they obey the order freely, because there is always the option of preferring death. But only if we thought that an order in which there are masters and slaves, and in which we are the slaves, were a wise order, would the fear of the master possibly be the beginning of our wisdom. But it is precisely this that Hegel says. So what does it mean?

I prefer to read the passages thus: Hegel is interested in the conceptual difference between (animal) desire and conceptually guided intention,

---

[5] This is my reading of "Aufhebung des Andersseins des Gegenstandes der Begierde bzw. des Willens."

between immediate appropriation of things (for example in catching and eating) and actions in which an immediate motivation by desires is inhibited.

In the end, Hegel's analysis of the sociality of reason goes much deeper than Marx, Kojève, Habermas, or Honneth think. For Hegel sees that without this sociality of reason there is no thinking and no intentionality at all. Marx does not seem to see this social grounding of reason and intentions. Like Hobbes, Marx starts with persons that are able to act intentionally, as if social institutions come later, as a kind of joint decision to cooperate in a certain way. As a result, the dependence of personal competence on the social surroundings is underestimated.

Hegel in Swedish

BRIAN MANNING DELANEY

In the realm of great philosophy Hegel is no doubt the only one with whom at times one literally does not know and cannot conclusively determine what is being talked about, and with whom there is no guarantee that such a judgment is even possible.

[*Im Bereich großer Philosophie ist Hegel wohl der einzige, bei dem man buchstäblich zuweilen nicht weiß und nicht bündig entscheiden kann, wovon überhaupt geredet wird, und bei dem selbst die Möglichkeit solcher Entscheidung nicht verbrieft ist.*]

Theodor Adorno
"Skoteinos, or How to Read Hegel"[1]

Hegel's language is—it has been said time and again—untranslatable.

[*La langue de Hegel est—on l'a dit maintes et maintes fois—intraduisible.*]

Alexandre Koyré
"Note sur la langue et la terminologie hégéliennes"[2]

The first thing to ask about translating Hegel might well be: why bother? Hegel's thought is so difficult, his writing, particularly in the Phenomenology, so complicated, that anyone interested in understanding him deeply

---

[1] Theodor W. Adorno, "Skoteinos oder Wie zu lesen sei," in *Gesammelte Schriften*, vol. 5 (Frankfurt: Suhrkamp, 1975), 326. In the collection of texts translated by Shierry Weber Nicholsen as *Hegel: Three Studies (Studies in Contemporary German Social Thought)* (Cambridge, Massachusetts: MIT Press, 1994), 89. I will be citing Adorno's text with two page numbers: the first the page number in *Gesammelte Schriften*, the second the page in Nicholsen's excellent translation. The English passages cited below are all from Nicholsen's translation.

[2] Alexandre Koyré, "Note sur la langue et la terminologie hégéliennes," *Revue Philosophique*, 1931. Republished in *Etudes d'histoire de la pensée philosophique* (Paris: Gallimard, 1981), 175. All page references are to the text published in *Etudes*. Translations of Koyré are my own.

may well need to embark on a multi-year journey of Hegel research, and anyone willing to embark on this multi-year journey who does not read German generally decides to begin first with the much shorter, easier journey of learning to read the language in which Hegel wrote.

And how many people are interested in understanding Hegel's thought "non-deeply"? Or more to the point: *can* one understand Hegel's thought non-deeply? In Germany one speaks of a particular kind of educated, though non-academic person: the "reader of Goethe" (*der Goethe-Leser*). In the English-speaking world the equivalent might be the "reader of Shakespeare." This is someone who enjoys reading brilliant, difficult classics despite not having the background to be able to plumb all their depths. Would the reader of Shakespeare, with no background in philosophy, be able to make sense of the Phenomenology, even if accurately translated into his own language? Would the reader of Strindberg? (Would, for that matter, as Siep asked, the reader of Goethe, who doesn't even need a translation?)[3]

The Phenomenology is famous for containing brilliant analyses of particular cultural phenomena and historical events whose brilliance is thought to be sufficiently self-contained that they can be enlightening to the reader of Goethe on their own—for example the comments on *Rameau's Nephew*, or the account of the significance of the tragedy element in *Antigone*. One might be able to benefit by reading these analyses in isolation, like reading a poem or two from *Leaves of Grass*, but it would be risky to say that any of these passages or analyses in the Phenomenology tell us much about Hegel's thought.

In fact, anything other than the whole of the Phenomenology (and, Hegel himself would be quick to add—the whole of his system) will fail to yield the whole of Hegel. Karl Popper, more than a mere "reader of Goethe," failed to grasp Hegel in his *The Open Society and Its Enemies* precisely because he based his diatribe largely on Scribner's *Hegel Selections*, not on a reading of any of Hegel's complete works.[4]

Obviously, the conviction of the translator is that anything can be translated, even the Phenomenology. The fact that it continues to be retranslated into the same languages on a regular basis shows that the

---

[3] Ludwig Siep, *Der Weg der Phänomenologie des Geistes: Ein einführender Kommentar zu Hegels "Differenzschrift" und zur "Phänomenologie des Geistes"* (Frankfurt am Main: Suhrkamp, 2000), 9.
[4] Or so claims Walter Kaufmann in *From Shakespeare to Existentialism: An Original Study* (Princeton: Princeton University of Press, 1959), 98–99.

challenge is enormous, and that success has so far has been regarded as imperfect. But this does not mean the book is, as Koyré claims, literally untranslatable. And translating Hegel into Swedish entails far fewer losses than translations into other languages. Here I'd like to explore some of these losses by way of a comparison to translation problems that arise in translating German texts, and, specifically, the Phenomenology, to English (with a few limited comments on translations to French added along the way).

Hegel's difficult language

Before addressing the difficulties specific to the translation of Hegel's German to Swedish or any other language, we should briefly look at why Hegel's language itself is so challenging.

As Terry Pinkard points out in *Hegel: A Biography*, Hegel's German wasn't always so tortuous. A change in his attitude towards writing took place rather suddenly when Hegel was approaching thirty years of age.

Hegel's initial career ambitions centered on his becoming what today might be called a public intellectual. He was an "activist of letters," inspired, as were so many of his friends and colleagues, by the French Revolution, and above all by modernity itself.

Hegel started to realize, influenced to a great degree by Hölderlin, that a new age required a new idiom, a new style of writing; in particular, it required a style that challenged the reader, made him work to create his own meaning, made him participate in the fashioning of this new, modern world.[5] Hegel did not want to be an essayist telling the people how and what to think. That wouldn't be appropriate for the modern age. "What [...] matters to the study of science is that one take the rigorous exertion of the concept upon oneself" (§58),[6] writes Hegel in the preface to the Phenomenology. What's more, Hegel came to see philosophy as an activity that not necessarily everyone could share in. (Perhaps, then, worrying about the reader of Shakespeare or Strindberg would be irrelevant either way.) Shortly after his arrival in Jena, Hegel wrote, in *Kritisches Journal der Philosophie*, the journal he started with Schelling, "Philosophy is by its nature something

---

[5] Terry Pinkard, *Hegel: A Biography* (Cambridge: Cambridge University Press, 2001), 82.
[6] All references to the Phenomenology in English are to paragraph numbers in Terry Pinkard's translation (2008), currently (2011-07-27) available online at: http://web.mac.com/titpaul/Site/Phenomenology_of_Spirit_page.html.

esoteric, neither made for the mob nor capable of being prepared for the mob."[7] Whatever his new kind of writing would be, it would not be unchallenging.

Another important influence was Schelling, who encouraged Hegel to move to Jena to take part in the burgeoning philosophical life at the university there. The decision to move to Jena marked the final abandonment for Hegel of the goal of being an essayist, a popular philosopher. Instead, Hegel would become a systematic, *wissenschaftlich* philosopher à la Fichte.

The systematicity, along with the abandonment of the popular style in order to force the reader to fashion his own meaning—his own new, modern world—are of course manifest continually in the Phenomenology (with the partial exception of the preface, which is in fact written in a style more popular than that of the rest of the book—even if the matters being addressed are of concern to a limited few). The systematic presentation of the self-education of consciousness was a new way of doing philosophy (even if much of the strategy of the Phenomenology came from Schelling and especially Fichte), and it itself required that the text be strange, and the demand that the reader participate actively simply added to the peculiarity of the work.

But while Hegel's turn to systematic philosophy and his forcing the reader to participate actively in the creation of meaning had an influence on his writing, the more important factor was of course speculative philosophy itself, which by its very nature is an attack on normal language use. Hegel is quite explicit about this, saying, for example, that the nature of the speculative judgment "destroys" the distinction between subject and predicate that is contained within the very structure of the normal judgment or proposition (§61). One might best put it the other way around: not that speculative philosophy is an attack on normal language use, but that abnormal language use, in the service of speculative philosophy, becomes the means of attacking traditional, non-speculative thought, or, in the Phenomenology in particular: the unnaturalness of Hegel's use of language is a way to attack the "naturalness" of the position of natural consciousness.

Hegel's (largely) intentional mis- or "other"-use of language, his obscurity, finds one of its greatest defenders in Adorno—himself, paradoxically, a master of crystal clear (if exceptionally challenging) prose.

---

[7] Cited in Robert Stern, *G. W. F. Hegel, Hegel's Phenomenology of Spirit and Logic* (London: Routledge, 1993), 198f.

In the essay "Skoteinos, or How to Read Hegel," Adorno contrasts the striving for certainty and clarity of Descartes with the obscurity of Hegel, lauding the latter.

Skoteinos was an epithet for Heraclitus, and means "the obscure one." For Adorno, the obscurity of Hegel's writing is a virtue, not just the virtue one makes of an unrelated necessity, but itself something necessary: there was no other way for Hegel to write, given the nature of his philosophy.

> There is a sort of suspended quality associated with his philosophy, in accordance with the idea that truth cannot be grasped in any individual thesis or any delimited positive statement. Form in Hegel follows this intention. Nothing can be understood in isolation, everything is to be understood only in the context of the whole, with the awkward qualification that the whole in turn lives only in the individual moments. In actuality, however, this kind of doubleness of the dialectic eludes literary presentation, which is of necessity finite when it unequivocally states something unequivocal. This is why one has to make so many allowances for it in Hegel. ("Skoteinos," 328; 91)

It is not simply that nothing can be understood in isolation, but that the very essence of Hegel's philosophy is process; Hegel's thought is always a think*ing*:

> [The form of Hegel's texts] is the complete opposite of Nietzsche's maxim that one can only write about what one is finished with, what is behind one. The substance of Hegel's philosophy is process, and it wants to express itself as process, in permanent *status nascendi*, the negation of presentation as something congealed, something that would correspond to what was presented only if the latter were itself something congealed. To make an anachronistic comparison, Hegel's publications are more like films of thought than texts. (ibid., 353; 121)

The substance of Hegel's philosophy is process, but, what's more, Hegel's own expositional method was "processual" in the sense that he, more than any other major philosophical figure, seemed always to be thinking aloud; he sought to capture the processual nature of his philosophy, but seemed also to want to express the very process of his own thinking, however halting, tentative, and, of course, self-correcting it may have been. This could naturally give the impression of sloppiness or inconsistency in the use of terms, or even a kind of "sovereign indifference" to language (ibid., 342;

109), but Hegel was partly just sharing with the reader the very dialectical activity that is at the core of his own philosophizing.

Adorno expresses surprise that language wasn't even more important for Hegel as an explicit theme, and, more specifically, as a manifestation of truth, given, in particular, that Hegel was a contemporary of Humboldt (ibid. 350; 117–118). Koyré, on the other hand, highlights those places—relatively few though they may be—where Hegel does indeed seem to stress the importance of language, for example where Hegel tells us that we can "see language as the existence of spirit" (§654, cited in Koyré, 187).

Whether or not language can be seen as the existence of spirit, it is the equivalence of history and logic—and, for Koyré, therewith the equivalence of history and language—that means that translation involves translating a whole history, a whole culture, into a different history and culture. This, finally, for Koyré, "is the reason we cannot translate Hegel," or

> at least why it is so difficult to do so. Not because his language is "imaginative and poetic" and full of emotional elements. Hegel himself did not take much to these forms of language that "suggest the ineffable and inexpressible." For him—and according to him—the ineffable and inexpressible did not have any kind of value. What he prized above all was the clarity, "the clear concept that leaves nothing unrevealed," and expresses what is deepest in man, his "very nature," which is thought and which is spirit. Synthesis and summation or, if one prefers, integration of moments (concepts, forms, *Gestalten*) of the past in the "present"—such is the Hegelian "concept." But if the history of humankind, to the extent that it realizes that the history of spirit is one, to the extent that it realizes itself, particularizes itself, differentiates itself, breaks apart. History is one, like thought and spirit, but the histories, like peoples and languages, are different. And that is why dialectical thought, the *concept*, representing a moment of this evolution, though representing it within the particularity of a language, cannot—generally speaking—be translated by a term of another language. Is it because history, the past that always becomes "present," would not be the same. That is the reason why "the abstract language of French philosophy" cannot translate the concrete language of the Hegelian dialectic. And this is also the reason why the best commentary on Hegel remains, for the time being, a *historical* dictionary of German.[8]

---

[8] Alexandre Koyré, "Note sur la langue et la terminologie hégéliennes," 204.

This extremely interesting claim by Koyré would actually take us into more general questions about the very possibility of translating any text, not just translating Hegel. Koyré was of course writing in a French context, and makes clear here, at the end of his essay, that his thesis about the impossibility or extreme difficulty of translating Hegel is about translating Hegel to French specifically. I will let our colleague Jean-Pierre Lefebvre comment on the challenges of translating Hegel into a language like French, distant as it is from German. (Myself, I may be too distant from French, too "Germanic," both historically and educationally, even to be able to grasp Koyré's thesis, without a historical dictionary of French.)

Translating Hegel into a Germanic language may be a very different matter. It may be that a "historical dictionary" of English or Dutch or Swedish would be so close to a historical dictionary of German as to render Koyré's concerns about French irrelevant to these other languages.

Let us turn to an exploration of how the close relationship of Swedish to German affects the quality and "feel" of translations into Swedish, by way of examples and comparisons with English (and some references to French).

Hegel in Swedish

Hegel claimed in 1805 that he wanted to "get philosophy to speak German, and German, philosophy."[9] The challenge of translating Hegel into Swedish could thus be understood as the challenge of getting the philosophy that Hegel got to speak German, his particular German, to speak Swedish.

In the second preface to the (Greater) Logic, Hegel himself makes clear that the match between his philosophy in particular, speculative philosophy, and German was exceptionally strong, and suggests that getting each to speak the other, whatever he might have thought the challenges were when he was younger, would be relatively easy. In part this is because German words have a rich breadth of multiple meanings, but, more importantly, because they often contain within themselves opposite meanings, which itself is something in which "one cannot fail to recognize a speculative spirit of language" ("ein spekulativer Geist der Sprache nicht zu verkennen ist")—

---

[9] Quoted in Will Dudley, *Hegel, Nietzsche, and Philosophy: Thinking Freedom* (Cambridge: Cambridge University Press, 2002), 234. In practice, this meant using words that many in Hegel's day would have taken *not* to be German.

and which permits a certain pleasure for thought, even if, for the understanding, such oppositions are nonsensical.[10]

There is the additional factor that the different meanings, and even the "constitutive" meanings of the words gleaned from their roots, and the way these roots relate to one another, are in general more obvious to a German reader, because German is, in Vico's sense, a highly "original" language, in the sense that the original, more concrete ways of expressing things are still evident in the words used today. One example is the German word for an object.[11] The normal word for a physical object in German is *Gegenstand*, which is made up of roots a German speaker knows, because the roots themselves are also words in German: *gegen* (against) and *Stand* (standing, position, etc.). So an object is something standing against one. English is an extremely non-original language, and the word *object* is a perfect example of its non-originality. For an English-speaker who doesn't know Latin, *ob* (against) and *ject* (part of the past participle of the Latin word meaning to throw, *obicere*) mean nothing.[12] The "speculative spirit" of language, especially the play between the concrete and the abstract, can indeed be missed in English and other non-original languages, at least in the case of many words.

We might expect these traits to be found, at least to some degree, in all Germanic languages. If they were, at least some aspects of translating Hegel to a different Germanic language would be easier than translating Hegel to non-Germanic languages. And so it is with Swedish, but, perhaps surprisingly, it is much less so with English.

Anyone who knows German, Swedish, and English will be struck by the similarity of German to Swedish. English almost seems like a Romance

---

[10] "Viel wichtiger ist es, daß in einer Sprache die Denkbestimmungen zu Substantiven und Verben herausgestellt und so zur gegenständlichen Form gestempelt sind; die deutsche Sprache hat darin viele Vorzüge vor den anderen modernen Sprachen; sogar sind manche ihrer Wörter der weiteren Eigenheit, verschiedene Bedeutungen nicht nur, sondern entgegengesetzte zu haben, so daß darin selbst ein spekulativer Geist der Sprache nicht zu verkennen ist; es kann dem Denken eine Freude gewähren, auf solche Wörter zu stoßen und die Vereinigung Entgegengesetzter, welches Resultat der Spekulation für den Verstand aber widersinnig ist, auf naive Weise schon lexikalisch als *ein* Wort von den entgegengesetzten Bedeutungen vorzufinden." *Werke*, vol. 5, *Wissenschaft der Logik I: Die objektive Logik* (Frankfurt am Main: Suhrkamp, 1979), 19–20.
[11] See Michael Inwood's interesting discussion on this in *A Hegel Dictionary* (London: Blackwell Publishers, 1992), 8.
[12] Earlier, a different word was proposed, for example by Luther, as a translation for Latin's *obiectum*: *Gegenwurf*, the roots of which correspond exactly to ob-ject.

language by comparison, especially if the comparison is between texts dealing with abstract matters, where the English text will tend to have many words of French or ultimately Latin origins. But, curiously, English and German are actually in the same subdivision of the Germanic language family, the West Germanic languages, whereas Swedish is in an entirely different subdivision, the North Germanic. These subdivisions are of course based on early historical developments, and ignore later divergences and convergences. In the case of the split between the North Germanic languages (Norse or proto-Norse) and the rest of the German languages, mutual intelligibility was lost perhaps some 1500 to 1200 years ago. The relative similarity of Swedish to German today is the result of later convergence between the Scandinavian languages (though this applies only to a very limited extent to Icelandic) and Middle Low and High German, primarily because of the trading activities of the Hanseatic League. Old English, on the other hand, started rapidly moving away from German, mostly because of the influence of Latin and Latinate languages. (Norse had also influenced Old English, but the influence on vocabulary was limited, and involved words for everyday objects, not abstract terms. Its most significant influence was in the dramatic simplification of the case system of Old English.) Estimates of the number of words in English that are of Germanic origins are generally between only 25% and 30%. More than half of the words in English are from Latin or a *Langue d'oïl* (including French and Norman). But when looking at words actually used—especially for everyday matters—as opposed to counting words in a dictionary, English does of course seem extremely Germanic. Take the following sentence: "I went to school. I saw my friend. We sat under an apple tree by the old house and talked." Every word is Germanic, and even recognizable as closely related to its contemporary German counterpart (aside from *tree*, which comes from Old Norse; the word for tree in modern German, *Baum*, is related to the English word *beam*). But while Hegel does speak of trees and houses—the meaning of "das Hier ist nicht ein Baum, sondern ein Haus," for example, could perhaps even be guessed at by a native English speaker who knows no German—mostly he speaks of extraordinarily non-everyday things, things that are thus often expressed with non-Germanic terms in English, especially once we leave the here and now of sense-certainty. This is why the challenges of translating Hegel into Swedish are so different from the challenges of translating Hegel into English.

Consider the first sentence of the preface, in its French, English, German, and Swedish variants.

> Les explications qu'on a coutume de donner dans une préface, en tête d'un ouvrage, pour éclairer les fins que l'auteur s'y est assignées, les motivations qui sont les siennes, et la rapport que cet ouvrage entretient selon lui avec les autres traités antérieurs ou contemporaines qui portent sur le même objet, semblent non seulement superflues s'agissant d'un ouvrage de philosophie, mais même, compte tenu de la nature de la chose, inadéquates et contraire au but poursuivi.[13]

> In the preface to a philosophical work, it is customary for the author to give an explanation—namely, an explanation of his purpose in writing the book, his motivations behind it, and the relations it bears to other previous or contemporary treatments of the same topics—but for a philosophical work, this seems not only superfluous but in light of the nature of the subject matter, even inappropriate and counterproductive.

> Eine Erklärung, wie sie einer Schrift in einer Vorrede nach der Gewohnheit vorausgeschickt wird—über den Zweck, den der Verfasser sich in ihr vorgesetzt, sowie über die Veranlassungen und das Verhältnis, worin er sie zu andern frühern oder gleichzeitigen Behandlungen desselben Gegenstandes zu stehen glaubt—scheint bei einer philosophischen Schrift nicht nur überflüssig, sondern um der Natur der Sache willen sogar unpassend und zweckwidrig zu sein.

> I en filosofisk skrift förefaller det inte bara överflödigt, utan enligt sakens natur till och med opassande och ändamålsvidrigt, att som brukligt är låta en förklaring i ett förord föregripa skriften, beträffande det syfte författaren förelagt sig, liksom bevekelsegrunderna samt det förhållande i vilket han anser sig stå till andra tidigare eller samtida behandlingar av samma ämne.

Though the fundamentally different word order of each of the four makes it difficult to see, the English sentence, at least viewed via the nouns and adjectives, looks more like the French than the German or Swedish. There are numerous cognates—*coutume/customary, préface/preface, auteur/author, motivations/motivations*, etc.—and many of the other words could easily

---

[13] G. W. F Hegel, *Phénoménologie de l'Esprit*, trans. Jean-Pierre Lefebvre (Paris: Aubier, 1991), 27.

have been exchanged for cognates (*inappropriate* could perhaps have been *inadequate*, or the French could have had *impropre*, the English *improper*.). On the other hand, of course, the more common words, the hammer and nails of the sentences—prepositions, articles, conjunctions, and common verbs like to be (*in, the, to, a, it, for, and, is*, etc.)—are all Germanic.

Beyond distant and, for non-linguists, likely unrecognizable Indo-European roots, the Swedish would appear to have almost nothing in common with the French, and surprisingly little in common with the English. In the case of the Swedish version, the similarities with the German are obvious in the nouns and adjectives, especially the more abstract or non-everyday ones (*Schrift/skrift, überflüssig/överflödig, Verhältnis/förhållande, unpassend/opassande*), and not in many of the more common words, especially not conjunctions, articles, prepositions, and everyday adverbs and adjectives (*nicht* is *inte*; *nur, bara*; *nach, enligt*; *wie, som*; *zu, till*)—the opposite of the situation with English. It's as if translating Hegel to English involves furnishing a basic Germanic structure common to English and German with a Latinized Hegel, whereas translating Hegel to Swedish involves building a new structure with uniquely Scandinavian materials, and moving Hegel's furniture, perhaps reupholstered in a few cases, directly into it.

Translating Hegel into Swedish is of course a bit more complicated than the above analogy suggests, as we will see shortly. But first, consider a list of words that are very similar, or—once one is aware of a few sound and stem equivalencies[14]—essentially identical in Swedish and German:

German	Swedish
Bildung	bildning
(Ausbildung	utbildning)
begreifen	begripa
Begriff	begrepp

(We thus didn't have to decide between *concept* and *notion*, and the original sense of actually physically grasping something is retained in the Swedish.)

---

[14] For example, German's *an-* is *å-* in Swedish; *auf-* is *upp-*; *aus-*, *ut-*; *ein-*, *in-*; *steh-*, *stå-*; *deut-*, *tyd-*; *gr(ei/i)f-*, *gr(i/e)p-*; and the German noun ending *-ung* is *-(n)ing* in Swedish, and German infinitive verb ending *-en* is *-a* or occasionally *-å* in Swedish.

bestehen	bestå
bestimmen	bestämma

(And related words; and note that there is no difficulty figuring out how to capture all the senses of destiny, determination, and so on in Swedish, since they are as present in *bestämning* as much as they are in *Bestimmung*.)

erfahren	erfara
Erfahrung	erfarenhet
Einbildung	inbillning
Erinnerung	erinring
Satz	sats
setzen	sätta
sittlich	sedlig
Sittlichkeit	sedlighet
(And related words.)	
Vorstellung	föreställning
Wesen	väsen
wirken	verka
Wirklichkeit	verklighet
Realität	realitet

For most of these words, the richness of the German is captured perfectly by the correlating Swedish word. Swedish's *väsen*, for example, means "essence," but also "being" in the sense of a creature, just as *Wesen* does.

And *Wirklichkeit* and *Realität* were straightforward choices for us, since Swedish has both *verklighet* and *realitet*, and *verklighet* has the same relation to the verb *verka* that *Wirklichkeit* does to *wirken*.

Our choice for the notoriously difficult to translate *aufheben* was also much easier than it would be for French- or English-speaking translators: *upphäva*, though *upphäva* is not as utterly perfect a choice as it might seem given the identity of the two words' roots. The two contradictory senses Hegel describes at the beginning of "Perception"—"a *negating* and at the same time a *preserving*" (§113)—are both present in the Swedish, as well as the meaning suggested by the roots: a "lifting up." *Upphäva* and *aufheben* are not entirely synonymous in all their senses, however. In *upphäva*, the sense of "preserving" might be a bit weaker, and the original sense of the word is still strongly present—lifting up in the sense of commencing something, as in raising one's voice to begin speaking. A German would likely express this sense of a commencing with *anheben*, not *aufheben*. In any event, these niceties are nothing compared with the difficulties faced by someone translating *aufheben* into French or English. As Pinkard points out in the glossary to his translation, "sublate," when it was first chosen by Hegel translators in the mid-nineteenth century, was a questionable choice, but the term has become established, and can't easily be changed now. Instead of simply declaring by fiat that "sublate" captured everything Hegel wanted to say with *aufheben*, which is what these early translators essentially did (for the word most certainly did not mean *aufheben* when it first started being used by translators), it might have been more useful, and perhaps no more bizarre, simply to have declared that a more etymologically related term, like "upheave," would capture everything Hegel wanted to say with *aufheben*. (And the standard noun form "upheaval" might have helped people see Hegel's revolutionary side.)

Swedish is also a relatively original language in Vico's sense, which makes the multiple meanings of Hegel's words more present, more concrete, to the reader. But while many of our translation choices might have been relatively easy, the multiple, transparent meanings are at times radically different from those present in the German. Koyré gives *gleichgültig*, which normally means "indifferent," as an example of a word whose roots (*gleich*, equal, and *gültig*, valid) yield a different sense of the word: "equivalent" ("equally valid"), which Hegel also intended to be understood by the reader. Here, the Swedish *likgiltig* has the same multiple meanings. But the situation is different with *Gegenstand*. While Swedish has an equally "original" word, *föremål*, as a translation of *Gegenstand*, its roots are quite different. Rather than something standing against one, *föremål* suggests more a target, or goal, or objective (*mål*) that is before one, in front of one (*före*). The Swedish word with similar roots to *Gegenstand*, *motstånd* (*mot*=*gegen*; *stånd*=*stand*), means resistance, not object. An object for a Swede is not something that resists, or stands against, but is rather a curious little thing in front of one that one wants to inspect, one sort of zeros in on it, picks it up and turns it around in one's fingers, holds it before one.[15] In a

---

[15] Swedish also has the Latin import *objekt*, which corresponds to German's Latin import, *Objekt*. But *Objekt* scarcely appears in the Phenomenology.

few passages this might actually help one understand Hegel better than one could in other languages, even German. For example, in the introduction, it is perhaps more natural to understand the goal (*Ziel, mål*) of the phenomenological journey as a correspondence of concept and object (§80) when the word for object contains a sort of teleological, goal-like, aspect to it (*föremål*). In Swedish, perhaps natural consciousness more easily overcomes its separation from the object.

Dasein and *Existenz*, like *Gegestand/Objekt* and *Wirklichkeit/Realität*, constitute another instance of a pair consisting of a "heroic" or original word and a newer import that has a corresponding pair in Swedish: *tillvaro* and *existens*. *Dasein* is of course a famously difficult word for Germans, let alone for translators, with many German philosophers assigning it radically different senses. For Hegel it often meant a determinate being, which is suggested by the roots: being (*Sein*) there (*da*). *Da* in the sense of "there" is "där" in Swedish, but the word *därvaro*—being (*-varo*) there (*där*)—means "presence," not "existence" (and *därvaro* is an extremely obscure word in Swedish; the normal word for "presence" is *närvaro*). "Presence" can of course also be heard in *Dasein*, and that sense was stronger in the word in centuries past. Etymology is not meaning—even if, from the outside, one might think it would be for heroic languages—and *Dasein* does indeed relatively unproblematically mean *tillvaro* in most of its uses, just like *Gegenstand* does indeed mean *föremål*, whatever the differences in the etymologies. But here we might once again expect there to be a slightly different valence to the translated word, even if Swedes and other speakers of heroic languages of course don't go around breaking down words into their constituent parts to understand what they really mean. *Till* in Swedish, like *till* in English, is etymologically related to the German *Ziel*, goal, yet it isn't precisely that *tillvaro* feels somehow more "teleological" than *Dasein*. But in certain contexts it does partly refer to one's immediate surroundings—whether they are healthy, auspicious, nurturing, etc. (the etymological connection might lie in their furthering the goal of my life, my living)—a sense that is not as obvious in *Dasein*. This difference in sense is one of the reasons why we occasionally translated *Dasein* as *existens*, not *tillvaro*. Consider, for example, the following sentence in the first paragraph of "Spirit" (§437): "Aber die Wahrheit des Beobachtens ist vielmehr das Aufheben dieses unmittelbaren findenden Instinkts, dieses bewußtlosen Daseins derselben." [However, the truth of observation is even more the sublation of this instinct for immediately finding things, the sublation of this unconscious existence of the truth.] An "unconscious *tillvaro*" sounds strange in Swedish, especially in the Swedish welfare state of today, where it might sound like Hegel is talking about the Swedish state's reflection on truth's "unconscious quality of life." So we chose *existens*.

Most German words, of course, are quite different in Swedish, and one realizes Swedish in many ways is more distant from German than English, precisely as its placement in historically based language groups would suggest. There's nothing that looks like "Zweck" in Swedish. *Ändamål* (literally: "end goal") captures the weightier meaning of *Zweck*, but we translated it with *syfte* when it meant a relatively temporary or provisional goal, as opposed to purpose, or ultimate goal. There are also extraordinarily many "false friends" (which were in almost all cases true friends many centuries ago). *Anstoß* looks like it would be *anstöt* in Swedish—the roots are identical—but *anstöt* means nothing other than offense (*ta anstöt av*: take offense at), so we chose *impuls* (impulse) for *Anstoß*. *Ding* and *ting* are not false friends, but *Ding* often had to be translated with *sak* (related to *Sache*), because the meanings of *Ding* and *ting* don't quite overlap. The German verb *werden* and Swedish's *bliva* (today usually used in the shorten form, *bli*) were a straightforward translation match for us, although they could be almost described, at least to the extent that becoming and remaining are opposed, as "false enemies": *bliva* has the same roots as German's *bleiben* (to remain), so one might think it means the same thing, and not becoming, but it has come to be the normal way to say *werden* in Swedish (an older Swedish word etymologically related to *werden*, *varda*, is now largely obsolete). *Werden* ultimately comes from roots meaning turn or twist, and *bleiben* comes from roots meaning to stick to something, as in to a place, that is, to remain in a place. The *bleiben* sense of *bli(va)* still remains, for example in the expression "låt bli honom" (let him be). Becoming might feel like less of a turning to Swedes, and more of an allowing something to become, if left alone, in the sense of allowing it to unfold as it would on its own, which would of course be more appropriate to a *phenomenology* of spirit. German's *dar-* is related to the Swedish *där-*, but *darstellen* is *framställa* in Swedish, not "därställa" (which doesn't exist in Swedish). On the particle "fram," the Brothers Grimm, in a strangely mournful tone, say: "For us [Germans], this ancient, venerable particle has long since died out" ("diese uralte, ehrwürdige Partikel ist uns längst ausgestorben"). Its sense is different from *dar*, "there." It means rather "forward," in the sense of going from one point to a different one (English's "from" has the same roots). So the teleological sense of the presentation of the dialectic might be more present in Swedish (to say nothing of its ancient venerability).

In Hegel, *ande* is the relatively unproblematic translation of *Geist* into Swedish, although *Geist* has many more shades of meaning than *ande*. (Some of these other shades of meaning – the German equivalents of "team spirit" or a "spirit of cooperation" – are captured by a different, though obviously related word in Swedish, *anda*. Indeed, one could argue that *Geist* in the Phenomenology does occasionally appear in a sense that's perhaps more like *anda* than *ande*, such as the "spirit of a culture," which is a borderline case between *ande* and *anda*. But the continuity with *Geist* qua *ande* required consistency in our translation choice.) *Geist* and *ande*, as well as *spirit* (and *esprit*), all ultimately derive from words denoting the movement of air in one way or another. But the earliest forms of *Geist* (like the Swedish *gast*, and the English *ghost*) meant primarily air moving in the sense of wind, often a wind whipped into a fury, whereas *ande*, like *spirit*, comes from words meaning the movement of air in the sense of breath or breathing (one of the meanings of *anda* is literally "breath"). Whether this means that readers of translations of Hegel—and the Swedish, English, French, Spanish, and many other translations translate *Geist* with a breathier word—sense something gentler in spirit, or in world spirit, than Hegel or his German readers did, is hard to know. (Hegel made Napoleon himself less "furious" or "gho/a/stly" in a letter to Niethammer, when he wrote that he had seen "Welt*seele* zu Pferde," not "Welt*geist*," though Kojève contends this was simply because Napoleon wasn't fully self-conscious, and thus couldn't be *Geist*.)

There are of course numerous challenges that result from figures of speech being different in different languages. Most of these are of little significance. But that, for example, common sense is "der gesunde Menschen*verstand*" in German posed a slight problem for us, since it's "healthy reason (förnuft/Vernunft)" in Swedish, which strips the term of a sense Hegel probably intended, certainly at the end of the perception chapter. We chose the normal Swedish expression in the preface, but used "vanligt sunt förstånd" ("normal healthy understanding"), with scare-quotes (because it sounds quite odd in Swedish), at the end of Perception, where Hegel clearly is adumbrating the transition to the understanding chapter.

There are a few curious things about Swedish (and other Nordic languages) that pose unique, if, for the most part, relatively minor translation challenges. All verb endings for a given tense are the same in Swedish, regardless of person and number, even for strong or irregular verbs (as it might look from the outside: "I am," "he am," "they am," etc.). When Hegel writes, in §102, "Ich ist nur allgemeines [...]" (directly translated into English: "I is only universal [...]") the Swedish translation, "Jag är bara något allmänt [...]" could be read as either "(the) I is only universal" or "I am only universal," the latter being of course, in other contexts, the much more normal way to read those German words, though here it is not the correct way to read them. It becomes clear in the context of the passage what is meant, but the Swedish doesn't work quite as well as the German.

Swedish has an extremely inflexible word order, one that differs substantially from that of other non-Nordic languages. Although this certainly bears on the difficulty of doing the translation, it generally has no bearing on the quality of the resulting translation into Swedish, with a couple of strange exceptions. Adverb placement is altered in dependent clauses, so that, for example, "I can not go" must become, in a dependent clause, "(he said that) I not can go." In a few cases this leads to potential ambiguity in the Swedish. For example, in §200: "[...] damit *durchaus*, in demjenigen, *was für das Bewußtsein ist*, kein anderes Ingredienz wäre als der Begriff, der das Wesen ist" becomes in Pinkard's translation (he starts a new sentence): "There would thereby be *for all intents and purposes* no other ingredient in *what is for consciousness* than the concept which is the essence." Unless we want to rewrite the sentence entirely—which can cause other potential misunderstandings—we can only place the "durchaus" ("for all intents and purposes") directly after "for consciousness," which could make it seem that it's modifying consciousness, not the verb "be."

Such problems are of course relatively minor. A bit less minor, and often much more frustrating, is the difficulty in Swedish of using a word such as "of" (or an article in the genitive, like *eines* or *des* in German) to mark the genitive. The genitive is the description of a particular kind of relation of one noun to another. The most common relations are relations of possession, partitive relations ("cup of coffee"), and relations of origin ("people of Europe"). English can choose between "of" or the possessive *s*, depending on the kind of relationship, French doesn't use *s* to mark the genitive, and Swedish has nearly the opposite limitation of French: it is generally necessary to use the possessive *s*, and not the word for "of" (*av*), except in certain expressions like "type of" (*typ av*); in partitive use it uses no marker of any kind (as in many other languages): "a cup of coffee" is expressed as "a cup coffee"). The genitive *s* is used in ways that seem very strange to non-Nordic ears: for example, one must express "The City of Stockholm" as "Stockholm's City" (though Swedish generally doesn't use the apostrophe, so in Swedish it's *Stockholms stad*). The title of our translation sounds, to foreign ears, like "Spirit's Phenomenology" (*Andens fenomenologi*)[16]. Different languages have different ways of saying the same thing, so there's nothing inherently limiting about this aspect of Swedish, except that Swedes generally avoid using the possessive *s* on long noun phrases, and, more importantly, the German genitive case covers many different types of noun-noun relationship, and figuring out how to render certain instances of German's genitive articles into Swedish can sometimes be quite difficult. Consider the title of the fourth chapter: "Die Wahrheit der Gewißheit seiner selbst." There are two genitives. Pinkard chose a noun compound, "self-certainty," for the second genitive, perhaps to avoid the clumsiness of two "ofs." For the first genitive he chose *of*. Lefebvre chose two "ofs" (as one is nearly forced to in French): "Le vérité de la certitude de soi-même." Noun compounds like "self-certainty" work fine in Swedish, but it wouldn't have been idiomatic here, so we chose "certainty about/concerning itself" (*vissheten om sig själv*) for the second genitive. But the first genitive is an example of where translating into Swedish is much harder than translating into English. "Of" has a breadth of meaning that more or less covers the breadth of the genitive "der," and can be chosen as a correct translation without having to worry about exactly what sort of noun-noun relationship exists between *Wahrheit* and *Gewißhet*. The Swedish "of," *av*, would be wrong here, as indicated, and the genitive *s*, while much broader in its use in Swedish than in English, isn't quite right either, partly because the relationship isn't one of possession or origin, even broadly understood, but mostly because Swedish frowns on the use of the genitive *s* at the end of long noun phrases—it would sound almost as bad as the corresponding construction in English: "certainty concerning itself's truth." We thus had to choose a preposition other than *av*. We chose *hos*, which means "at" in the sense of "chez," ultimately coming from the Swedish word for house, in the same way that French's *chez* comes from Latin's *casa*. So the feeling of our translation of the chapter title is partly "the truth chez self-certainty." There is of course something fundamentally

---

[16] Translated word for word, it's actually "The Spirit's Phenomenology"—the *n* in *Anden* is "the." But explaining that will take us into even more obscure territory.

right about the "chez" aspect of our choice here, and it might even aid the reader in seeing that the question is how much truth there is "in" self-certainty, not whether self-certainty is true or false (which might be suggested by the English). But one criterion of a good translation is that it point back to the original in an unambiguous way, and our translation points to some degree in two directions: "Die Wahrheit der Gewißheit seiner selbst" and "Die Wahrheit *bei* Gewißheit seiner selbst."

Let us leave these obscure aspects of translating Hegel and return briefly to Adorno. As we noted, Adorno says the substance of Hegel's philosophy is process, and that it presents itself as the "negation of something congealed." Normal language use can only be stretched a small amount before it ceases being challenging and interesting and becomes nonsensical. One way to write with an anti-congealing effect in English that wouldn't necessarily seem like a bizarre experiment with language is to use more gerunds where one would normally use a "congealed" noun: "the thinking" instead of "the thought," "the transitioning" instead of "the transition," and so on. The equivalent in German is the nominalized infinitive.[17] Anyone reading the Phenomenology in German will be struck by how often Hegel uses nominalized infinitives. Of course, German is much more permissive with nominalized infinitives than English or Swedish, to the point where they are almost synonymous with their congealed forms. For example, in talking about the relation between the soliciting and solicited force in "Force and the Understanding," Hegel switches to "Übergang" at §139 then back to his normal non-congealed "Übergehen" at §140. To insist on a consistent translation into English of *Übergang* with *transition* and *Übergehen* with *transitioning* would be to insist on a distinction Hegel himself might not have been making. There is of course the additional problem that "the transitioning" sounds much stranger in English than "das Übergehen" does in German. In the case of *Übergehen* and *Übergang*, the translation challenge in Swedish is similar to that in English: the nominalized verb form in Swedish that corresponds to English's "-ing"[18] (*övergåendet*) sounds too strange in Swedish for us to have used it consistently, though it's not quite

---

[17] The German nominalized infinitive can of course also be translated into English as a nominalized infinitive in some cases, which wouldn't sound as "anti-congealing" as the nominalized gerund—"to think" instead of "thinking." But in the Phenomenology, the vast majority of nominalized infinitives are best understood as the equivalent of gerunds in English.

[18] Technically, this is not a gerund in Swedish, but its function is more or less the same.

as strange as "the transitioning" is in English. We did choose *övergåendet* a few times, however, where it seemed that *övergång* ("transition") really would have been congealed in a way Hegel would not have endorsed.

There are numerous other uses of nominalized verbs in the Phenomenology, but one that was slightly unusual two hundred years ago, and posed a tremendous translation challenge for us, was "das Erkennen." Today this non-congealed form has taken on a congealed meaning, much like "writing" is a normal noun that doesn't necessarily refer to a person's actual activity of writing. But two hundred years ago it was not in common use, certainly not among philosophers. Fichte and Schelling almost never used "Erkennen" in this way in their published writings.[19]

In most of the contexts in which Hegel uses it, "das Erkennen" means literally "the knowing," or "the process of knowing or coming know," "the process of acquiring knowledge" about something, etc. (though there are other senses to the word, like "discern," and in everyday use today it has many other meanings, including "realization" or "recognition"). "Das Erkennen" was unusual, but not a bizarre usage in Hegel's time. In English, "the knowing" (or "coming to know," "coming into awareness of," etc.) would produce more of a *Verfremdungseffekt* than Hegel would have intended, this is why *cognition* in English makes sense as a translation here. Unfortunately, *kognition* in Swedish does not work as well as *cognition* in English: the use of *kognition* in Swedish is too restricted to the cognitive sciences to feel right for the Phenomenology. Swedish's version of "the knowing," on the other hand, presents other problems. German has two verbs that mean to know: *erkennen* and *wissen*. Swedish has only one normal verb to mean "know" in the sense of *wissen*: *veta*, which is the obvious (etymologically and otherwise) choice for *wissen*. It could also function, if imperfectly, as a translation of *erkennen*, but we could not of course use it for both *wissen* and *erkennen*. There is an older verb, *kunskapa*, that means, or used to mean, to know in the sense of *erkennen*— to acquire knowledge about something (in the sense of bringing something into one's "ken"). Today the word is used, if it's used at all, to mean to

---

[19] Fichte uses it only once, in *Grundlage der gesammten Wissenschaftslehre*, and, there, it is used only as a contrast to what is known (das Erkannte): "Zuvörderst einige Worte über die Methode!—Im theoretischen Theile der Wissenschaftslehre ist es uns lediglich um das Erkennen zu thun, hier um das Erkannte." J. G. Fichte, *Gesamtausgabe der Bayerischen Akademie der Wissenschaften / 1. Reihe: Werke: Werke 1793-1795*, vol. I, 2 (Stuttgart: Friedrich Frommann, 1965), 416.

"spy," to gather intelligence, etc. We considered reviving its more philosophical use, but it would have been an uphill battle. The dictionary of the Swedish Academy (*Svenska Akademiens ordbok*) gives an example of its use to mean "to know" from 1808, and another example from 1936, but the text from 1936 puts "kunskapade" (a past participle form) in scare-quotes, since by then the word's use as "to know" had already become obsolete, or nearly so. Hegel doesn't need to be made more mysterious than he already is, so we chose the unfortunate though necessary compromise of "kunskap" (which, alas, is also the translation of *Erkenntnis*) in many cases, and in some cases, where the aspect of knowing, or gaining knowledge seemed particularly essential, something more like "acquiring/to acquire knowledge of" (*att få kunskap om*).

While "das Erkennen" posed a great challenge for us, "das Wissen" is, as indicated, straightforward for Swedish translators. The verb *wissen* is *veta* in Swedish, and the nominalized verb, which is completely normal in German (and was in Hegel's time), means the same thing as the nominalized verb in Swedish (*vetande*), which is also completely normal in Swedish. In English, the choice is not quite so straightforward. All the translators, from Baille to Pinkard, choose "absolute knowledge" for "absolutes Wissen." But there are other possibilities, above all the less congealed "absolute knowing." It's interesting that many native German speakers, when speaking or writing about Hegel in English, use "absolute knowing" for "absolutes Wissen." This, of course, may mean little more than that there are risks to writing in foreign languages. But it may mean that these native German speakers sense a progressive or processual aspect to *absolutes Wissen* they feel (perhaps incorrectly) isn't captured by the word *knowledge*. Yet *Wissen* is an entirely normal noun in German, and translating it with anything other than "knowledge" would make Hegel's text more alienating than it already is. The only downside might be that Hegel is pushed, ever so slightly, towards Kojève, where the goal of the Phenomenology is seen as bringing the reader to a state of total knowledge, of making one "wise" in Kojève's sense, instead of simply bringing consciousness to a *way* of knowing, as a preparation for Hegel's actual system. On the other hand, if one of the possible etymologies of *knowledge* is correct, its roots mean, essentially, to create or produce knowing,[20] making it, in a sense, even less congealed than the word *knowing* itself would be.

***

Translations are generally called "interpretations" when they are translations of poetry, but all translations are interpretations. The limitations pointed to by Koyré are in fact a rich resource, one that makes translations of Hegel into languages with different linguistic histories new texts, new Hegels—as in the Swedish Hegel, where the subject might more readily see itself in the object, where becoming might be letting be, where *Geist* itself might seem less ferocious, lending Hegel an almost Nietzschean *Heiterkeit*.

The reason to translate Hegel, and to keep translating him every decade or two, even into the same language, is thus not so much to introduce Hegel to the "Reader of Strindberg" (or Shakespeare or Cervantes or Proust), or to introduce Hegel to undergraduates (though this latter goal is important). The reason to translate Hegel is perhaps more fundamentally a matter of continuing to produce new interpretations, from new perspectives—something a modern Skoteinos surely would have endorsed.

---

[20] *-Ledge*, from *-leche*, is a suffix meaning to become, or produce, what is specified by the first element of the word.

French Losses in Translating Hegel
A Heuristic Benefit?

JEAN-PIERRE LEFEBVRE

> Philosophy invents its concepts in opposition to its time and always comes to shake up language.
>
> Gilles Deleuze

1.

The translation of German philosophical works into French always encounters all the problems attending the passage from a Germanic to a Romance language, and furthermore, it does so under the conditions of the particular expectations of the reader of philosophy, and of the implicit interpretative contract set up between him and the translator.

The French reader of philosophy does not generally have access to the German language, but of all readers of translations, he is undoubtedly the one who will most often try to compare the translation he is reading with the original (which, for instance, very few readers of novels will do). This is why we find German-language editions of the great philosophical classics in the Parisian philosophical bookstores.

The philosophical reader is vigilant with regard to the letter, a vigilance rooted in an old, conflicted history, the history of conflicts over translations, stemming from the great theological conflicts, above all in the Christian world. And furthermore, he has a potentially critical relation to the translator, who is accused of not providing sufficient help to the reader to understand, a critical relation sometimes identified with the procedure of philosophy itself—in brief, a heuristic disbelief. Thus, there is a tradition of bilingual editions of the great texts of Descartes, Spinoza, Cicero, and sometimes Kant and Hegel.

This has consequences for the translator: he is not necessarily intimidated by this vigilance on the part of the reader, which can even function as positive stimulus, but he has interiorized this conflict, and has often received his philosophical culture in this (polemical) universe: he has been this critical reader of translations, and it is to this critical relation that he owes becoming a translator.

In France, the translation of German philosophical texts is a fairly recent phenomenon, and more or less coincides with more than a century of antagonistic relations with Germany, including three brutal wars. To be sure, it was in at the beginning of the nineteenth century, with Kant (when it was France who entered Germany with Napoleon), that translation of German philosophical texts had its true beginning. Yet, it must be said that it was also around that time, at the end of the eighteenth century, German-language philosophy itself began. Hegel was first translated in the mid 19th century, beginning with the *Lectures on Aesthetics*, and, a bit later, extracts from the *Encyclopedia*. Systematic and philological translation dates from the mid twentieth century.

These translations are also from the very start over-determined by less directly visible political issues, in which the great ideological forces of the State and the Church have played a discreet and yet decisive role. The mere look of a translation can pull Hegel either towards the religious side, or the revolutionary atheist side.

In the twentieth century translations occasion contradictory debates, partly due to translation errors that have been uncovered by scholarly work on the texts. From these errors, one then passes over to specific difficulties (inevitable losses, and makeshift solutions).

This historical dimension finally produces strategies, sometimes of an agonistic character, for imposing general principles, as well as series of standard solutions, above all onomastic ones, that unfortunately are not regulated by international standardization committees, and above all do not pose the question of the nature of philosophical language.

The stakes are seen as universal, the solutions often hand-crafted.

Intellectuals in France are well aware of the problems posed by the translation of Freud, and it has been the topic of articles in the press with titles such as "When will they finally translate Freud?" as if there were a pathology to be cured there, as well. In January 2010 the copyrights to the works of Freud will have expired, and the flood of translations that are bound to appear will undoubtedly change this state of affairs. But for the moment some of these works are translated on the basis of a *strategy* that can be understood as an interesting symptom of the combination of constraint and anxiety that has a hold on the translator of theoretical texts. And this symptom also has its bearings on the translation of Hegel (whose strong presence in Freud is pointed out by many authors, beginning with Lacan)

This strategy—which, it is true, is partly due to the practice of collective translation—first of all consists in always translating a German word with one French word, a principle which I a priori consider to run against the economic essence of language, and whose effects are further aggravated in the case of the transition from German to French.

Cases of this would include the following:

Phantasie is for instance always translated by *fantaisie*.

Hilflosigkeit by the neologism *désaide*.

Seelisch by *d'âme*.

Seele by *âme*.

Traum, in compounds (for instance *Traumarbeit*), is translated by *de rêve*, although French spontaneously turns to the adjective *onirique* for compound concepts—even *Traumdeutung* has sometimes been translated by *oniromancie*....

I invoke the case of Freud not because I don't know what conference I'm attending, nor because I happen to be focusing on the translation of Freud at the moment, but because it opens a window onto the practical objective of the reading of translation and the practical resources of systematizing when one wants to convey a coherent body of thought, especially because some of the current translations of Hegel into French appeal to the systematic character of Hegel's philosophy in order to proceed in the same way that he does.

In the background of all these prefatory remarks, there is an anxiety that something might get lost in translation. I myself have experienced this from the point of view of the author: a novel that I wrote in French was translated and published in Germany.

This fear certainly presupposes that the reader of the German text never loses a thing when he reads the text in his own language, something which is by no means certain. Today we will postulate this.

Technically, this fear is based on the fact that many translators of philosophy in France have a non-linguistic understanding of German, principally based on philosophical texts, and are often unable to speak in German on other subjects. They read German like they read Latin or Greek. They sometimes look upon it as a sacred icon, a sibylline prime matter. Conversely, many French Germanists, dread the difficulty and abstraction of philosophical texts. Here, there is a cultural syndrome that weighs heavily on the work of the translator. I just wanted to mention this issue before moving on to the actual topic of our conference. The philosophical translation is a kind of writing that takes place under a double constraint.

2.

I now, without further ado, turn to the subject of our conference, by commencing with the notion of the object. I take this up in order to illustrate what I mean by "French losses."

German uses, as you know, the Germanic term *Gegenstand* for this notion and the Latin term *Objekt*, as well as their adjectival derivatives: *gegenständlich, objektiv*. In the *Phenomenology of Spirit*, *Gegenstand* has a very important topical status. *Der Gegenstand* is what stands in front of consciousness, or if you will, in front of the subject *Bewusstsein*. There is no symmetric rhyme with *Gegenstand* (as with the occasionally synonymous pair, subject-object), if not another *Gegenstand*.

What is lost in the French translation will then be this absence of symmetry, since the French reader faced with *OBJET* will always think of SUJET in petto. As a result of this interior rhyme, consciousness is not the natural counterpart of object. Thus, to translate *gegenständlich* with "objectif" constitutes another loss, since in current usage this French adjective connotes the method of a subject that is not "subjective" but rather *sachlich*, neutral, impersonal. One speaks of an objective vision of things, sometimes even of an objective judge. Obviously, we can hope that the philosophical reader, endowed with a sharpness of reason, will permanently make the correction, but this means imputing to him a power of near superhuman attentiveness.

What is lost is the permanent reference to the intended topic via the other distinguishing marks: *für sich seyn, seyn für anderes*. Unlike the French *pour, für* always elicits *vor*, and is located in the region of *gegen*. The solution I have adopted is one that I would like to call a modest neologism, which liberates the term from its primary parasitical relation—or, as we say in French, *parasitage*—and signals the singularity of the corresponding concept in German. I have spontaneously translated *gegenständlich* as "objectal," and subsequently discovered that the translators of Husserl had made recourse to the same neologism.

This sole example compels me to return once again to the concept of *parasitage*, a phenomenon that a word, in its own language, exhibits in relation to its semantic and thus cultural periphery. What is lost in translation is therefore:

Firstly, the semantic periphery of the German concept: for example, *Selbstbewußtsein* and *selbstbewusst* both mean, in German, self-consciousness and the fact of being conscious of oneself, but also a certain psychological and even existential modality: a self-confidence that can go as far as arrogance, a self-assurance about one's own knowledge. The concept also contains the conjugated root of the verb *wissen* (*wusst*). Finally, it is subsumed under the category of a being (Hegel thus writes it with a "y"! *Seyn*). This entire complex periphery works on the meaning, labors patiently on the memory of the reader. The assemblage is never arbitrary.

Secondly, the very presence of a periphery, if one makes use of it, as one translator does, produces a complex neologism such as "*autoconscience*." The French concept is then "outside-of-language," like certain religious categories. The same thing could be noted in the case of the concept of *Aufhebung*, the trivial character of which, in German, is abolished by the use of neologisms, or puns (as in the case of Derrida's translation, *relève*)

This first loss is seen and commented upon often, nonetheless, the loss is significant because it is permanent. Its permanence means that its strength is more significant than the vigilance of even the reader who is most aware of the difficulty. In Hegel, it concerns a majority of the concepts to which I have dedicated an appendix at the end of my translation.

Let us take some key concepts: *meynen* in German designates a very intimate, almost sentimental, relation to the object, which in the first chapter echoes *sinnlich*, and which can almost mean "love." All of this is lost in the French equivalents, although it would have helped the reader to understand this type of relationship of a consciousness to an object.

Wahrnehmung is traditionally translated into French as "perception." What is lost is the relationship to the "truth," to which the text alludes, but also the disengagement from the sensible, for the French *perception*—and the verb *percevoir*—still has a strong connotation of simple sensation. The same problem no doubt exists in English, where philosophical language very often is of Latin origin and close to French.

Verstand is a category that Hegel treats with a critical distance. *Verstand* is nothing but *Verstand*, in the same way that *der Gedanke* is only the product of the understanding, which is not yet reason, *die Vernunft*. It is still very close to *Vorstellung* and even to *Anschauung*. Hegel plays on its presence in the expression "der gesunde Menschenverstand" which almost has characterological significance.

The French language, which necessarily reserves "raison" for *die Vernunft*, thus regularly has recourse to the word, *entendement*—as do I. Unfortunately, this noun is completely alone in the paradigm: there is no accompanying verb *verstehen* (*comprendre*), which, by the way, does not appeal to Hegel very much, nor adjectives such as *verständlich*, *verstandesmäßig*. For these latter adjectives one might tempted to translate as "rational" (particularly given the tradition of the critique of rationalism). Unfortunately, one must retain "rationnel" for *vernünftig* because the French "raisonnable" does not have the same rational content and means rather an ethico-psychological quality connected to the concept of moderation.

The play with the semantic periphery is by definition, so to speak, lost when philosophy itself engages in wordplay, for example *mein*, as a possessive, and *meynen*, as a verb; or *seyn*, as a verb, and *sein*, as a possessive. But Hegel doesn't play too much with these homophones, and here, the translator's notes are sufficient.

Behind these notions of periphery and play there is the fundamental fact of the economic character of language, which means that a term is also specified by its context. A dominant sense is here defined, yet accompanied by other possible, but less probable senses. Unfortunately, the French language cannot preserve the same term, it must choose: thus, the adjective "allgemein" sometimes inclines towards that which we call "universal" (as opposed to particular) and sometimes towards *gemein*, a notion of community which is less radical, and for which we would rather say "général," and not solely in the case of Rousseau's "volonté générale." And yet this very word *général*, in French, plays host to the parasite *genre* (which is used as a translation of *die Gattung*).

With *Sein* and *Wesen*, the "Spanish" solutions *ser* and *estar* would be useless, and this situation is pretty desperate. Very often, the translator is tempted to translate *das Wesen* by the noun "être" in French, and not only in the case of *das höchste Wesen*, *l'Être suprême* of the French Revolution. Similarly, *Wesenheit* is not always *l'essentialité*, but can designate that which we call an instance. This is to say nothing of *Dasein*, and that which happens with that word in Heidegger. What is permanently lost in this pair is the highly idiosyncratic characteristic of *das Sein* in German, which is always understood as an infinitive verb form used as a noun for speculative purposes, while *un être* in French is a sponge-noun, welcoming all the parasites of the earth....

This is only one category of loss, but it is the most abundant and visible. It concerns concepts as important and common as *Anschauung, bestehen, erfahren/Erfahrung, entfremden, Erscheinung/erscheinen, die Sache, die Sittlichkeit, das Tun, der Zweck*. For each of these terms there is a rich profusion of French conceptual resources, and the solution that makes use of one single term creates a purely formal continuity, but one that is, with regard to its content, false.

Finally, it affects the homogeneity of the grand semantic networks that support the German text thanks to the visibility of the roots of the words, for instance *wissen*, present in *Gewissheit, bewusst, Bewusstsein, Selbstbewußtsein, Gewissen, Wissenschaft*.

3.

Another category of loss (and of difficulty for the translator) is of a syntagmatic nature, particularly noticeable in Hegel, whose syntax is very linear; allow me to explain.

There are three German genders (der, die, das) and several cases (nominative, accusative, dative, genitive). In French there are only two genders (male, female), and there are no cases. Via pronouns, the German language can therefore refer, in a very precise and discriminating way, to nouns used earlier, sometimes even at the very beginning of the paragraph, without having to repeat them. When pronouns are translated systematically into pronouns in French, the text becomes horribly imprecise, and Hegelian philosophy resembles the typical caricature that has been made of it. The French translator must therefore—via rational interpretation—make an effort to attribute these pronouns to the previously named concepts, and then express these attributions through precise references. This exercise is at times difficult (which explains why even certain German readers use foreign translations in order to understand obscure passages).

This procedure inevitably makes the text expand, and makes it heavier: that which was intended to facilitate the reading becomes a source of difficulty. What is lost is the benefit of density, which makes possible the occurrence of the concepts in proximity to one another. And of course, what is lost is a certain quality of the poetic genius of the pair language-thought, a poetic genius that is connected to this density.

In addition, the plasticity of German syntax is lost, a syntax which can progress from a nominative to an accusative, and then begin again from this accusative at the beginning of the phrase and return to a nominative, and then begin once again from that nominative, and so on. In French, the tendency to restore the standard subject-verb-complement order in the phrases destroys this linearity and disperses the elements even more. Very often we must go back to the beginning in order once again to find the thread. The baggage is heavy enough as it is. Reading becomes slow, wearing.

4.

On the other hand, there is perhaps less difficulty translating the astonishing conceptual constructions used to parody Hegelian discourse: being-for-self, being-in-itself, being-in-and-for-itself, etc. with their verbal forms *fürsichseiend, ansichseiend, anundfürsichseiend*. The morphological singularity of these notions authorizes the translator to use a parallel strategy in his own language. He might even be tempted to leave these shibboleths of Hegelianism in the original, in order to add a little local color.

But, in this case, other problems would arise. I raised the matter of the topographical echoes of *für sich* previously. There is an even more radical difficulty with *an sich* and *an sich sein*. The conventional translation is *en soi* and *être en soi*. Unfortunately, *en soi* calls to mind a topography of interiority which is not at all that of *an sich*, where "an" signifies a completely different type of proximity by contact and tangency, one we find for example in *Anschauung*. *En soi* would then correspond more to *in sich*, which we, by the way, also see in Hegel's text. But the tradition of the speculative use of "en soi" in French, somehow saves this translation. However, in other cases, *an* should be translated as "à même" and never as "en."

5.

This chapter of new difficulties that we have opened here, is that of small syntagmatic tools such as *Ich, selbst, gleich, nur, erst*, which appear very frequently, and some of which have a conceptual form (e.g. *das Selbst, die Gleichheit*). One of the linguistic effects of the German *Bildung* of French philosophy has been to make possible what was previously forbidden. Not only can we substantivize the infinitives: *le rêver* (the dreaming), *le penser* (the thinking), etc., which have come to be added to everyday substantivations such as "le boire et le manger des auberges"—"(the) drinking and eating at a country inn," but it is also possible today to write *le Je* (*das Ich*) instead of *le Moi*, as was done in the earlier tradition. It is easy to see what is at stake philosophically in this difference. Not only for *Ich* and *mich*, but also for *Sich* and *Selbst*, which must be differentiated even though the French philosophical tradition translates both with *Soi*, and relies on the context to make the distinction clear. Myself, I have maintained this differentiating signal by translating *das Selbst* as "Soi-même."

On the other hand, I have differentiated the translations of *gleich* and *Gleichheit* depending on the context, reserving the paradigm of equality for contexts that are quasi-juridical or political, while often respecting the abstract sense of identity that is often that of *Gleichheit*.

What gets lost here is precisely the initial indeterminateness, which is a result of the frequent appearance of the word in Hegel's phraseology, and all associative or speculative play thereby permitted. Or, if you will, the support that philosophy draws from language, the "speculative move of language."

The result of these disjointed remarks would then be rather pessimistic, if one didn't count on the exceptional contextualizing power of the Hegelian procedure and the integration that always begins afresh in each development or each phenomenological pronouncement of the totality of the experience of consciousness. Even a faulty translation functions in a positive way. The reader advances, he is pushed away and pulled back. He progressively recognizes a entire realms of his culture, his history, his world. Here, I am speaking only of the Phenomenology. The book contains highly poetic and eloquent moments; the abstraction is made vivid by this cadence, and, in my view, it is this that authorizes the impertinence of the translator and all the accumulated loss. Many things are always in the process of dying, but rebirth is always possible.

In this way, the philosophy of Hegel has, as Deleuze says, "shaken up" the French language via the German language. There is a way of a philosophizing in French that has inherited, among other things, this disruption, and resounds in the language and thought of the anthropological school, be it Lévi-Strauss (who himself recognizes this), Michel Foucault, or the Hellenist Jean-Pierre Vernant. It was they whom I had in mind in the last paragraph of my introduction to my translation, which I will read to you here in English, thanks to my fellow translators:

> What is important is not to accumulate more or less successful tricks, which are fully justifiable, even necessary, in an explanatory comment, but to respect the linguistic ethos at work in Hegel's way of proceeding. The Phenomenology is, in fact, a great book of translation, an immense, supple glossary appropriate to the mission of communication. It is not merely this original and pure treasure that others would attempt to transport to their own language, but it is itself a dialectical anthology of the treasures possessed by these others, the placing into a regional idiom of universal philosophy and the discourse of History. In this sense, we can once again compare Hegel and Luther. This is the "common sense" of his singularity, the essence of his difficulty: just as he does not explicitly cite those of which he speaks, but himself speaks in them and in their texts, Hegel—in a way which undoubtedly is ultimately artificial, and which in the end failed (despite the epigonic burst of Heidegger) since in 1807 we were no longer in 1517, and since it was a question of philosophy—expelled the "cosmopolitan" vocabulary of European philosophy from his discourse, eliminated or assigned the terms of Greek or Latin origins to the phases of the movement of thought that had been overcome. The following year, Fichte, the great disciple of the cosmopolitan Kant, in parodying the title of an address by Luther, "To the Christian Nobility of the German Nation," held before a swooning audience his famous "Address to the German Nation," where he justified, among other things, this practice of thinking in one's mother tongue. But at the same time, he bade farewell to this practice. And thus it is, in the awareness of the limits of this unprecedented experience that we must admire the intensity and rigor in Hegel, and attempt to translate him with the same orientation: the orientations that are at home in the rivers and hills of our own idiom, whose very beauty depends, just as the English landscapes painted by Turner or Monet, on the intrusion of a historical artifact that comes to challenge its nature.

Translation by Brian Manning Delaney and Sven-Olov Wallenstein.

Authors

ROBERT B. PIPPIN is the Evelyn Stefansson Nef Distinguished Service Professor in the Committee on Social Thought, the Department of Philosophy, and the College at the University of Chicago. He is the author of several books and articles on German idealism and later German philosophy, including *Kant's Theory of Form*; *Hegel's Idealism: The Satisfactions of Self-Consciousness*; *Modernism as a Philosophical Problem*; and *Idealism as Modernism: Hegelian Variations*. Additional books include *Henry James and Modern Moral Life*, *Die Verwirklichung der Freiheit*; *The Persistence of Subjectivity: On the Kantian Aftermath*; and *Nietzsche, moraliste français: La conception nietzschéenne d'une psychologie philosophique*. His most recent book, *Fatalism in American Film Noir: Some Cinematic Philosophy*, was published February, 2012 by the University of Virginia Press.

WALTER JAESCHKE is Professor of Philosophy at the Ruhr-Universität in Bochum, and the director of the Hegel archives. He is the general editor of Hegel's *Gesammelte Werke*, published by the Nordrhein-Westfälischen Akademie der Wissenschaften, as well as of Friedrich Heinrich Jacobi's *Werke* (together with Klaus Hammacher), and Jacobi's *Briefwechsel*. His publications include *Die Suche nach den eschatologischen Wurzeln der Geschichtsphilosophie: Eine historische Kritik der Säkularisierungsthese*; *Die Religionsphilosophie Hegels*; *Die Vernunft in der Religion: Studien zur Grundlegung der Religionsphilosophie Hegels* (Eng. trans. *Reason in Religion*), and *Hegel-Handbuch*.

TERRY PINKARD is Professor of Philosophy at Georgetown University. His field of research includes German philosophy from Kant to the present, particularly the period covering the development from Kant to Hegel, philosophy of law, political philosophy, and bioethics. Some of his recent books include *Hegel's Phenomenology: The Sociality of Reason*; *Hegel: A Biography*, and *German Philosophy 1760-1860: The Legacy of Idealism*. In 2012 he published *Hegel's Naturalism: Mind, Nature, and the Final Ends of Life*. He is currently completing a new translation of Hegel's Phenomenology for Cambridge University Press.

SUSANNA LINDBERG earned her Ph.D. from Université Marc Bloch in Strasbourg, 2000, with the thesis *Heidegger avec Hegel: une explication philosophique*. She is Associate Professor of Philosophy at the University of Helsinki, and a postdoctoral researcher of the Academy of Finland and the University of Helsinki. Her current work deals with ideas of "life" and the "elemental" in German idealism, contemporary phenomenology, and deconstruction. She recently published *Heidegger contre Hegel: Les irréconciliables*.

CARL-GÖRAN HEIDEGREN is Professor of Sociology at Lund University. His research areas include the history of ideas, sociology of philosophy, and sociology of culture. His publications include: *Hegels Fenomenologi: En analys och kommentar* [Hegel's Phenomenology: Analysis and Commentary]; *Johan Jakob Borelius – den siste svenske hegelianen* [J. J. Borelius: The Last Swedish Hegelian]; *Det moderna genombrottet i nordisk universitetsfilosofi* [The Modern Breakthrough in Nordic University Philosophy], *Erkännande* [Recognition], and *Ernst och Friedrich Georg Jünger: två bröder, ett århundrade* [Ernst and Friedrich Georg Jünger: two brothers, one century].

SVEN-OLOV WALLENSTEIN is Professor of Philosophy at Södertörn University in Stockholm, and is the editor-in-chief of *Site*. He is the translator of works by Baumgarten, Winckelmann, Lessing, Kant, Hegel, Frege, Husserl, Heidegger, Levinas, Foucault, Derrida, Deleuze, Agamben, and Adorno, as well as the co-translator of Hegel's *Phenomenology* into Swedish. He is also the author of numerous books on contemporary philosophy, art, and architecture. Recent publications include *Essays, Lectures*; *Thinking Worlds: The Moscow Conference on Art, Philosophy and Politics* (co-ed. with Daniel Birnbaum and Joseph Backstein); *The Silences of Mies*; *Biopolitics and the Emergence of Modern Architecture*; *1930/31: Swedish Modernism at the Crossroads* (with Helena Mattsson); *Swedish Modernism: Architecture, Consumption and the Welfare State* (co-ed. with Helena Mattsson), and *Nihilism, Art, Technology*.

STAFFAN CARLSHAMRE is Professor of Philosophy at Stockholm University. His research has focused on the foundations of the human sciences, and questions of meaning and interpretation. He is the author of *Language and Time: An Attempt to Arrest the Thought of Jacques Derrida*, as well as the co-editor (with Anders Petterson) of *Types of Interpretation in the Human Sciences*.

VICTORIA FARELD is associate senior lecturer in the history of ideas, Stockholm University. She completed her Ph.D. in 2007 at University of Gothenburg, and her dissertation, *Att vara utom sig inom sig: Charles Taylor, erkännandet och Hegels aktualitet* [Being without oneself within oneself: Charles Taylor, recognition, and Hegel's actuality], deals with the notion of recognition in political philosophy. She is currently Co-Director of Studies at the Centre for European Studies at the University of Gothenburg.

BRIAN MANNING DELANEY is completing a dissertation on the relation between Hegel and Nietzsche. He has taught at Berkeley, has guest-lectured at several Stockholm area universities and colleges, and sits on the editorial board of *Site*. He has co-translated Hegel's *Phenomenology* into Swedish, and recently translated Daniel Birnbaum and Anders Olsson's *As a Weasel Sucks Eggs* (*Den andra födan*).

JEAN-PIERRE LEFEBVRE is the director of the German section the École Normale Supérieure in Paris. He is the translator of works by Hölderlin, Heine, Rilke, Brecht, and Celan, as well as of Marx's *Capital*, Hegel's *Phenomenology*, and the three-volume edition of Hegel's *Lectures on Aesthetics* (together with Veronica Schenk). He is also the author of *Hegel et la société* (together with Pierre Macherey), as well as of the novel *La nuit de passeur*. He recently published a translation of Freud's *Traumdeutung* into French.

Södertörn Philosophical Studies

Södertörn Philosophical Studies is a book series published under the direction of the Department of Philosophy at Södertörn University. The series consists of monographs and anthologies in philosophy, with a special focus on the Continental-European tradition. It seeks to provide a platform for innovative contemporary philosophical research. The volumes are published mainly in English and Swedish. The series is edited by Marcia Sá Cavalcante Schuback and Hans Ruin.

www.ingramcontent.com/pod-product-compliance
Lightning Source LLC
Chambersburg PA
CBHW031257110426
42743CB00040B/696